25/"/
15/1:
4/
0.

6 880 877 000

No Surrender
in Burma

No Surrender in Burma

Operations Behind Japanese Lines, Captivity and Torture

Frederick C. Goode

Pen & Sword
MILITARY

First published in Great Britain in 2014 by
Pen & Sword Military
an imprint of
Pen & Sword Books Ltd
47 Church Street
Barnsley
South Yorkshire
S70 2AS

Copyright © Peter Frederick Goode 2014

ISBN 978 1 47382 378 5

Typeset in Ehrhardt by
Mac Style Ltd, Bridlington, East Yorkshire
Printed and bound in the UK by CPI Group (UK) Ltd, Croydon,
CRO 4YY

Pen & Sword Books Ltd incorporates the imprints of Pen & Sword
Archaeology, Atlas, Aviation, Battleground, Discovery, Family
History, History, Maritime, Military, Naval, Politics, Railways, Select,
Transport, True Crime, and Fiction, Frontline Books, Leo Cooper,
Praetorian Press, Seaforth Publishing and Wharncliffe.

For a complete list of Pen & Sword titles please contact
PEN & SWORD BOOKS LIMITED
47 Church Street, Barnsley, South Yorkshire, S70 2AS, England
E-mail: enquiries@pen-and-sword.co.uk
Website: www.pen-and-sword.co.uk

Contents

Acknowledgements		vi
Foreword		vii
Introduction		viii
Chapter 1	The Bush Warfare School	1
Chapter 2	To the Thai Frontier	5
Chapter 3	The Bombing of Taunggyi	17
Chapter 4	A Rich Grave	31
Chapter 5	A Trap Well Laid	40
Chapter 6	Race to the Irrawaddy	47
Chapter 7	The Separation	57
Chapter 8	The Return of Lacey	68
Chapter 9	Father McGovern	80
Chapter 10	Attack by Bandits	91
Chapter 11	The Confrontation	100
Chapter 12	A Tempting Offer	112
Chapter 13	On to Tengchong	124
Chapter 14	Fortress Sima	137
Chapter 15	Betrayal in Sadon	150
Chapter 16	Ruthless Barbaric Animals	164
Chapter 17	Torture in Myitkyina	182
Chapter 18	Rangoon Central Jail	194
Chapter 19	Cholera and Bombs	210
Chapter 20	Forced March to Freedom	220
Postscript		232
Notes		236
Index		244

Acknowledgements

by Peter F. Goode

There are many people to whom I would like to offer my gratitude, not least my wife Yayoi Faith, a Japanese national who transcribed my father's notes onto disk and translated Japanese Kanji documents, and who through it all has been patient, enthusiastic and courageous in reading of the atrocities committed by Japanese forces during the occupation of Burma. Stephen Fogden is by far the leading expert on the POWs held in Rangoon Central Jail, and his contribution of sharing documents with me is greatly appreciated. With him I was able to identify many characters from my father's notes. Nick Collins of the Commando Veterans Association was kind enough to post on their website (http://www.commandoveterans.org/site) a brief resume of my father and SSDII, a post to which we received many responses and links, one of which was from Alan Weeks, of the Swythamley Historical Society in Staffordshire, who is researching the history of the Brocklehurst Estate. To Alan, too, I am very grateful for support and assistance in my research. Michael Rawlinson, a fellow retired Hong Kong Police officer with whom I had the pleasure of working on many complicated cases during our long careers was an inspiration when it came to historical research and review of the draft. Finally I would like to thank Patrick Newman for his help, advice and tremendous encouragement.

Having made these acknowledgements, I would like to point out that the story told here is my father's own, and I have made no attempt to alter it in any way. It is also not a historical account of my father's unit, which basically was in existence from September 1941 to July 1942. It is one man's story of personal survival against all odds.

Foreword

by Major General Corran Purdon CBE MC CPM

This is a gripping, true account by a Commando during the Burma campaign. He and the members of his Commando were sent from the Middle East to assist Chiang-Kai-Shek in his guerilla war against the Japanese.

On arrival in Burma the Commandos were posted to the Bush Warfare School at Maymyo. Here they were instructed in how to live in the jungle by local Burmans, in the use of explosives by the famous, later Brigadier, Mike Calvert DSO, and in the rudiments of Urdu and Mandarin. Frederick Goode alone of his comrades was very successful in learning these languages, which knowledge was to prove vital in the future. The Commandos carried out attacks against Thai/Japanese positions, but were eventually cut off behind the Japanese lines. Their CO decided that he and his Commando should split into small groups and make their way towards India and safety.

Frederick walked 2,000 miles towards India, but was betrayed to the Japanese when only twenty miles short of his destination. They were captured, tortured and held in Rangoon Central Jail until the end of the war.

This forceful and vivid account is compelling reading and should be among the epics of the Burma Campaign. Frederick Goode was a Corporal at the time and had his deeds and powers of leadership been officially known then he could well have been decorated and commissioned.

Introduction

by Peter F. Goode

Frederick Charles Goode was born in Birmingham, England on 22 July 1918, one of nine children of Gertrude and William Goode in the Lozells district of the city. He was educated locally until the age of 14, and worked as a labourer until the age of 17, when he joined the 1st Battalion, The Duke of Cornwall's Light Infantry, as a private with the army number 5108868. Fred's first posting overseas was to Lahore, then still part of India. With the outbreak of war in 1939 his regiment was sent to Libya and based in Tobruk, where it saw action against German and Italian forces. When the British Army then called for volunteers for Commando units in late 1940 he joined No. 8 Commando, and after initial training in the UK arrived at the Bush Warfare School in Maymyo (now Pyin Oo Lwin), in the Shan Highlands of Burma, some forty miles east of Mandalay, in September 1941.

The school was set up in early 1941 following the success of a similar school established at Wilsons Promontory, Victoria, Australia, to train elements of the Australian Army Independent Companies (AAIC), by Mike Calvert, DSO (and Bar), also known as 'Mad' Mike Calvert, and Colonel F. Spencer Chapman, DSO. After training Commando detachments in demolition techniques there and in Hong Kong, Calvert commanded the school at Maymyo, while Chapman was posted to a similar school in Singapore. Elements of the AAIC were already in Maymyo when the British contingent – some 100 men, including Fred – arrived. The new arrivals were assigned to two newly formed units: Special Service Detachment I (Middle East), or SSDI, and Special Service Detachment II (Middle East), or SSDII. Fred was one of the fifty men assigned to the latter.

SSDI was initially led by Orde Wingate, then a captain, but subsequently was commanded by Major Milman. SSDII was commanded from the outset by Henry C. Brocklehurst, initially a captain, then a major, then finally a lieutenant colonel.

SSDI and SSDII were set up under the codename 'Mission 204', also known as Tulip Force, their mission being, alongside elements of the AAIC, to secretly go into China and train Chinese troops in demolition and guerilla tactics to use against the occupying Japanese. However, following the Japanese attack on Pearl Harbor on 7 December 1941, the two units' orders were changed, and they were directed to assist in the defence of Burma, with SSDII assigned to the 1st Burma Division. In early February 1942 the C-in-C West Pacific – Earl Wavell – ordered that Orde Wingate co-ordinate irregular warfare in the theatre. SSDI and SSDII therefore came under the direct command of Wingate, now a Brigadier.

SSDI were deployed to Loimwe in Shan, and SSDII to the Taunggyi area of the state. The majority of SSDI eventually crossed the Irrawaddy River into India and safety. Milman was then assigned to Kunming. The same, sadly, was not true for the men of SSDII, who reached the Irrawaddy at Shwegu in February 1942 to find the far bank swarming with Japanese.

These men then split up. Two groups attempted to cross the Irrawaddy near Shwegu, while another two, one of which included Fred, attempted to go the long way round. Heading northeast, Fred and colleagues embarked on an arduous 2,000-mile trek on foot across jungle-clad mountains in a desperate attempt to reach India and safety. Many Burmese and Chinese villagers helped them on the way, at great risk to themselves, but Fred was finally betrayed to the Japanese in October 1942, just twenty miles short of his goal, and later incarcerated in Rangoon Central Jail. In April 1945, all the POWs held in the jail were force-marched away from the advancing 14th Army until after a week their Japanese guards abandoned them and they were liberated at last near the village of Waw. Those British POWs well enough to travel, including Fred, were airlifted out by Dakota and then transported by train, ship and air back to the UK

After discharge from the army, Fred returned to Birmingham where he gained employment as a plastic-moulder in a local factory. He married Dorothy Woodward in St Paul's Parish Church, Lozells in 1947. They had one child: me.

My father began writing about his wartime experiences towards the end of the 1950s. He had read fellow SSDII survivor John Friend's 1957 book *The Long Trek*, in which my father appears as 'Sam Beddall', and my gut feeling is that he wanted to set the record straight. (Friend and my father never did quite see eye to eye …) I well remember him coming home from work and sitting at the dining-table in the kitchen of our house in Great Barr, Birmingham and writing in longhand, with a pencil. It took him a long time, and he would ask me to take the resulting pages to my English teacher at school to review for him. Each time she handed them back for me to give to my father I would see sadness in her eyes. I, being so young, did not understand and was not allowed to read them.

My father died on 1 November 1993, never knowing that he, along with other surviving Far East POWs, had succeeded in obtaining compensation from the British Government for the ill-treatment they received at the hands of the Japanese. He was one of a group selected by 'The Burma Star Association' to be examined on an annual basis in a military hospital in London to determine the amount of disability that could be attributed to his incarceration. Payments to the survivors or next of kin began in January 1994.

It was not until 2012 that I got around to reading his reminiscences. I immediately wished I had read them while he was still alive. There were so many unanswered questions. It was then that I decided I should review them, put them in some order and undertake research into the men of SSDII.

It soon became obvious that there was indeed very little known about them. SSDI, by contrast, is well reported on, with copious photographs and documentation. My curiosity was piqued, and I determined to find out all I could about the men who split up on the banks of the Irrawaddy, only eight of whom, I eventually discovered, survived the war. It was the start of a roller-coaster ride of emotions that led to this book.

This, then, is my father's story.

Chapter One

The Bush Warfare School

I was a lance corporal in a party of one hundred Commandos sent to Burma from North Africa in September 1941. We had all volunteered for a special job; what, we did not know.

We had travelled first by sea to Ceylon, then on to Calcutta, and from there by French tramp ship to Rangoon. We stayed in Rangoon for two nights before boarding a train northward to the old Capital of Mandalay, from where we travelled by trucks up the Burma Road that links China with Rangoon. The journey took us nearly five hours around the twisting and winding bends, sometimes climbing over hills, sometimes going down into valleys. The engines of the trucks groaned against the hard climbing that was asked of them. Then suddenly we were upon a plateau with rising hills on either side. We continued on through the small town of Maymyo, and some way past the town we turned off the main road and followed a well-worn track until we came upon a clearing. On the fringe of the clearing bamboo bungalows were set out. That was our destination, the Bush Warfare School.

Other troops were here already and had prepared a meal for us. After getting our kit from the trucks and making ourselves comfortable in our new home we settled down for the night. All of us asked the same question. What were we doing out here? Not one scrap of information had been given to us from the beginning of the journey from North Africa. Four commissioned officers had travelled with us – two captains, Wingate and Brocklehurst, and two 'one-pip' lieutenants, Gardener and Lancaster – but any instructions from them came through the two sergeants with our group, Cobham and McAteer, Cobham being the senior. Breakfast would be at eight the next morning, and we were told to parade at nine, where we would be sorted out into two detachments.

Sleep came very easily that night as the long and tiresome journey had taken its toll upon us. Most of us made for our beds early as there was not much to do in the strange camp which, by the time we had got our kit sorted out, was in darkness.

At nine the next morning we formed up into two ranks with the two sergeants taking up positions in front. Shortly after, the four officers came. After the usual 'present and correct' from the sergeants, the two NCOs were told to take up posts away from us. Then the two captains called names out from sheets of paper they were holding. Captain Brocklehurst called for men to form up on Sergeant McAteer, and Captain Wingate called out men to form up on Sergeant Cobham. I was called by Captain Brocklehurst and so fell in on Sergeant McAteer along with the rest.

After the separation of the two detachments, Captain Brocklehurst told us that, as from now, we would be known as ME Detachment II, while Captain Wingate commanded ME Detachment I. The next thing was to get our kit sorted out so that we were all together in one bungalow. It was Friday and payday, after which we had the weekend to ourselves to explore Maymyo.

Monday morning began with PT at 06.30 hours, followed by breakfast, then parade at nine to be marched to one of the larger bamboo bungalows which served as a classroom. Here we were introduced to a man named Calvert. He was a captain in the Royal Engineers and was going to teach us about explosives and demolition in general.

Captain Calvert – 'Mike' to his friends – was a dark-haired, black-steely-eyed and flat-nosed man about five-foot eight-inches tall, with very broad shoulders. His appearance was as if he was almost square, as broad as he was tall. He talked to us about what we would be learning and what we would be doing, but he would not tell us why. He talked for nearly an hour, and in that time he had got the admiration and the confidence of everyone in the room, so much so that had he at any time said 'Follow me to hell' I am sure that every man there would have got up and gone without question, such was his impact upon all of us.

Our lessons from him would be twice a day, five days a week, with an examination on what we had learned, both written and practical on Saturday mornings. Our first lesson was to begin at nine o'clock the next day.

The next introduction was to two 'one-pip' lieutenants whom we had never seen before. Their uniforms looked very new, as if they had just been drawn from stores. The pips on their shoulders showed also that they had never had a button brush put across them, so we gathered that these two were really green to the service. Captain Brocklehurst introduced them as Mr Robinson and Mr Moore. Then came the first big surprise. These two officers were going to teach us all to speak and understand Mandarin, the standardised Chinese language. A wry smile spread over the captain's face as he glanced along the rows of faces staring at him in sheer amazement.

Mr Robinson was something of a lah-di-dah sort of fellow, not very old, about twenty-two. He told us that he spent quite a good deal of time in China working with the Shell-Mex company. Mr Moore was an entirely different person. He was a little older, in his thirties, short and a little untidy, but his speech and manner were much more to our liking. He too had worked for Shell-Mex, but it seemed that he left the majority of things for Mr Robinson to say. It appeared to us that Mr Robinson had already assumed seniority.

Chinese lessons were to be undertaken twice a day, five days a week, beginning at eleven o'clock the next morning, with written and speech examinations on Saturdays.

After the final introductions and talks by our instructors, Captain Brocklehurst told us that we should now be formed into three sections, with an officer and sergeant in charge of each section. So, there and then, two senior corporals, Friend and Baker, were made up to sergeants. Two more junior officers were to join us at a later date to make up the full complement, we were told. (In fact, Captain Brown, the adjutant at the school, later joined us as the head of the third section.) Brocklehurst and Wingate were also promoted to majors, and the two 'one-pippers' to full lieutenants.

The first week went by with most of our work taking place in the classroom. We were getting on quite well with the Chinese language, and Captain 'Mike' Calvert was keeping us hard at work on different types of explosives and how best to use them.

We still could not find out for what purpose we were there, though many rumours floated about, as is usual in any of the services.

Sporting events such as football and hockey were arranged between units. Sometimes at weekends we went out on exercises. During these exercises we were instructed by Burmese, who taught us how to use the jungle and build rafts and small lean-to huts that would give us shelter in an emergency, how to make string and rope from bamboo, how to use the male bamboo for cooking-pots and so on, what grass is suitable for human consumption, what berries and plants and snakes and rodents we could eat, and if the worst came to the worst what type of tree bark would sustain us.

In October there were more promotions among the officers. Wingate and Brocklehurst were made colonels while Gardener and Lancaster were made up to captains. These sudden rises in rank had no effect on any of us, and we carried on with the jobs that we were given.

Towards the end of October there was, however, a rift between the two colonels about who was the senior. Brocklehurst had been an officer in the Royal Flying Corps, so even to us that made him the senior. This, we understood, upset Wingate, and he suddenly left. We heard rumours that Wavell had recalled him to New Delhi and put another officer in his place.

Things went on as normal without Wingate. 'Mike' Calvert was putting us through some very rigid exercises, and so were the two Chinese-language teachers.

Then, about the middle of November, we got measured for civilian clothes and also had our photographs taken – but we still could not find out why.

Chapter Two

To the Thai Frontier

It was a misty damp Monday morning, December 8th about eight thirty, as we emerged from our bamboo huts to make our way to breakfast. Someone somewhere shouted, 'The Japs have bombed Pearl Harbor!'

'Pearl Harbor?' I asked, 'Where the hell is that?'

'I don't know, but it means that the Yanks will be in the war with us now,' someone answered.

After a hurried breakfast and plenty of chatter we all gathered around one of the wireless sets that we had for communications. There we heard the President of the United States make his speech to the people of the USA, saying that they were at war with Japan.

Overnight the whole situation had changed. Instead of the utmost secrecy surrounding us, everything was now out in the open. We learned that the original intention was for us to go into China as civil advisers or technicians to assist the Chinese in the war against the Japanese in an effort to try to keep them a little more occupied in that area. With the altered situation we were told that we could proceed across the frontier in our own uniforms and trucks marked with the Union Jack flags. The Australian contingent who were also in training with us were the first to move out. They were destined for the Canton region as they had been learning Cantonese. It was well after Christmas when we moved to the southern Shan state of Burma to set up a base at a town called Taunggyi.

Things were really looking black for us. Hong Kong had fallen on Christmas Day, and the Japanese had swept down the Malay Peninsula. The battleships *Prince of Wales* and *Repulse* had been sunk by Japanese planes, and the 'impregnable' fortress of Singapore had fallen. The Japanese had also taken Indochina and were well into Thailand. Meanwhile, back in North Africa Rommel had taken Tobruk and was pushing up the desert towards Alexandria.

We left our heavy kit back at the school, and only carried necessities. Our lorries had been packed to capacity with all types of ammunition and explosives, and we moved into bamboo bungalows just outside the town of Taunggyi, where we made a supply base. After a couple of days' rest we set off in the lorries, leaving two men to look after the base, and headed in a southeasterly direction towards a small town called Kentaung. Here we rested for one night, then we

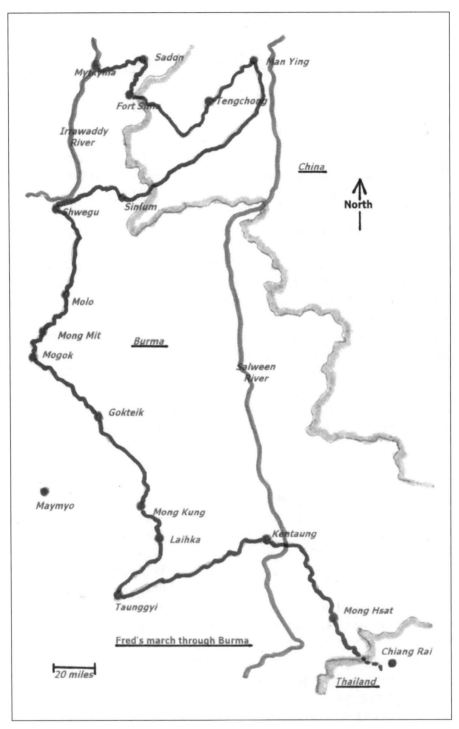

Fred's march through Burma.

travelled further southeast to a very small town called Mong Hsat. Here we had to leave the lorries, as the motor road ended. We picked up mules to carry our gear, and also bid farewell to Captain Gardener and his section, as they were moving on to the southern tip of Indochina.

From then on we were on foot, leaving behind another two men to make another supply base. We moved out of Mong Hsat with just enough supplies loaded on the mules. We marched until well into the afternoon before making camp for the night.

Around the camp fire and after our meal, the Colonel gave us our instructions for the following day. Beginning at dawn we were to split up into parties of five or six, with two Chinese muleteers and six mules. The parties were to set out at intervals of four hours. Our party consisted of Corporal Robert 'Jock' Johnson, Private Harry 'Ginger' Hancock, Private Thomas Morgan, Lance Corporal William Bland, and me. We were given a reference point on the map, marking an old Buddhist temple about sixty miles from the Thai border, which, without any mishap, should take three days of marching to reach. There we would all collect and wait for everyone to arrive. Our party was the third away, setting off at about two thirty in the afternoon.

We marched at a comfortable pace with the mules bringing up the rear. We took turns at going forward, having two men in front, one link man and two at the rear in close contact with the mules. It was left entirely up to Jock to call the halts, except when we made camp for the night. Then the two front men picked the best place where we could not only get water for cooking and cleaning, but at the same time be under cover.

Each one in the party knew where the rendezvous was, so that should anything happen, the others could carry on. We saw signs left by those ahead of us that told us that we were on the right track, but we did not always stop where they had made camp. In some instances we were a few hours ahead.

It was midday when we came to the Salween River. The only way across was by a large bamboo raft that would take three men with their gear plus one mule.

The raft was handled by two natives. One of them paddled until it was well into the current, while the other, on the opposite bank, pulled on a thick bamboo rope tied to the raft.

This was repeated about six times before all our kit and the mules were across. We did not hang around as we knew we could be spotted by any passing aircraft.

After leaving the river and being very pleased with ourselves at crossing without trouble, we camped deep into the thickest jungle, with the knowledge that we would, bar anything going wrong, reach the temple by noon the next day.

It was a little after that time that we were met by a couple of the men who had taken a quiet stroll out of the camp to meet us, 'just in case,' they said, 'we had suffered any casualties.'

We found on arrival at the temple that we had been most fortunate with our mules who had behaved very well in comparison to the other parties. We heard that some of the mules had just bolted at the river's edge off into the jungle, while others, once their loads were taken off, would not have them back on again. One mule flatly refused to go on the raft, so he and his handler were forced to swim the river.

Of the original fifty other ranks, we had now got three officers and twenty five men. We had left two at Taunggyi, two at Kentaung and two at Mong Hsat and, of course, Captain Gardener's section.

We rested for two whole days at the temple. Dawn was just breaking when we set off on the third day with two scouts in front and two men bringing up the rear.

At about four in the afternoon the two forward men reported some movement of what looked like uniformed troops. The column was halted. The colonel, Sergeant McAteer and two men went forward. It seemed that the colonel had expected this, as we had been told that some Chinese troops were being sent to this area.

After a short while the colonel and others returned. Under his orders we moved on for about another five miles before making camp. The colonel wanted no friction with the Chinese troops, as they had a reputation for stealing kit and equipment.

We broke camp the next day, and except for short stops marched for another two days until finally reaching our objective, which was no more than a spot on the map, just six miles from the Thai border.

Before making camp, the colonel had us unload all the mules, kept only six and sent the rest away with the muleteers.

We made the camp well and truly camouflaged from the air. We were within strolling distance of a beautiful clear running stream with wild peaches, bananas and other tropical fruits, and exotic tropical flowers growing all around it. It gave one the feeling of paradise. Had it not been for the job in hand it could well have been paradise, with the beautifully plumaged birds and the antics of the gibbon apes as they swung about in the trees to our amusement.

We then had two days of rest, lounging in the sun and swimming in the stream. On the third day, at about ten in the morning, the colonel called us all together. A sand table had been made with two large mounds, which represented hills. The colonel pointed out that these two hills were our objectives for an attack. 'We shall have to march six miles to the border,' he said, 'then about two more miles to get near enough to observe our targets, making our assault on them in the early hours of the morning. They are two gun emplacements that cover the whole of an escarpment and are manned by both Thai and Japanese troops. To get there well before dusk and get a good view, we must set out this afternoon.' He paused for a second, and then went on. 'There will be two parties. Captain Lancaster and Sergeant McAteer will take one, and Captain Brown and I will take the other. Sergeant Friend, you will stay with four men and guard this camp.'

I was in Captain Lancaster's party. Eight of us were told that we would be carrying the packs of prepared charges of fifty pounds of gelignite each, plus the instantaneous fuse and primer. The sergeant would be carrying the 'time pencils' which would act as detonators.

With two men out in front and the colonel leading the main party, we set off at a leisurely pace, but at the same time keeping on the alert for any danger.

The sun was well behind us, as we were travelling in an easterly direction. Our path took us up the side of a small mountain and along a grassy ridge, which led us onto a tree-covered plateau. Then after some distance we went down into a valley and up another hill. There we rested. The three officers and the sergeant went on forward further up the hill. After some time they returned and told us to go forward in fours, lending us two pairs of field glasses so that we could see for ourselves the targets.

Looking through the glasses we could see another range of hills. To the left, at ten o'clock, there was a large hump, and at two o'clock there was another. These were our targets. The whole of the range was covered with trees, while below was a rich green valley, the trees and scrub coming only part of the way down, thus giving the defenders a clear view of the whole of the valley and also the range of hills that we were on. With the aid of the glasses one could make out camouflaged earthworks through the trees on each of the humps.

The positioning of these emplacements had been well thought out, as they could cover the escarpment. We talked among ourselves as we returned to where the rest were waiting. When all had seen the targets we set off again, but with even more caution being taken.

Once again we halted. This time it was for the two parties to separate. Watches were synchronised. The time to move on to the targets was set for 2 am. The colonel led his team off. We had a little further to go to get opposite of our target. It had become quite dark when the captain called a halt. The order was given for no smoking and no talking. We lay in the cover of some trees, awaiting the order to move off.

A strong breeze had come up and was pulling at the trees, causing them to make a rustling sound. The night had become a little chilly, and we huddled closer together so as not to lose contact with each other. The wind was, I thought, in our favour. It would not only make the defenders keep their heads down, but also cover any noise we made as we approached.

It seemed no time that a whispered 'let's go!' came down the line of huddled men. The captain led the way over the crest of the ridge. Part of the way down we left Morgan, the Bren-gunner, and Scanes, his number two, to cover our withdrawal should we need it.

At the bottom of the hill and moving across the valley to the other side the signal was passed along to fan out. The captain and sergeant were in the centre with two pack men on either side of them, and on each flank was a Thompson machine gunner.

Slowly and steadily we began the steep climb, sometimes on the wet dewy grass. The heavy pack seemed to be trying to pull me back down the slope. We climbed for about two hundred yards before coming to the scraggy brush near the top. Here we halted, for in among the short brushwood, sticking out of the ground and pointed towards us, were shin-high spears of sharpened bamboo. Known as 'dragon's teeth,' these had not been visible through the glasses and were placed at intervals and not in any straight line. We therefore had to take more care how we went, as there may have been some sort of warning system attached to any one of them. As we picked our way through these spears we wondered if the other party were in the same predicament, as time was the major factor between success and failure. Should one discharge go off too soon, then the other party stood the chance of being detected before they had even got into position to set their own charges.

Everyone seemed to be making headway in their own time and method. At the top we all closed on to the centre to check that everyone was there.

Our target was about twenty feet in diameter and about eight feet high. It had a covering of brush and other material. From where we were, the nozzle of a gun was just visible. Above the noise of the wind in the trees we could make out voices some distance away.

The drill was for the four pack men to go two on each side and about six feet apart, dig into the mound about three feet from the ground, fit in the prepared charges and bring back the fuses to the sergeant, who would be waiting in front of the mound. He would then connect all the fuses together. Then, at the correct time, which was four o'clock, he would set the time pencil. This should set off all four charges at precisely the same instant. This again was in conjunction with the other party doing the same.

The sergeant gave me the signal to go, and I tapped Jock on my left. We both moved forward. As I neared the large black mound the voices became much clearer. They were slightly to our left and above. Jock came near to me. As we got under the mound he tapped me on the shoulder to let me know that he was moving further round.

The newly grown grass at the base of the mound was wet and quite cold. I slipped off the heavy pack and put it to one side. Then, on my knees, I marked out an area that would be large enough to take the prepared charge. I began to dig away at the earth with the small-handled trench tool. Luckily, underneath the first layer the earth was quite dry and fell away easily. When I thought that I had gone in deep enough, I took from the backpack the charge, which was in a sandbag, and pressed it into the cavity that I had made, then scooped up the dirt with my hands and pressed it in with the charge. All this time, although it was quite cold, I had broken out into a sweat. I smoothed over the dirt. With the fuse wire dangling, I picked up the now empty pack and my trench tool, and with the fuse wire slipping through my fingers returned to where the sergeant was sitting at the front of the mound waiting for us. After I handed over the fuse wire to him he waved me to go back to the shelter of the scrub. Jock was not long after me.

Waiting under cover in the low scrub it seemed hours before the sergeant joined us. Then the signal was given for us to make our way back down the slippery grass slope, avoiding the dreaded 'dragon's teeth'. We climbed back up to where we had left Morgan and Scanes, who gave a wave as we passed them. Then we all took cover among the trees behind the ridge. We were about to settle down to a well-earned rest at just before four o'clock when there was a terrific explosion, followed by some smaller bangs at our left. Then from where we had placed our charges came a large explosion followed again by some smaller ones. We looked towards both directions and could see two pink and red glows in the sky.

We jumped with joy and shook hands, congratulating each other on the night's work. It was the captain, although very pleased, who brought us back to reality and got us moving back along the trail towards the meeting point with the other party.

With some short rests we followed the same track back. It was beginning to get light. The enemy had by this time set up a number of mortars, for we could hear bombs exploding in rapid succession over on our ridge. Then, as the light improved, we heard the drone of aircraft coming in our direction. We lay perfectly still, not even looking up to see what sort they were. The planes dived and began strafing at something and dropping a couple of bombs. The mortars also renewed their attack near to where the planes had dived. Eventually the planes separated and went in opposite directions, flying low over the top of the trees, no doubt trying to spot us.

It was not until the aircraft were out of both sight and sound that we began to move. We had done very well in not having any casualties so far, but the main topic of conversation was how the other party had fared.

Sporadic mortar fire still continued, but none came near us, so we pushed on to where we were to meet up with the other party.

While we waited at the meeting point, the two aircraft returned from opposite directions and once more made sweeps over where we hid. After a time they flew away. By now it was about eight o'clock in the morning and the sun was well up in the sky. We must have waited at least an hour before the other party came along.

We were relieved to find that they, too, had no casualties, but from what they told us they had had one or two narrow escapes with both the mortars and the aircraft.

The colonel took charge and set off at a good pace, saying, 'We ought to get a good rest, and above all, a good hot meal inside us.' It was rather funny but the march back did not seem to take as long. There was much chatter and very few rests.

Back at the camp we found that they, too, had had to take precautions against being seen by aircraft, which had come very close and very low. However, the base team had managed to get a good meal ready for our return.

The next day until noon we spent cleaning our kit ready for the next mission. After our midday meal we were all called to sit in a half circle. The colonel gave us the outline of our next target. This was much further away and would take about three days to reach, so this time we were to take the mules to carry food and gear to do the job. Once again four men, including a sergeant, would be left to guard the camp. This meant that Sergeant McAteer would be staying behind.

My role along with five others was to be a muleteer. In the late afternoon we loaded up the six mules and set off in a northeasterly direction, following a track that ran almost parallel with the Thai border. We were going to march by night and rest and feed during the day until we had covered one hundred miles, make a camp, then from there make the assault on the target.

We had taken our second rest when the sun began to set behind the high mountain ridge to our left. In no time it seemed that a large blanket had been drawn across the sky. At times it seemed darker than normal as we passed beneath the thick and dense canopy of trees, shutting out even the stars. Then, just as soon, there would be a gap in the trees and there above us once more were the stars and clear sky. We were descending a hill as the grey light of dawn began to creep slowly over the high hills to the east. In the half-light we saw, spread out before us, a lush green valley dotted here and there with large clumps of bamboo and banana trees. As the light got better we could make out tall teak trees on the slopes of the hills beyond the valley, appearing almost black.

A small but fast-running stream cut through the floor of the valley, disappearing now and then as it passed between the clumps of bamboo and banana trees. It was the ideal place to make our camp. In one of the larger bamboo copses we secured the mules, taking them two at a time to water, while the others settled down. After eating, we slept. Everyone took turn at being on guard, even the officers.

I was woken up at about four in the afternoon. After freshening up in the stream and getting a meal we got on our way once more, again clearing up and hiding any sign that we had been there.

It was estimated that on our first night's march we had covered about thirty miles. So if we could maintain that, we should be near our destination by the morning of the fourth day. But as usual we met obstacles that were not foreseen. The second night we encountered some very rough country. This slowed us down quite a lot, besides having to cross a river that was more difficult than we had imagined, especially in the dark.

The third night was much the same, except instead of a river it was a village. We had to make a detour of some miles. Because of these delays we did not reach our destination until after midday of the fourth day.

We made camp in a well-covered area, and with fresh water and plenty of wild fruit around cooking was kept down to a minimum. Only water for tea was heated. Food was from tins.

We rested there all that day and night. At about nine in the morning the colonel informed us of the coming operation. He told us that the target was still a good distance away and that he, Captain Lancaster and Sergeant Friend would go and reconnoitre the ground, and that they might be away for about twenty-four hours. They wanted to know exactly how long it would take to get to the target and observe it.

They set off at three o'clock in the afternoon. All three were armed with Thompson submachine guns and a few hand grenades. We carried on our usual duties, looking after the mules and so on, but keeping on the alert at all times and keeping under cover as much as possible.

It was almost twenty-four hours later when we were alerted by one of the lookouts that someone was coming towards the camp. It was the two officers and Sergeant Friend.

The colonel told us that the next morning we would load two of the mules. Lance Corporal Homans and I were picked to go with the animals. The idea was to load the mules with what gear was required, go most of the way, then leave us two with the mules while the demolition party went on to the target.

We set off at noon, leaving three men with the rest of the mules and equipment that was not needed. We marched until it became dark. We settled down in the thick jungle, but one could hardly call it resting, for we seemed to have camped in a place that was infested with all types of insects, and quite a number of wild animals came sniffing around.

We were up and awake early. The jungle was quite damp and cold with a heavy mist covering the trees. It was suggested that we move further on to a more comfortable place. This we found after about a quarter of a mile of marching. Here the others made preparations to go forward, while Homans and I busied ourselves with brushing the mules down with handfuls of the stiff grass that grew around.

The party set off with all their gear just after midday. The mist had by this time cleared and the sun was at its hottest. Homans and I kept close to the mules, mostly to keep them quiet in case anyone should come into the area. We took it in turns to keep watch for both unwelcome humans and also any animals that got the scent of the mules. We armed ourselves with long forked sticks to defend the mules, as we dared not use our rifles for fear of alerting the enemy.

It seemed ages and ages before dusk began to fall, and time seemed to drag even more. The sun had gone down, and darkness had closed in upon us. The mules began to get a little restless. We both had to stand at their heads giving them a reassuring stroke and pat, but they continued to shake their heads and stamp their feet. Whatever it was that was unsettling them, neither I nor Homans could see or hear.

It had been dark for quite some time. Not having a timepiece between us, we had lost all knowledge of what the hour was. With our time being spent calming the mules, I think that I must have dozed off. I had one arm over the shoulder of the mule and was holding the stick in the other hand. Suddenly the night came alive with the noise of gun fire. First there came the rat–tat–tat of automatics, then some smaller bangs, followed closely by some rapid louder bangs, then more automatic firing. From where we were it seemed that our party had run into some opposition and was having to fight their way out.

The firing continued, together with the crump–crump–crump of either artillery or large mortars, which we already knew the Japanese used to good effect. The noise of the firing kept on for what seemed hours to us, and yet perhaps it may have been only one or two hours. We both thought that it was about three in the morning. As we had not been included in the operation we had no idea at what time the attack was to begin. Neither did we know how far the party had had to travel after they left us. Here again we could only judge from the sound and make a guess that they were about three miles away. But even then, with the sound carrying over the trees, it could have been more. So we reckoned that without accident and no hold-ups, they should be back in about an hour and a half or perhaps less.

Homans and I were pacing around, looking and listening for any noise that would tell us that they were coming. As the light began to tell us of the approach of dawn over to the east we heard the slow drone of aero engines. We kept well under cover and kept hold of the bridles of the mules. I had my rifle slung across my back, but Homans and I were concerned about not giving our position away more than anything else.

The planes swooped down with all guns blazing away at some distant target that we could not see. We did see, however, that this time there were three planes. They turned in small circles, going over the same area, and also dropped a number of bombs again and again. They swooped low, strafing at something.

Homans and I looked at each other. We both must have felt the same. What could we do? We both stood there helplessly. Then, just as suddenly as it had begun, it ceased, except for the slow drone of the planes as they flew away into the distance. All we could hear was the chattering of the monkeys and the twittering of the birds as they seemed to be protesting at the noise that had disturbed them. Both Homans and I were discussing whether we should go out to try to find our friends or stay put as we had been told to. They might return by a different route. We were still talking when we heard a shout. 'Bring the mules, bring the mules!' It was Jock Johnson. We recognised the Scots accent. Then he appeared out of the trees and came towards us. 'Quick! Follow me!' he said breathlessly, as if he had run for a few miles. 'We got caught as we were going in', he panted out, gasping for breath. Quickly getting the mules, we followed Jock. We were almost running as we tried to push our way through the thick jungle. We were not following any track, but Jock had marked a tree here and there, as well as treading down the undergrowth. We were forced to stop for a short while to give Jock a chance to get his breath. We asked him to ride one of the mules, but he refused, stating that it was not too far now. Two more of our men came to meet us. They told Homans and me to carry on while they and Jock went back the way we had come.

Some hundred or so yards further on we came upon the rest of the group. The colonel came to us and said, 'We have four casualties. Two are able to walk, but the other two are in too bad a shape. So, we shall have to do the best we can, but,' he continued, 'I want to get away from here as soon as we can before those dammed planes return.'

The walking wounded had gone on with a couple of others, while the rest of us made two cradles out of bamboo and fitted them onto the mules. After making the wounded men as comfortable as we could, we set off at a steady pace.

A number of times the sound of aircraft came to our ears, and we made sure that we were always under cover. When we reached the three men whom we had left to look after the other mules, we wasted no time to push on. The colonel decided that this time we would not avoid the village, but make use of what assistance we could get from there, both for food and to be able to dress and make the wounded more comfortable.

From what the men told us during the march back and in between rest stops, they had not only come across the 'dragon's teeth' but had also triggered some kind of anti–personnel detonators that were threaded with twine connected to the bamboo spikes. This had signalled exactly where they were, so with guns set on fixed lines in any position they were almost sitting-ducks. They had not had a chance to lay any charges. All they could do was return fire and throw grenades as they withdrew, using the darkness as cover. The mortars had done the most damage. Once again, the aircraft were well off target.

At the village we were treated very well, as they had no idea who we were, or where we had come from. The colonel gave them money to make litters for the wounded men to be carried back to our base camp.

On arriving at the base camp we rested with the wounded for one night, then transported them again on the litters to Mong Hsat. There they would be transferred to motor transport and back to Taunggyi and into hospital. We had quite a bit of air activity in our area which came very close at times, but none of the planes were ours.

As we were completely cut off from any radio and the outside world, we knew nothing of what was going on elsewhere.

It was about the third day after the wounded had gone that an Indian of a mounted regiment rode into our camp. He had brought an urgent message for the colonel. We invited him to have some tea and any food he wanted, but he only took the tea as he was a Sikh and a vegetarian. He then told us that he had met up with the wounded and their escort and that was how he had managed to find us as quickly as he had. Then came the most surprising news. 'Rangoon had fallen some days ago,' he told us in the lilting way that Indians have of speaking English. He went on to say that the Japanese were pushing northwards towards Pegu and the oil wells at Prome. This meant that we were almost behind the Japanese forward troops. Should the Japanese decide to come over the Thai border we would be really in trouble!

Chapter Three

The Bombing of Taunggyi

The colonel did not have to give us a speech. We knew what we had to do, and we did it fast. Luckily we had the six mules, so things that could be loaded on the mules were loaded and everything else was destroyed. Less than two hours after receiving the bad news we had begun our return journey to Mong Hsat. We reached the temple on the morning of the third day. We made a meal and rested until noon, and then we pushed on towards the Salween River, which we crossed without any trouble. It was now a day and a half's journey to Mong Hsat. There we met up with those we had left behind. They looked at us in amazement, for none of us had shaved since we had left them. Some of us had a really good growth of beard. Ginger Hancock was more noticeable than any of us, for his beard was of almost deep red.

Motor transport had been arranged for us to move out as soon as we were ready. The small town was in utter confusion, and refugees, most of them Chinese, were pouring in from all directions. The fear of what might happen to them showed in their faces. As we walked along the dusty main road towards where our lorries waited, they tugged at our clothes and begged us to help them in some way. There were old men and women and young women, some with four or more young children, all trying to carry what belongings they had managed to grab in the rush to get away from their hated old enemy. Some had hand carts, some bullock carts, and some bicycles with their belongings strapped on the back, but most were walking.

Our transport consisted of five three-ton trucks, civilian Fords that had been commandeered by an army major who was stationed in the district. We piled our gear into them and set off northwards. At first we made very little progress because the road was jammed with refugees. We must have gone barely ten miles when the noise of aircraft was heard. The refugees scattered in all directions. Our convoy pulled off the road and into the cover of the trees. We had our guns ready as the aircraft swept down the road strafing at anything. They turned and came down again. We opened up with everything we had. Some of the refugees had not even made it to the trees and were falling like ninepins, screaming and shouting, both in fear and in pain.

Small children sat screaming by their injured or dead mothers. Others were walking around crying and looking for someone to comfort them, but there was no one.

We had little time to consider as the planes swept down again, one after the other, blazing away with all that they had while we hammered back at them. Finally the planes flew off. We had a roll call. We did not have one casualty, and yet there were dead and wounded all around us, young and old shattered to pieces. Some were hardly recognisable as human beings, as they had caught the full fury of the attack. We could do nothing but sympathise.

The colonel got the trucks on the move once more. The road remained a little clear for a time until the shock had worn off, then once again became choked. However, we had made some headway and made it to Kentaung just as darkness was approaching. Here again was panic and confusion. We did not stay long, just long enough to pick up some of the base gear and the men that we had left there. Then we were on our way back to our main base at Taunggyi.

The moon had set and the sky was a little darker, although the stars in the clear sky were doing their best to give some light.

We rumbled into the sleepy town at about two o'clock in the morning. Here there was no panic at all. There were even lights on in some of the buildings and huts. It seemed just the same as when we had left it. How long ago was it? It seemed ages.

A hot meal was waiting, and it was not long before we were hitting the sack, as we had had a really rough time in the last few days. It was very nice to get a hot bath and shave off our beards, and also clean our guns and equipment and be ready for any action that would be required of us.

We were really taking things easy. We had been back in Taunggyi for two whole days and had made good use of the rest. It was Thursday and market day in the town. We were doing our usual tasks and the time was about ten o'clock in the morning when we heard the dull drone of aircraft engines at a very high altitude which caused everyone to look up. 'Air Raid, Air Raid!' someone somewhere shouted out loud enough for us all to hear. We made for our slit trenches well away from where we had stored our demolition and explosives. The drone of the engines came nearer and nearer until they were right overhead. Looking up we could make out a formation of eight bombers.

Suddenly there was the scream of falling bombs. They fell right across the small town. There had been no warning signal and no anti–aircraft fire. From where we were we could hear the screams and wailing of people who had been injured in the crowded market place. We watched as the planes turned, keeping in formation and still keeping their altitude. Once again there was a scream of falling bombs onto the small town. The planes then turned and went off towards the east.

We clambered out of the trenches, stood there for a while and saw a pall of black smoke and dust rising from the direction of the town. Then the siren sounded the all clear, as if to mock what had taken place.

Together we all raced down the hill towards the town. Halfway down we came upon a Gurkha soldier lying by the side of the road. Being able to speak Urdu, I asked him, 'Kia bart hai?'

'Idder, idder', he answered, pointing to his thigh.

Sergeant McAteer had followed us down the hill. 'Stay here with him', he said, 'there must be a stack of other injured like him,' then ran back up the hill.

In what seemed no time the sergeant came back with a lorry he had commandeered. It had been delivering foodstuff. We had dressed the Gurkha's wound with field dressings, and carefully lifted him on to the lorry.

As we turned onto the main road Scanes, who was driving, suddenly stopped the vehicle and jumped out of the cab. Two of us followed him to where a man was sitting beside a small Ford saloon car on the grass verge. He looked as if he was asleep. Scanes tapped him on the shoulder, and as he did so the man fell sideways. He was dead. In the centre of his forehead was a small jagged hole, but what was remarkable was that the windscreen of the car had also got a hole in it, right opposite the driver's seat. From the hole, cracks were going in all directions like long spider's legs. The man must have subconsciously got out from the car before he died.

We left him and went looking for those who needed help. We had not gone far before we had almost twenty very bad cases on board. Some way into the town we stopped in front of a large woman dressed in the usual black garb of the Shan women. In her arms was a young girl of about ten years old. The woman was sobbing and swaying from side to side. The child was lying still and looked very pale. Down the front of the woman's black robe was a stream of blood running into a pool at her feet. Quickly Jock Johnson and I went to her and took the child and laid her on the ground. We saw that the artery in the child's wrist had been severed by a fragment from a bomb. The artery was still flowing blood. Jock squeezed the girl's arm and stopped the bleeding while I made a tourniquet with a strip of the woman's black cloth and twisted it tight by using the handle of my knife. We handed the child up to Morgan who cradled her with utmost affection and gentleness, and tears could be seen in his eyes.

Jock shouted to Scanes to get to the nearest hospital as soon as we could, which was the military hospital. Scanes drove straight up to the door and steps of the veranda. There we were met by a nurse who, without looking at any wounded, said, 'Take them away from here! We only accept military casualties.'

'But Sister,' we pleaded, 'we have a young girl here who has lost quite a great deal of blood. She is a very urgent case.'

'I'm very sorry for that,' she answered, 'but I have my orders.' She then waved her arms for us to go.

We dropped off the Gurkha, who was the only military casualty we had. Then Scanes turned the lorry around, went down the drive and turned to the right and up the road to the civil hospital which was about another quarter of a mile.

Here there was utter chaos. People of all races and religions had made their way here. Some had died in the attempt and just lay on the grass at the side of the driveway. Others had made it to the steps of the wooden veranda and died there. The veranda leading to the main ward was littered with wounded men, women and children. Blood from at least two hundred was oozing onto the wooden veranda and seeping through onto the earth beneath.

The lorry pulled up in front of the main doorway, and for a brief moment we, who had seen much blood and wounded in different spheres, stopped and looked down on that pitiful scene.

Someone shouted, 'Come on lads, let's get cracking!' We jumped from the lorry and some began helping those we had brought from the truck, while some of the others and I went inside to offer our help. In the meantime another truckload of casualties had been brought in by some more of our chaps. With them was Sergeant McAteer who began to organise us into sections under the guidance of the matron, who was a half-caste woman.

We, that is our section consisting of Morgan, Bland, Hancock, Edwards and myself, began cleaning and dressing the worst cases who were on the veranda, trying to stop the loss of blood. We also took part in being stretcher-bearers and getting those that could not walk off the veranda into the wards.

Casualties seemed to arrive as quickly as we got rid of them, but we seemed to be coping and making room. There were not enough beds, so we had to make do with laying them in between beds on the floor.

The colonel came along with the other officers and some of the civil officials who, to us, did not seem to be too put out at the misery and the suffering that was happening in front of their eyes. The colonel showed more compassion by saying, 'Carry on lads, you are doing a grand job.' Then they drove off and left us to it.

It was rather funny, I thought. How many times throughout my army career, which was nearly seven years, had I worked among squaddies and heard them moan because they had not had a bite to eat, or a drink of tea, or even time to have a smoke? Yet here were about thirty hardcore blokes, who had not had a bite to eat or a drink of tea since eight o'clock in the morning, and it was now coming up to about three in the afternoon and not one had moaned.

It was well after six in the evening before things began to quieten down. Some of the men had been asked to get the dead to the mortuary, as there was the fear that prowling jackals would feed upon the corpses if they were left out on the streets.

As they brought in the dead, Morgan and I stood at the side and counted them. Among those from the hospital was the young girl. She had not recovered from the loss of blood. The trucks searched the roads and the back streets of the town, which was now almost deserted. How many more dead lay in the jungle to be eaten by either jackals and hyenas or vultures which were surely waiting their chance to pick the bones of the unfortunate victims of the indiscriminate bombing by the Japanese?

Sergeant McAteer came and asked for volunteers to do night orderly duty. I think everyone wanted to do it. So he picked out four to return at ten o'clock. Morgan, Bland, Ginger and I were to stay until those four came on at ten. We carried on doing minor dressings and helping to clean the place up a little. We had paired off. Ginger was with me on the women's wards.

We were asked by the matron to bring a Chinese woman to the theatre for a foot amputation. Bland and Morgan were standing outside the operating room when Ginger and I came out after taking the woman in and putting her on the table. I turned to the others and said, 'I have never seen an operation performed, have any of you?'

'No!' they replied almost together.

'Well, now's our chance,' I said. We quietly walked into the room and stood behind a waist-high screen that was there for students to watch. I leaned over to whisper in Morgan's ear. 'They say that the first time you see anything like this you may pass out.' He glanced sideways at me and gave me a sickly grin, then nodded his head.

From where we stood we could see the surgeon cutting the flesh from around the shin bone about halfway from the knee. The matron standing on his right handed him a bright shiny stainless-steel saw. As he took it he blocked my view, and then all that I could hear was the teeth of the saw as it dug into the bone.

In that instant the room began to spin like a top. I felt my knees go weak, and then everything went blank. I came to outside the room, with Morgan, Ginger and Bland pouring water on my face and slapping me. Morgan with his usual red face and beaming wide grin asked, 'What happened, Fred?'

'It was that saw,' I said, shaking my head to clear the dizziness, 'it must have grated on my teeth.' We all laughed! 'I'm going back in there,' I continued, 'it's not going to beat me!' They tried to persuade me not to go, but I went in.

Just as I entered, the matron dropped the half limb into an enamelled bucket and, turning to me, said, 'Take that outside, will you please.' I picked up the bucket and went out to where Bland and Morgan were having a smoke.

'Where do I put this?' I asked. They both looked down into the bucket, and the colour drained from their faces. Both fell to the floor together. Ginger came outside, and seeing what had happened burst out laughing. He took the bucket from me and I returned inside to watch as they stitched the skin around the stump and then dressed it. Ginger and I then took the woman back to the ward. While she was still unconscious we placed a pillow under the bandaged stump.

The four for the night shift came on and we told the matron that we would return sometime after breakfast the next day, if we were allowed.

News was coming to us that the Japanese were making a real push up the country, so the colonel gathered us together to tell us that whatever job we were doing at the hospital or anywhere else, we were to drop it and return to our real function, that of fighting men and not hospital orderlies or anything else. We said that we understood.

We four went to the hospital that morning but stayed only a short while as we were picked for night duty.

Morgan and I went down there early to find out what the matron wished us to do. Ginger and Bland came a little later. Darkness was falling when the matron wished us goodnight. Morgan and I did the first of the rounds, going to every ward. Morgan carried a hurricane lamp, as there were no lights.

We had made the operating theatre our headquarters or meeting place, to sit and talk. When we returned, Ginger and Bland called us out onto the veranda. There were, they said, a couple of fires that had started just outside the town. We looked and could see the pink glow in the sky. As we watched, two more started, one at each point of the compass. Then to our ears came the sound of planes, and we knew what the fires had been lit for.

We all split up and went to the darkened wards. The patients had heard the approach of the aircraft and had begun to get panicky. Fumbling my way around the beds I tried to keep them quiet with some words of comfort which most of them could not understand anyway. It was the women who took the most consoling and trying to tell them that they were safe. The bombs were now falling, it seemed, all around the hospital, and creating a terrific noise as they exploded. The raid lasted about ten minutes, although it seemed longer.

The matron came to see if there was any damage done after the aircraft had gone. Being a very strict and stern woman, she soon had the women quiet and back to normal. She was a large-built woman with jet-black hair and black wide eyes. Her hair was done up in a bun at the back of her head. It was hard to judge her age but we reckoned that she was about thirty or perhaps a little older. She was quite good looking in some sort of way, although not too attractive because of her large size. After a while she left us, and we sat in the operating room and drank tea, two of us going off at intervals to see that all was well.

At about half past eight the next morning the matron came. Before we left to return to our billets, she asked, 'Would you lads like to come to my house for dinner tonight?'

'Yes please!' we all answered together.

'Right, then I'll see you at about eight. Oh, you do know where I live, don't you?' she asked smiling. She pointed her finger directly opposite the hospital. 'It's over there. I'm sure you will find it.'

We returned to our bamboo hut and settled down to sleep after we had eaten. We slept through till tea time which was about five in the evening. All of us took a shower after eating, and then began to get spruced up for our dinner date. It was about seven thirty that we set off towards the hospital. We did not hurry for we did not want to be there too early, as no doubt the matron would have quite a lot to do before she could leave the hospital. It was a good twenty minutes' walk. We arrived at the house, which was illuminated with candles and small oil lamps, and the matron met us at the door. She had arrived just before us. To our complete surprise, some of our mates were already there. They were as surprised as us, but, like us, they had said nothing to anyone else. Others were arriving after us, and this caused a little bit of chatter among us, calling each other 'crafty so and so's.'

Eventually the room was quite full of us men. The matron was the only woman, except for the Shan servant woman who had prepared the meal. We were invited to sit at the table. This was set for ten, but there were more than ten in that room.

Suddenly there was a loud banging at the door, and Captain Brown pushed his way inside, followed by Sergeant McAteer. 'Come on! All of you outside!' they shouted, 'come on, duty calls.' We all trooped out wondering what had happened.

As we piled into a truck they had brought to collect us we could see the red glow of fires in the sky. As we moved off, another fire blazed up on the outskirts of the town. The sergeant who was driving turned in the direction of where the new blaze had started.

Driving the vehicle at top speed the sergeant swung the truck first right then left as he negotiated the bends in the road, then turned the truck up the first road that ran at right angles to the fire. As we turned a bend in the road another fire was just showing above the trees. The sergeant made directly for this fire. It was a bamboo bungalow that was on fire. Some of the people there were trying to put it out. We jumped from the truck, and Captain Brown ordered us to split up into fours and scout around for any suspicious characters who may be responsible. The only arms that we had with us were our knives. Morgan, Ginger Hancock, Jock Johnson and I were now right on the outskirts of the town and soon in among the shops and wooden buildings.

We all stood still as we heard the drone of planes coming nearer. In no time at all we seemed to be right in the middle of falling bombs exploding all around. I dived into a deep ditch to take cover from the burst of explosives and flying shrapnel. Crawling along the bottom of the ditch, I waited until the planes had gone. Then, crawling out, I searched for my companions. I stood still and in silence, waiting for them to shout. I was about to cup my hands together to call to them when a man appeared as if from nowhere. He darted in and out between the wooden buildings into a lane on the other side of the houses. Now and then he stopped as if he were listening. I followed as quietly as I could, hiding behind the houses whenever he stopped. He was not going fast, and I could hear the pit-a-pat of his feet on the hard ground. Suddenly he vanished, and instead of a pit-a-pat of running feet I could hear the crunch of more than one pair of army boots. Coming towards me were two men of the King's Own Yorkshire Light Infantry, or KOYLI. They wore arm bands of the Regimental Police.

'Hallo Corporal!' they called out, 'what are you doing here?'

I answered them with a question. 'Have you seen a Burmese passing you two?'

'No Corp, we haven't. Are you chasing one?'

'Yes,' I replied, 'and he isn't very far away, either.'

They were armed with Lee-Enfield rifles. 'Come on then', they said eagerly, 'we'll have a look around.'

As we turned to go back to where I had last seen the man there was some movement in the shrubs at the side of the lane. The three of us dived through the hedge, and there squatting down was the man I had been following.

The two MPs began questioning him in Burmese after bringing him back onto the road. One of the MPs told me that he said he had gone there to relieve himself so, leaving one MP to guard him, the other MP and I went back to where he had been. Squatting and striking a number of matches to give us light we searched to find any excreta, but could find nothing. Going back to the man the MPs questioned him further, asking where he had come from. The man pointed towards some buildings on the right hand side of the road. The MP who was doing the questioning told us that the man had said he lived with his uncle on that side of the road. So we escorted him back to show us where his uncle lived. The man pointed to a wooden house high up on stilts. 'Alright,' I said, 'go on up!' I pushed him up the stairs which led to the doorway. There was a chink of light coming through a crack in the door. I rattled on the door and waited with the man by my side and the two MPs behind him. I could hear some whispering going on inside, and the door slowly opened just a little, enough for an old man to poke his head out. He held an oil lamp high above his head. He was a Chinese. Here I put my Chinese to the test, greeting him with 'Nee how'. At the same time I pulled our suspect forward into the light of the lamp so that the old man could get a good look at his face. 'Nee jour dow shur nager wren?' ('Do you know this man?') I demanded.

'Wor boo jour dow shur nager wren,' ('I do not know that man') was his answer.

I turned to the two MPs and said, 'That's good enough for me.' After thanking the old man we pushed our suspect down the steps.

'We'll take him back to our CO and let him deal with him,' I said to the two MPs, and they agreed. As we escorted the man along the road a large car pulled up. An officer poked his head out of the window and asked if we needed any help. 'Yes sir!' I answered. 'We think we have got one of the firebugs here sir, and we are going to take him back to my CO.'

'Get in the back, all of you and we will drive you there,' he ordered. There was another officer in the front passenger seat. He asked, 'Who is your CO, Corporal?'

'Colonel Brocklehurst, sir,' I answered. 'Do you know him, sir?'

'Yes, we both know him very well,' he replied, turning his head towards me. The driver introduced himself as Captain Thompson and his passenger as Captain King. On the drive I explained why we were bringing the man in.

Both officers agreed without any hesitation that the suspect was a possible arsonist who had set fires to guide the Japanese bombers. We were driven into the main police station. There we all got out of the car. Our CO was outside, talking to a rather large fellow in uniform. We marched the suspect over to them. They asked, 'What have you got here, Corporal?' Once again I related what had transpired, adding that we three thought it worthwhile to bring the man back for questioning.

'You did quite right, lads,' said the colonel. 'We'll soon find out if he is a firebug or not.' The large man stepped forward, and then I saw that he was the

Chief of Police. Immediately he began to ask the suspect rapid questions in Burmese. The suspect was getting nervous and began to look around him for a way of escape.

The police chief stopped his questioning, then turned to the colonel and said, 'He is one, alright.'

The colonel turned towards the two KOYLI and said, 'Take him away and shoot him.'

The two men stepped forward to grab him, but he made a sudden dash past them. I chased after him and got near enough to grab the long flowing black hair on his head. He stopped and I ran into him. He turned around and got his hands around my throat. Without a second thought my hand went to my knife and drew it and plunged it into his side, below the ribs, while I still held his hair with my other hand, pulling his head back away from me. Suddenly he went limp, and the whole weight of him fell against me, forcing me to take a step backwards. It was then that two red-turbaned policemen came and held him as he slipped slowly to the ground. They dragged him back into the station building.

The whole episode had not taken more than a few minutes. I walked back to the group of officers and men. The colonel said, 'Well, let's hope that it is the end of a night's work. I think we can stand down now.'

'Can I give anyone a lift?' Captain Thompson asked.

'Could you drop me near the civil hospital, sir?' I asked.

'Jump in, Corporal,' he replied, 'We'll soon have you there.'

The car halted right at the entrance to the matron's quarters. I wished the officers goodnight, and then knocked on the door loudly, for there was the noise of a piano playing and some singing going on. The door opened, and as I stepped into the room I had to shield my eyes from the bright lights. Suddenly a deadly hush fell on the room. Everyone was staring at me, especially my clothes. I looked down and saw that my trousers and parts of my tunic were saturated in blood.

'Blimey! Fred! What have you done?' they all seemed to ask in one voice. The matron and her servant came forward and began to sponge me down in an attempt to remove some of the crimson stains while I related what had taken place.

'So, you reckon you caught one of those bastards then, Fred?' Scanes asked.

'I think so,' I replied, 'or why should he try to run away.' I sat down and ate the food that had been saved for me. It seemed that I was the last to return.

The next day, all those available were detailed to help with the evacuation of the military hospital. Most of the equipment had already gone. It was mostly bedding and the iron bedsteads. Lorries had been commandeered. Morgan, Bland, Ginger Hancock and I had this job. Morgan, Bland and I were having a rest while we waited for some of the lorries to return from the railway station, when up strode the colonel. 'Come here, lads,' he beckoned us towards him. We stood in front of him in a half circle. 'Have you three got any strong beliefs about religion?' He eyed each one of us.

We stood silent for a moment, taken aback by the question. Then one after another we answered, 'No, sir!' At the same time a grin had come to all our faces, wondering what the next question was going to be.

'Well lads,' he paused before going on, 'I am going to ask you,' and he emphasised the word 'ask', 'not order you, and you can refuse if you wish, to do a very unpleasant job for me, a most unpleasant job.' He paused as if he wanted his words to sink in. 'I shall not hold it against any one of you if you say you don't want to do it. Is that clear to all of you?'

'Yes sir, we understand,' we answered.

He turned and asked us to follow him. He led us to his car and told us to get in, and then drove us down the road to the civil hospital. He turned into the drive and stopped the car at the rear of the wards. Here we all got out. We followed the colonel towards the small brick-built mortuary. Just before we got to the double doors he halted, turned and faced us. 'What I want you to do, and you can still refuse if you wish to, is to get all the corpses out of there, get them onto a lorry, then take them out of town to a place for burning.'

None of us had had any reason to go to the morgue since the first day of the bombing. We knew then that there were about eighty bodies stacked inside, but since then many more had been taken in. The mortuary was a small brick building, about twelve feet long and eight feet wide, with six-foot high walls. It had a steep sloping roof and no windows, the only ventilation being through the double doors. Drawn up in front of the entrance was a three-ton civilian lorry with its tailboard down. The colonel moved forward to the doors. We three followed him. He turned the handles of the double doors and pulled them open. For a moment we all stood still, as the stench from the rotting bodies hit us full in the face and made us step back a few steps. Slowly we went inside, trying to hold our breath against the deathly smell that enveloped us. The sight was appalling. The bodies had been chucked in an untidy heap, so there was hardly any room to move. Rigor mortis had also made them into horridly contortioned shapes, with legs and arms twisted in different positions.

The colonel was the first to break the silence. 'Will you lads do it for me?' With hardly any hesitation from any of us we all said that we would.

Morgan boarded the lorry, while Bland and I, with handkerchiefs around our noses and mouths, went inside and began to carry the corpses out to Morgan, who dragged them into some form of order on the lorry. Now and again one of us had to clamber onto the lorry to help Morgan pile them on top of each other.

We had counted thirty when the colonel said that was enough for one load. The driver of the lorry had all this time stood well away. He was an Indian, of what caste or religion we had no idea, but when the colonel tried to call him to drive the lorry he shook his head and flatly refused even to come near. 'One of us will drive it, sir!' Bland said.

'No, lads,' the colonel replied, 'I want you three on the back, just in case there is any trouble as we go through the town.'

'Shall I try to talk to him, sir?' I volunteered. 'I do speak a little of their lingo, sir.'

'Alright Corporal, do your best,' the colonel said.

I walked to where the driver stood. 'Kia-toom-ou-gay?' I pleaded.

'Nay-sahib,' the driver answered, shaking his head and looking down at the ground, moving from one foot to the other like a frightened schoolboy.

Spreading my hands in front of me to emphasise my words, I said in a more pleading voice, 'Esco-hath-mutt-lee-gow. ('You don't have to touch them') Toom-driver-bust!' I went on, 'Hum-keerin gay!' ('We will do it, you only drive').

For a moment he stood and thought, then with a nervous grin he said, 'Teek-hai-sahib.' Patting him gently on the back we walked back to the others.

'Well done, Corporal!' The colonel shouted, clapping his hands. 'Now, follow me!'

During the daylight hours many of the inhabitants returned to the town and some of the shops were open, so the colonel made a detour trying to avoid the built-up areas as much as possible, but here and there quite a number of people were still coming along the roads. At first they just stood and stared, then as we got near to them and they realised what our cargo consisted of they turned their backs on us and the women covered their heads and faces.

The colonel led us in his car to the western side of the town and about two miles out until we came to a large refuse dumping pit. Here we stopped, and no sooner had we done so than our driver ran for his life and hid behind some trees about a hundred yards away.

We three were only too glad to climb down and get clear for a while from the horrible stink that was coming from the dead bodies.

From the colonel's car came a nurse, the police chief who had questioned the fire-raiser, the colonel and another man dressed in a white suit. The four came towards where we had stood. 'I want you to put the bodies down into that pit,' the colonel said more as a request than an order.

'Are you going to burn them, sir?' Morgan asked.

'That is our intention,' the colonel answered. 'We shall soak them in petrol and set fire to them,' he added hesitantly.

We had finished putting all the bodies into the pit. The colonel came and gave us each a cigarette, but the stench from my hands after handling the corpses made me want to vomit. I glanced at the other two and they had both turned a shade of green.

We returned to the pit with another load, using the same route. These were even more ghastly for they were from the first bombing raid and had been dead longer. It was nearing noon when we began unloading. The sun was beating down, making us sweat, and the smell of our sweat seemed to mingle with the stench from the corpses, which were harder to handle and carry because of the different postures to which rigor mortis had stiffened them. My sweat-soaked clothes also seemed to be absorbing the stench that arose as we disturbed the now blackening and rotting corpses. The flies had also been at work on them, clustering around the dried blood of the wide open wounds.

Morgan went to the matron as we began our third load. He came back with three gauze face-masks saturated with some chemical. These were of great help and an improvement on our handkerchiefs, but still not good enough to stop the smell from getting up our noses.

We had got about twenty onto the lorry when Bland came running out of the building shouting, 'Fred! Fred! There's one alive in there!' He pointed towards the mortuary. Morgan and I jumped from the lorry and dashed inside the mortuary.

'Where?' I called to Bland who stood outside.

'There!' he pointed to a body, 'can't you see him breathing?'

Morgan and I went closer. There was movement under the blood-stained shirt. We both went and lifted the shirt, and then we could see that a large gaping wound in the man's chest was a mass of moving yellow maggots. The sight made all three of us vomit into our face masks. I staggered to the door pulling at my own mask. Morgan was beside me leaning on the side of the lorry with his head cradled in his arms. Bland was not so bad. He rushed off and returned with the matron, who brought us a large jug of sweet tea.

The three gruesome loads had emptied the small mortuary. When the last body was dumped into the pit we were more than relieved that the horrible task was finished. The colonel came to thank us, and gave us the rest of his cigarettes.

On our return to the billet some of the men greeted us with, 'Hello! You three are in some trouble. Sergeant Friend wants to know where you have been.' Then without giving us a chance to explain, they went on to say, 'We came back from the station and had to do your dirty work.'

'Wait a minute! Wait a minute.' I said, putting up my hands to stop any more outbursts. 'Listen to our story before you say anything about dirty work.'

I went on to tell them the whole sordid story. They listened intently to what I had to say, with Bland and Morgan speaking now and then and adding to the story.

When we had finished they were all apologies. Bob Sharp said, 'Hey! That will shoot Friend up the jacksy, won't it, when he comes to tear you off a strip?'

Ginger suggested that we all keep quiet and let Friend rant at us before we told him. Everyone was in favour of this and started to have a good laugh even beforehand.

It was after tea when Sergeant Friend came. 'I want to see you,' he said. He pointed at me and glared, his face going red with temper. He then pointed at Bland and Morgan and shouted, 'And you and you.'

'Yes, Sergeant,' I said in as calm and quiet voice as I could, and looking a bit surprised.

'I want to know,' he blurted out, 'where you three have been all bloody morning. In fact, where have you been all bloody day?' He stood staring at each one of us in turn, his legs astride and his hands on hips. Behind us I could hear Ginger stifling the sniggers. What the rest were doing I could only guess. 'Well!' he demanded, 'what have you got to say?'

I began, 'Well Sergeant, it was like this.' I went on to tell him what had happened.

I had got about half way through when he stopped me, saying, 'Hold it! I've heard some tales in my time but that takes the cake. You must think that I am stupid, even to listen to you. You!' he pointed at me, 'you ought to know better. You'll all be in front of the colonel tomorrow and you can tell him the same story.' He turned to go.

'Sergeant!' I shouted after him. He turned and stood, glaring at me. 'The colonel knows. He was there with us.'

For a moment he was speechless, and then slowly he walked back towards me until he was very close. 'Do you want insubordination added to your charge?' he asked, pushing his face close to mine.

I shrugged my shoulders and said, 'Alright Sergeant, please yourself.'

Needless to say we heard no more about the charges.

Chapter Four

A Rich Grave

Morgan, Ginger and I were getting ready to go to the hospital and relieve three others who had been there all day when in rushed Corporal Murray and Amey. 'Where are you two going in a hurry?' I asked.

'We've been invited to dinner at the matron's,' they replied. 'Why don't you come with us?'

'I have already promised to go on night shift with these two,' I said, pointing down the hut to Morgan and Ginger.

'You could come over at about ten,' Murray shouted as he lathered up for a shave. 'They have an assistant surgeon on duty now. He arrived today. That's why we left there early.'

The three of us walked out of the hut leaving them still getting ready. We made our way slowly down towards the main road, along which we passed the now closed and deserted shops. It was about seven in the evening and still quite warm. As we climbed the steps of the hospital veranda the matron came out to meet us. Just behind her was a young Burmese girl. She was small, about five feet in height. Her black hair was done up in the usual top-of-the-head 'bun' style. She wore the usual Burmese women's lace blouse of white with the long dark sarong-style skirt, doubled over at the waist and tucked in. It almost covered her feet, which just peeped out at the hem. The girl looked even smaller against the matron, who had taken her hand and pulled her forward. Taking off our hats, we all said 'Hallo!'

The matron said, 'This girl has come to help you boys.'

I turned my head and glanced first at Morgan. He was grinning widely with his blue eyes gleaming. Then I glanced at Ginger, whose face was as red as his hair. His broad smile lit up his face even more. I could not help smiling at the expressions on their faces.

As I turned my head back to the matron, I heard her say, 'I know that I can rely on you boys to give her all the help she may need. I know that I am leaving her in good and capable hands.'

The matron continued to talk, but we three just stood there mesmerised as we stared at the young girl. She had a pretty oval face with almond dark eyes slightly slanted. When she smiled she showed a perfect set of white gleaming teeth that shone even whiter against her ruby red lips. It took quite an effort to take my eyes off her, back to the large buxom figure of the matron, who was saying, 'Well, I'll leave you then, and I will see you in the morning.' We all bid her goodnight.

The young girl went into the hospital with us following, and led the way into the operating theatre. For a moment we all stood silent. I broke the silence by saying, 'Well, if we have got to work together, we might as well get acquainted. This,' I said, putting my hand on Ginger's shoulder, 'is Ginger, and this,' I said, putting my other hand on Morgan's shoulder, 'is Morgan.' (Neither ever liked to be called by their first names.) 'Me,' I said, patting my chest, 'you can call me Fred.' I gave her a big smile and she smiled back. 'Now, what's your name?' I asked, still smiling.

When she spoke, it was a very meek but tinkling voice, the way Orientals have of seeming to sing their words. In broken English she began, 'Meeah, namah iss Hohi-Sloh.' She continued with a very serious look upon her face, 'Een ingliss, dat meenss, meah iss awll prittee.' She put her hands to her face and began to giggle in the shyest way that I have ever seen. We made her laugh even more as we tried to say her name.

It was getting quite dark, when there was a commotion outside. Three Indians had a bullock cart drawn up in front of the women's ward. When they saw us, they came to us and said that they had come to take the wife of one of them away. At first I refused, but Hohi said that as it was the husband it was best to let her go. The woman they wanted had been wounded in the chest. Ginger and I got a stretcher and took her to the bullock cart. 'Where are you taking her?' I asked the husband.

'Many miles away, to my father's village in the mountains,' he replied.

We four stood and watched as the bullock cart trundled away into the darkness. 'Come on!' I said, 'Let's go inside.' Ginger made some tea, while Hohi, Morgan and I sat at the operating table and made gauze pads and cotton wool swabs. I glanced up at the clock on the wall and said, 'One of us should go around the wards. Would you like to come with me?' I asked Hohi. She readily agreed. I glanced at Morgan and Ginger and they were both grinning. Morgan winked, and the girl got up from the table while I got a hurricane lamp and lit it. I strode along the veranda with Hohi following.

Suddenly she caught hold of my arm and in her sweet tinkling voice said, 'Pliss Frred, doont walk soo quick.' I slackened my pace, and as I did she slid her hand down my arm and gripped my hand. I was a little taken aback by this, as most of the women and girls had given us the cold shoulder and hardly spoken to us. I looked down at her. Her head came just up to my shoulder.

'Have you been around the wards with matron?' I asked, making conversation and looking down at the sweet oval face.

'No Fred,' she answered, 'I had only just arrived before you came.' She was still finding it difficult to say some of the words properly.

We made a good inspection of all the wards and returned to Ginger and Morgan. They had made some fresh tea, and both of them jumped up to get Hohi a clean cup, but she stopped them, saying, 'I don't take milk or sugar.' We three sat and watched as she moved around the theatre, going from cabinet to cabinet and bringing things out as if she knew where everything was.

When she sat down again, I asked, 'You are a nurse, aren't you?'

She looked up from what she was doing. 'Well, I am partly,' she answered shyly, lowering her eyes.

'Well, you know a lot more than we do,' I replied.

'No!' she said shaking her head. 'You must have had much more training than me,' she said in that tinkling voice.

We three burst out laughing at this.

With a serious look upon her face, she asked, 'What have I said that makes you all laugh?'

Morgan, still laughing, said in his Lancashire accent, 'None of us have ever worked in a hospital before we came here.'

'That's true, Hohi,' Ginger said, grinning.

After that, we must have sat talking for about two hours, still making the swabs and gauze pads. Hohi told us about her childhood, how she had grown up in a village not very far away and her father being the *saubur*, or chief, of the area around their village.

Although we had had many hot baths and changed our clothes, there were times when the deathly smell from the corpses came up into my nostrils, as though it was coming out from our own bodies. As Hohi talked, this was one of the times, and I began to feel quite sick. Without saying anything I got up from the table and walked outside into the fresh air. Somewhere nearby there must have been a eucalyptus tree, for the scent of it came to me. As I took some deep breaths to clear the horrid stench from my lungs, a sound of music also drifted across to me. It was coming from the matron's house. A movement near me made me turn. It was Hohi. She was standing very close to me.

'The lads seem to be enjoying themselves,' I said, nodding in the direction of the house.

'Yes,' she said, 'I suppose one of them is dancing with the matron.'

'Yes, I suppose so. Do you dance?' I asked her.

'Not your type,' she replied, giggling.

Our conversation was suddenly interrupted, by three Gurkhas. Two were almost carrying one who had a large patch of blood on his shirt. I shouted to Ginger and Morgan to get a stretcher. We took the wounded Gurkha to a bed while Hohi went and fetched the two assistant surgeons from their quarters. According to the other Gurkhas there had been a duel between the injured man and another who was now under guard.

After a quick examination of the man the two doctors told me to go and get the matron, as an urgent operation was needed. I made my way to the matron's house as fast as I could. Nearing the house the music became louder, and I could hear someone singing. I knocked on the door, but without waiting to be called in I entered. For a moment I stood there, and then Murray saw me and came to me.

'Come for a drink, Fred?' he asked.

'No!' I replied, 'I've come to tell the matron that she is needed urgently.'

I looked around the room, but there was no sign of her. Sergeant Friend was the one who had been singing. He had stopped as I entered. He came towards me drunkenly.

'What's up, Corporal?' he asked, slurping, in a loud voice.

I shouted, 'Where's the matron? There has been a shooting, and she's needed for an operation.'

This seemed to get through to them. The sergeant walked to a door which I presumed was the bedroom door. He knocked and shouted, 'Betty, Betty, you are wanted urgently.'

From within came a faint, 'Alright, I'm coming.' She opened the door. As soon as I saw the state that she was in, I knew that I was wasting my time there.

I explained what had happened as quickly as I could.

'It's not one of your boys, is it?' she asked.

'No!' I answered thankfully. And if it were, you'd still be of no use, I thought to myself.

'Tell them that I'm not up to it tonight,' she managed to reply.

As I turned away I thought, You can say that again! in disgust.

I made my way back to the hospital. Hohi met me at the steps. She was already dressed for action and looked even prettier with a white headpiece covering her black hair, and over her black skirt and blouse a white gown which came right up to her chin.

'Is she coming, Fred?' Hohi asked as I climbed the steps.

'No, I am afraid she isn't,' I answered as we walked into the operating theatre.

There were two men scrubbing their arms at the sink, one I recognised as a Mr Farrier. He had been at the hospital from the first air raid. I went to them and told them that the matron was not coming. The other man introduced himself as Mr Bell. He was the senior of the two. He said, 'Oh well, if she's not coming, you will have to assist.'

'Me?' I asked, taken completely by surprise. 'I couldn't do it, sir.'

'If you don't, then I shall have to ask one of those men.' He pointed to Morgan and Ginger. 'After all, you are the senior,' he snapped. 'Now, go and get scrubbed!'

Hohi took me by the arm and led me over to the sink, saying, 'Come on, Fred, I will help you.' This gave me a little bit of confidence, but not much. As I scrubbed my arms and hands, Hohi kept up with, 'Don't worry, Fred. You'll get through it alright.'

With rubber gloves and long white smock I really looked the part, but I thought, what if I passed out halfway through, especially at the crucial moment? Ginger and Morgan were getting the trays of instruments ready under the supervision of Mr Farrier. I was standing and looking down at the swabs and pads that we had made that night and thought what a coincidence that we should need them so soon.

Morgan and Ginger were told to go and get the patient. While they were gone Mr Bell gave me instructions on what I had to do. He was going to perform the operation and Mr Farrier was to administer the anaesthetic. Hohi was to hand Mr Bell the instruments on his right hand side, while I was to swab away the blood on his left. 'Blood is the surgeon's worst enemy,' he said, 'so swab as quickly as you can, as soon as I say swab. I will give you further instructions as we go along.'

The patient was brought in, semiconscious and totally naked, and laid on his back with his legs hanging over the end of the table, at the head of which Mr Farrier proceeded with the mask and chloroform. At my left rear there was a bowl of hot water with a large towel in it. 'When the intestines come fully out,' Mr Bell was saying, 'wring out the towel and drape it over them to keep them warm until I give the word to remove it.'

That was the end of my instructions, for Mr Farrier gave a nod. Mr Bell got a needle and thrust it into the patient's arm to make sure he was under. I jumped, but the patient never moved.

The surgeon pushed his mask into position and held his right hand out to Hohi who handed him an instrument. Holding it like a pen, he put the point just below the solar plexus and drew it down in a straight line to and through the navel to about six inches below it. I waited with cotton wool swabs for the word to swab. I dabbed away as fast as I could as the blood oozed out of the now gaping canal. Once more the silver blade traced a line, now deeper into the gaping wound. This time the blood flowed even faster. Clips were inserted on each side of the wound and the blood eased off slightly. I was amazed at the thickness of the skin in that region, which was now beginning to dry. I was also amazed at myself at not feeling sick or faint at the sight before me.

Mr Bell paused for one moment before making another cut, then I realised that as he made that final sweep with the blade he was waiting for the stomach to deflate, so that he would not injure the intestines below the now thin divide. As the blade travelled down, out oozed the yellow coloured mass of intestines. Quickly I wrung out the towel and draped it over the moving mass. The surgeon took a slight breather, and then through his mask came a muffled, 'Right!' I snatched off the towel and dropped it back into the bowl.

Mr Bell then took hold of the intestines and turned them over in his hands. He found two punctures. He then searched some more and found another puncture. His deft fingers searched among the tubes for the bullet, but there was no sign of it. 'He'll pass that out in a couple of days,' he said through his mask, making us all smile. I raised my eyes to Hohi, but as hers met mine she coyly dropped her gaze in embarrassment.

It did not seem to take us so long to get everything back in again. The most awkward was getting the intestines to stay beneath the stitches as they were pulled together. Once that was done it was fairly easy going, taking off the clips from the main arteries as the wound was sewn together.

Hohi and I finished dressing the patient. Ginger and Morgan, who had watched the whole proceedings, brought the stretcher, and with a drip to his backside we put the patient to bed. On our return to the theatre the two surgeons came and thanked me for the help that I had given.

Morgan, Ginger, Hohi and I cleaned up and got the place back to normal. With Hohi gone now to look at the patient, Ginger volunteered to go and cook an early breakfast. It was about four in the morning when we sat down at the operating table and ate a good meal of bacon, eggs and sweet tea.

At about seven thirty in the morning, the matron came. She looked haggard, as if she had not had any sleep. Hohi and I took her and showed her the new patient. We explained what had been done.

We three left the rest for Hohi to tell and made our way back to our billet. On our arrival back there we found quite some excitement. The whole of the men had been split into three parties. Two of them had already been sent out to destroy installations and anything that may be of use to the enemy, who, we were told, were less than twenty miles away. We three were ordered to get our arms and ammunition and get onto one of the lorries. On board there were explosives, fuse wire, hand grenades and other gear needed for destruction. Our two lorries followed the colonel's car out of the camp and down the main road that led towards Heiho Aerodrome, which had been used for refuelling and reloading of bombs to our planes. So, we were at this moment going south towards the advancing enemy. The 'drome' was about eight miles from Taunggyi.

As we went along, we three were told that we were going to the 'drome' to destroy anything that had been left behind by the RAF units that had been evacuated some three or four days before. As we had not been present when orders were given out, we were now told that we would split up into two parties. One was to put charges on the wooden structures of the hangar to wreck it completely, and another party would collect all the drums of petrol, put them onto the runway and set fire to them. This 'drome' would be of the upmost importance to the enemy in that it was near enough central for planes to strike across the Irrawaddy to the west and also strike to the east into China.

It was a hazardous drive as the lorries followed the colonel's car down and around the winding hills, sometimes going at a snail's pace to manoeuvre the sharp bends in the road. At last we turned up the driveway that led to the airfield. The lorries kept on to the far end where the hangar was. The place was absolutely deserted. We got out and went and viewed the hangar. It had wooden uprights with wooden crosspieces. The roof was covered with corrugated iron sheets. The timber uprights were five by three inches. It was decided that gun cotton slabs lashed to the uprights and using a ring main fuse with a short slow-burning fuse would give us time to get clear. We worked in pairs, strapping two slabs of the gun cotton, one on each side and one higher than the other, so as to have a cutting effect. Sergeant McAteer and Corporal Murray were the two left to light the fuses. We watched from a safe distance as they walked clear, then we all got down. There was a terrific bang, and as we looked up it seemed that the whole structure jumped. And as it came down, it just crumbled and fell flat, sending up a huge cloud of dust. Leaving that we went back to where the other party were assembling all the petrol drums into a huge cartwheel across the runway. The drums were stood upright. We had stripped to the waist, as by this time the sun was getting quite hot. I was very glad that we had eaten that early breakfast, for we had not been given the chance of even a cup of tea.

'Right lads,' the colonel said, 'you can get some shooting practice in.'

Getting away from the huge circle of drums at about two hundred yards, some knelt, some lay down and some stood, picking off selected drums. Between us we must have put about sixty or seventy rounds into the drums. Petrol was pouring out of holes in all directions, but not a single one ignited. 'Well! What do you think of that?' said Bob Sharp. 'If Errol Flynn had been here, he would have done it with one shot,' he joked. We all laughed.

'There is only one thing to do, Corporal!' the colonel called to Murray, who had a Thompson submachine gun. 'Go in a little closer and see if that will have any effect, but come away quickly if it does.' Murray went forward, gave one burst, and the whole lot seemed to go up in flames, sending a thick black cloud into the sky.

We all boarded the two lorries. The colonel got into his car and followed it around the outer side of the airfield, to where a stack of about fifty 500-pound bombs were. Into these we pushed sticks of gelignite at various intervals, together with the necessary primers and detonators. These again were all linked up to a main fuse so that they would all go off at the same time. Our last job was to set booby traps in any concealable places. The charges on the bomb stack would go off when we were well clear.

We had left a lookout at the entrance to the airfield just in case of any enemy forward troops coming before we had finished our task, but he reported that there was no sign of them. As we left we looked back onto the raging inferno that we had created. Drums were flying into the air as they exploded. As we climbed the steep hill following the colonel's car we could hear the sound of gunfire further down in the valley. When we turned onto the main road that would take us into Taunggyi, our trucks were forced to slow down because of the hundreds of refugees that had jammed the road.

All the tooting of the horns made very little difference to them, but eventually we did manage to get through, then our drivers increased speed and made our way back to the camp. Here we heard the latest news. The Japanese were making two thrusts, one in pursuit of the British on the west side of the Irrawaddy, and the other to the east, chasing the Chinese forces towards Lashio. So we were more or less cut off from our own forces, as we were on the east side of the Irrawaddy.

On going into the camp the colonel had decided that we would be more comfortable if we moved into Brigade HQ, which had been evacuated some days before. The place had been left in a shambles. Furniture had been smashed, there were broken lamps and slashed bedding, and torn-up papers were still burning outside in an incinerator. We used this to boil some water for making tea. Among the rubbish, Sharp found an old gramophone, but he could only find one decent record and that was cracked. Someone also found some half bottles of spirits and was drinking from them. Sharp got the gramophone going after coming back from sorting in the rubbish. 'What do you think?' he asked.

'There are about fifty bleeding records out there, and only one that we can play.' The needle was not much good either. One side of the record was 'In the still of the night' and on the flip side was 'Tonight I see the message in your eyes'.

We sat around on the floor in the darkening room with the lone record being played over and over. I felt a little relieved when Sergeant McAteer came in and asked for six men. I got to my feet and with the others followed him out. While we had been resting, one of the other sections had returned. They had been to the Treasury, with Captain Brown and Sergeant Friend. There they had loaded up twelve bullock carts with sacks of rupees. Then with six men as escort they had been sent on ahead to make a rendezvous with us later. At the same time they had loaded one of our three-ton trucks with sacks of rupee coins. This truck was standing outside, loaded down onto its springs. The sergeant told us to climb in, and with Captain Lancaster driving we headed towards the town. At the main road we took a left hand fork which brought us to the military cemetery. Here the lorry turned slowly and carefully through the gate, almost bringing it down. We stopped there and dropped one man off to keep watch for any Japanese patrols that may be getting near. The lorry then continued on its way, rolling from side to side as it weaved between the gravestones in the meagre light of the shaded headlamps. The captain drove it to the far left hand corner under the shadow of an overhanging crag and hill.

We got down and began to dig out a rectangle the sergeant marked out. We worked in pairs, the sergeant and captain taking their turn. It was a rather large grave and much deeper than usual. When it was ready we placed the bags of coins at the bottom then filled the grave back in with soil and sods of turf. The empty lorry was driven out to wait for us as we brushed away any signs of the lorry being in there.

At the gate of the cemetery we stopped to pick up the lookout, who reported that he had seen lights that looked like a motorised convoy down in the valley. We made our way back the way we had come. As we neared the HQ we could hear the gramophone still playing its well-worn tune.

Chapter Five

A Trap Well Laid

At about two in the morning our convoy of four lorries and the colonel's car moved off out of what had been the Brigade HQ. First we visited the civilian hospital to say our goodbyes. Hohi came out and so did the matron. I jumped from the lorry, and Hohi ran to me with her arms outstretched and flung them around my neck. I was taken aback by this, but I put my arms around her. 'Come back, Fred!' she pleaded, 'Do come back!'

I looked at her in the darkness. I could see she was actually crying. 'Don't worry, we'll be back!' I told her.

The others had got off from the lorries also to say their goodbyes. Then the order to get back on was given. We waved to them all as they stood there in the half light of the hospital.

Our route, the only one left open to us, was in a southeasterly direction. Thus we were going towards the advancing Japanese. A small town called Psipaw was our first objective. The leading truck was a 10-cwt and was acting more as a scout car. It had a Bren gun mounted on the canopy. Psipaw was about forty miles from Taunggyi. This meant that we had to make a quick dash before turning north-northwest towards the Irrawaddy River, which we hoped to cross.

The road was little more than a track used only by bullock carts and mules over many centuries, thus the ruts on either side were of no great help to the lorries as they went from side to side, into one rut and then into the other. There was also dense jungle on either side. Sometimes the trucks were forced to leave the track and make their way as best they could through the jungle. This was done by two or three men going in front and literally cutting a path for them. But when the jungle became too dense we had to make back for the track again. Our progress was very slow. Dawn was coming when we came near to a Kachin village of some four or five bamboo huts. Men from the village came out to meet us. They seemed very agitated and excited as they informed the colonel that they had seen a small party of Japanese to the south of the village before darkness had fallen the night before.

Leaving the trucks well concealed and with guards, the rest of us with the colonel and one of the villagers leading made our way as quietly as possible to where the Japanese had last been seen. After about a quarter of a mile or maybe less, the Kachin signalled us to take cover. He with his keen ears had heard something. He told the colonel it was voices. The colonel told three of us to go forward about twenty yards and conceal ourselves, engage the enemy, draw their fire, and then pull back to where the rest were waiting. The only thing that worried the colonel was how big the party was.

We three were well spread out but in sight of each other. I could now hear the swishing of someone brushing against the trees on either side of the track. We looked at each other and gave a nod to let each other know that we had heard. Then I saw them. There were three of them, about twenty-five yards from us. When we opened fire the one in front stopped dead in his tracks, then fell forward. The second threw up his arms and fell sideways. The third man stood still as if in shock for a split second. He then turned as if to run, but one of the others put him away with a shot that hit him in the back of the head. There were no moans or groans from any of them, but raising myself up slightly I could make out the lifeless bodies in among the ferns. All this had happened in a matter of a few seconds, but the jungle had come alive with animals, birds and many other creatures crying out and making some very weird sounds. Then, just as suddenly, all was quiet again. We lay still in our positions. The sweat began to run down the side of my face. Flies began to gather and settled on my face and nose. They then tried for my eyes. I began to blink my lids to get rid of them.

Then all hell was let loose as in front of us the jungle seemed to be full of the enemy. Giving a nod to my two companions we crawled through the undergrowth until we were near to where our friends were. Then keeping down and firing from the hip we joined them. They immediately opened up at the oncoming Japanese, who were shouting and screaming. As I took up a position lying down I saw one of the enemy in a white shirt push forward with a sword held high, then suddenly stop when a burst of fire caught him across the middle. His white shirt turned first red then pink with blood, then he fell out of my sight.

The colonel, knowing that the Japanese always made a frontal attack and then tried to outflank, had put all the quick firing guns out on our flanks. The first attack stopped. There was an eerie silence, except for the noise of the birds and scared animals. During this short lull the colonel had us move to another position. The second attack came but with less vigour. As they came at us we caught them in a crossfire. They fell screaming and shouting, then once again all was quiet. We kept our positions for a few moments, then the colonel called us to group and check for any casualties on our side. There were none. We reckoned that there had been about twenty-five to thirty Japanese dead. If there were any survivors, we did not care. We made our way back to where we had left our trucks.

As we boarded our trucks we glanced up skywards. Already the vultures were circling high in the sky above, preparing to dive and take their pick.

Once more we got underway towards Psipaw. The track had begun to rise slightly and the jungle was getting a little thinner. Our speed had increased also. It was around noon when we came to a river, lying in a dale between two lines of hills and about ten feet wide. There was a wooden bridge spanning it, but it was doubtful if the structure would take the weight of the loaded three-tonners. The colonel decided to take his car over first then try the 30-cwt. Both went over with a little groaning from the latter. It was decided to try to reinforce the bridge before sending over the heavier vehicles. Some of us stripped off and began rolling some large boulders beneath the wooden bridge, where the river was three to four feet deep. Some of the men were taking the loads off the lorries while others were cutting down trees and lashing the logs to the bridge to give it extra strength. Three of the lorries went over with some difficulty with much creaking and groaning. The fourth got to the middle and stalled.

The driver, George Amey, calmly got out of the cab, opened up the bonnet, peered in and tinkered about as if he was in the main street of town. We were all shouting to him to hurry, as we could see that the build-up of water upstream was getting so great that it could sweep away the bridge and the truck with it, but he kept on until he was satisfied and calmly got back into the cab, started the engine and slowly drove the vehicle forward. The bridge creaked and groaned. The rear wheels had just reached solid ground when the bridge was completely washed away.

It took us some time to get the gear back onto the trucks, wading back and forth in the river, and we reached Psipaw in the dark, at about nine in the evening. The place was crammed with refugees. Our bullock carts were there, having made good time with no hold-ups. Also in the town was a large force of Chinese troops. The colonel did not like the look of things, for if they found out what we were carrying it could cause no end of trouble. Also, there were probably some right rogues among the refugees. So the colonel decided to move further on outside the town, and asked us to keep well on the alert.

We left Psipaw before dawn. The bullock carts had gone on ahead as the men who were with them could easily get their heads down while they were on the move. Our next objective was a small town called Laihka, about one hundred miles to the north. The bullock carts had about six hours start on us. They could make camp at anytime and anywhere, as they had got their own rations.

If they kept up the pace that they had been going, which was about six miles an hour, they would have done a third of the journey as we began.

We were making very good time from Psipaw. At about four in the afternoon we topped a rise and were looking down onto a wide dusty plain, across which the track ran before entering some sparsely growing clumps of trees. It was about a half a mile across to the other side. Once on the flat, all the drivers including the colonel in his car put their foot down and made it hell for leather across the open ground, thus sending up great clouds of dust which we were sure could have been seen for some miles from the air.

As we neared the trees our fears came true for the drone of aircraft came to our ears. The trucks were pulled well under cover as we all dismounted and waited. It was a single Japanese fighter. He had spotted us and was making a run very low over the trees. He came at us with all guns blazing away. We returned fire but he seemed more interested in our trucks than us. He went out wide and turned for a second run. Again we returned fire. He had set the first truck in the column on fire. Again he came around for a third run. Some of our chaps near the burning vehicle were scooping up sand in their hats and chucking it on the fire, stopping only when the plane came down again on its run. After the third run the aircraft turned south and went out of sight.

The burnt truck was one of the three-tonners. It was a complete wreck. Another three-tonner had its windscreen smashed and its radiator punctured, and the third one was damaged about the same except it had a slug embedded in its engine casing. Before setting off again we salvaged as much as we could from the wrecked truck and cut pieces of wood to plug the holes in the damaged radiators, but after a few miles we found that the slug embedded in the engine casing had caused a huge crack. We had reached about halfway when we were forced to abandon that vehicle and transfer as much gear as we could on to the other two three-tonners and the 30-cwt, which mainly contained the sacks of rupees. These, when we reached the halfway camp, we loaded on to the bullock carts, which set off as soon as we had finished loading.

We cooked a hasty meal and got our heads down for a well-needed sleep. We were woken at four in the morning, and prepared to move off in the two three-tonners, the 30-cwt and the colonel's car.

At about two in the afternoon, about fourteen miles from Laihka, we caught up with and overtook the bullock carts. We had gone about another three miles when the three-tonner I was on suddenly stopped. The engine had gone completely dead. I said to Jock, Morgan and Bland, 'Come on, let's walk for a while. They will catch us up when they get it going.' They agreed with me, and we set off. It was quite a change from sitting in the back of the truck. After we had been walking for about two miles the truck came alongside and slowed down to allow us to get on board again. We pulled up at a ramshackle bungalow. The colonel, who had gone on ahead, came out to tell us that the Japanese had been attacking Mandalay and at the same time a large force were engaging the Chinese Sixth Army at Maymyo.

Laihka was completely taken over by the Chinese. Once again the problem was the plight of the hundreds of refugees who had come into the town to find shelter for the night. It had begun to rain, and one had to feel pity for the refugees, old and young alike, who had most probably been walking for perhaps weeks already. Most of them were Chinese, but they seemed to get very little pity from their fellow countrymen, and seemed to expect none. Once again the colonel decided to move further on outside the town, more for our own safety than for anything else. 'We will keep to ourselves, and they can keep to themselves,' he said. We left Sergeant McAteer and six men as extra escort to bring the bullock carts through the town to where we made camp.

The rain by this time was really pouring down, and the track was fast becoming a quagmire of red mud. The ruts on each side of the track had now become small rivers in themselves. The trucks were slipping and sliding, with the front wheels stuck in the ruts and the back wheels spinning, sending up streams of red mud. So we had to get off and find large rocks and chuck them beneath the wheels to give them some grip, and then push. Although we cursed and swore at our predicament, we also found it rather funny and at times burst out laughing at the sight of each other as we were covered from head to foot in the red slimy mud as it was thrown up by the spinning wheels. It was like looking at a Charlie Chaplin film as we tried to scrape off the thick mud from our faces.

We had gone about three miles when the colonel, who was also in a little trouble with his car, called a halt. Finding a suitable spot and getting the vehicles well under cover, we split into pairs and began erecting bamboo shelters, grateful now for the training we had received at the Bush Warfare School. In less than an hour we had a large shelter under which we could do the cooking, and three smaller ones under which we could all shelter for the night.

A meal of stew was soon dished out together with mugs of hot sweet tea. The bullock carts arrived and, like us, their drivers were soaked to the skin. Following behind them came eight mounted Sikhs of the Frontier Force. Behind these on foot came about one hundred Indian troops of different regiments. Sergeant McAteer said that these had followed them from Laihka.

The colonel's immediate concern was for the bags of rupees on the bullock carts, firstly that they did not fall into enemy hands, and secondly that it would not start a war between rival factions, with us in the middle, if any of them found out how much we were carrying. It was with this in mind that he, with his two officers and the senior NCOs, ordered the Indian foot troops to move on, to make a camp of their own. But he let eight mounted men stay with us, as he thought that at some time in the future they might come in useful.

The escort on the bullock carts was trebled. Sixteen were detailed, four heading the column, four on each side and four bringing up the rear. We worked it between ourselves that the four in front would leapfrog in pairs. This went on for two hours, then four from the side would push on and take over at the head, while the four from the head rested and took up the rear position. In this way, all escort had rest but the carts were kept on the move. We had set off at 4 am. At midday we all took a rest and brewed up some tea. We reckoned that we had covered about twenty-five miles. The trucks passed us as we set forth again. It looked as if they had had a rough time, for they were plastered with mud. One of the trucks was gushing steam, no doubt from the leaking radiator. We were all of the opinion that it was to be the next casualty.

Our next objective was a small place called Mong Kung, fifteen more miles away. We had covered about three miles after the midday break when we came upon the three-tonner with the leaking radiator. It had run dry again. As we passed, Sharp, who was sitting on the rear, shouted, 'We have stopped to water the horses!' The rest had carried on to get a meal ready for us on our arrival.

We passed through the village of Mong Kung at about five in the afternoon. There we heard that there had been a great deal of air activity during the last hour or so. Also there were reports of parachutes seen coming down earlier to the north.

The colonel got hold of the eight mounted Sikhs, sending two of them to scout up the left-hand fork of the track, which was to be our route. This was heading due north, while the right-hand track went in a northeasterly direction. He sent two more of the riders along that track to see if there was anything along there.

The rain had stopped. The lorry which had broken down arrived. Following it came a large column of Chinese troops and the Indian foot troops. The colonel contacted the commander of the Chinese troops and told him of his anxiety with regard to reports of a large force of Japanese being in the area, but the Chinese commander ignored him and continued up the northeasterly track that would take them to Lashio and the China border. When the Indian troops and the refugees heard the news about the Japanese they immediately vanished into the jungle. By this time the mounted men came galloping back down the left-hand fork to report that they had bumped into a large force of Japanese who seemed to be regrouping for an attack, so our progress up the northern track was blocked.

It was obvious what the Japanese intention was. This second column was to push north and join up somewhere with the force that was engaged with the Chinese around Maymyo, thus cutting off their escape route up the Burma Road to China.

The colonel decided that to try to take the money any further was useless. His first thought now was to get ourselves out of this hopeless situation. First we unloaded all the bullock carts. After paying off the driver we all set about carrying the bags of coins far into the jungle, where we dug a huge pit, buried the bags in it and covered the place with brushwood, at the same time noting where it was. We then destroyed the colonel's car and the broken-down three-tonner, and got rid of any unwanted gear and equipment. This left us with one three-tonner and the 30-cwt truck.

It was very tough going up the track, which was taking us in a northeasterly direction and away from the Irrawaddy. The vehicles had taken some stick and were showing the strain. The rain of the past few days had not helped either. We were making slow progress over a winding track that took us up and around a mountain when suddenly the three-tonner went dead. Try as we might, we could not get any life out of it at all, so we decided to put all the gear into the 30-cwt and push the larger vehicle over the side of the mountain. The truck was only going at walking pace, and as it was now crowded some of us decided to walk. Now and again those who were riding swapped over with those walking.

We still had the mounted Sikhs with us, but had lost the Chinese. The Indians and refugees had vanished altogether. After a time the 30-cwt truck also began to give trouble. We came to a village, and while scouting around there for food one of the sergeants found a number of mules. This was reported to the colonel who immediately set about buying all twelve of them, with the 30-cwt thrown in as part of the deal.

From now on it was all on foot. Where we would end up was anyone's guess. Our whole plan had gone awry. Even the colonel was now at a loss. All that we could do was to keep ahead of the Japanese, keep going north and make for the Irrawaddy further on.

Chapter Six

Race to the Irrawaddy

We stayed the night at the village and obtained as much food as we needed. At dawn we set off with our gear strapped on the mules. Now we did not have to stay on the roads but could cut across country when and where the terrain suited us, until we hit the Myitnge River. After crossing that we would make for the ruby-mining town of Mogok. The colonel had pointed out that by then we should be ahead of the two Japanese columns that were chasing the Chinese towards the east. He also pointed out that this was not going to be a picnic, that we must at all times be on our guard and not falter. We would rest when we could but should be on alert at all times, he said, and above all trust no one else.

Some of the others and I had handled mules before, but when it came to crossing rivers with them, that was another matter. I considered myself quite a good swimmer, but with a mule? That posed a problem. Still, I thought to myself that I would worry about that when we got to the river.

We marched all that day and all through the night with a half-hour rest every four hours. We stopped for our first big break at about eight o'clock in the morning. We reckoned that we had covered about forty miles, which left us about sixty more miles before we came to the Myitnge.

After restarting from our much needed long rest, our route took us once again into the hills. The pace now was beginning to slow down after the hard march of the previous day and night. It was taking its toll on all of us, but we knew that we must try to keep up a steady pace if we were to succeed. The eight Indian horsemen, not being affected by fatigue, rode on slightly ahead of us and did a kind of scouting job, thus giving plenty of warning of any danger.

And so it turned out, as we approached the Myitnge the Sikhs warned us that they had seen uniformed troops on the opposite bank of the river. With great caution we went towards it. On closer inspection by a couple of our men who had gone forward they found that it was a section of Gurkhas who had come up the river from the south on that side.

The river was very fast flowing and about eighty yards wide, with steep banks on both sides. On our side the current ran slightly faster to some jagged rocks that stuck up out of the water about two or three hundred yards downstream, over which the river tumbled, causing white foam and spray to fly in the air, before falling down a waterfall, the roaring of which we could hear from where we were.

A small dugout canoe was moored on our side. To it was tied a long length of rope. By sending the canoe out into the strong current and keeping the rope on our side, the current swept the canoe over to the other side. We then hauled the canoe back over to our side. In this way we managed to get all our gear over in a dry state, with some of the men going over with the gear.

The next thing was to get the mules across. The Sikhs were already getting their saddles and equipment off their mounts. So we, who had to get the mules over, stood back for a while to see how they coped with the strong-flowing river. I had already stripped off to my gym shorts, and so had some of the others. The Indian horsemen began to take their horses over in pairs, swimming alongside them. The first two pairs went over quite easily, but among the next two pairs was a huge grey who, when just under halfway across, decided to turn around. The fast current caught it and turned it over, with its legs threshing the air and its head below the water, taking it at great speed down the river towards the rocks and waterfall. We all watched helplessly as the animal was dashed against the rocks and thrown like a log over the waterfall and out of sight. Its rider kept on swimming and made it to the other bank. The last we saw of him was running down the bank as fast as he could, no doubt to see if he could save the animal further downriver.

I was attempting to get my own mule into the water when I saw two of our men get into difficulty with their mules. They had gone into the water too close to each other, bumped, started to flounder and got caught in the current. The mules were swept down onto the rocks and were gone, while the two men kept swimming and made it to the other side. This made me decide to go further upstream to give both of us a chance, and also wait till it was clear of anyone else. I was quite confident of getting across myself, but to take a mule across was another matter.

I picked my spot where we could enter the water. When all was clear I lashed him across the flanks with a piece of brushwood and forced him into the water. Sharp had been in a cavalry unit and told me that when a horse swims it leans slightly to the right with its legs paddling on the left. 'So swim on his right side,' he said, 'or you may get a kick.' The mule entered the water and I plunged in after him. Swimming on his right side I was soon alongside his head. I grabbed the hair on his neck and began to shout encouragement into his ear. We were going very well until just under halfway where he decided that he had gone far enough and tried to turn around. I grabbed his ear with my left hand and at the same time struck out as hard as I could with my right, forcing him the way I wanted him to go. His head came around as he sensed what I wanted him to do. About halfway the current seemed to be pushing instead of pulling, and in no time we were touching bottom and walking up the bank to safety. I scrambled up the bank and stood for a while to get my breath back. The mule stood with his back feet still in the water, shaking his head to get rid of the water and blowing his nostrils. He looked at me and came forward, then tucked his head under my arm and rubbed his nose across my chest, almost pushing me backwards. I am quite sure that it was his way of saying thanks. From that moment on I would refuse to have it said that mules are stupid animals.

It was getting dusk when we were ready to move off. We were forced to leave more gear behind because of the two lost mules. The Sikhs had decided to stay with the Gurkhas, and were glad to take some of our gear. Our path took us straight up the side of the mountain from the river bank, the track, if it could be called that, leading up through the trees. The incline was almost upright and was covered with pine needles, while the roots of the trees stuck up out of the ground, making it very slippery. The trees in some instance were so close together that it was difficult for the mules to go through with their packs on.

The first man led his mule up the steep slope, working in and out of the trees. At intervals we followed behind, giving plenty of room for the one in front. The bank rose up to about fifty feet from the river's edge. I had got about halfway up when there were shouts from above. We could hear some noise coming down towards us. I moved my animal to the side. Peering through the creeping darkness in between the trees, I saw what looked like a huge black ball rolling down, smashing into trees and going from side to side as it went downwards. It was only now and then that one caught a glimpse of the animal's legs as it went tumbling down, screeching and snorting as it tried to regain its feet, but the heavy pack pulled it over and over downward. Two of the men followed it down. I tied my animal to a tree and followed down after them. The colonel, who had just begun the climb, was already there. Besides other injuries the mule had suffered a broken leg, so the colonel gave the order to kill it. The only way was to cut its throat, as we did not want the noise of a gunshot being heard.

I turned away and went back up to my animal. I patted and stroked him for some reason that I cannot explain. Perhaps I had become attached to him. Anyway, I did not want the same thing to happen to him, so I took a little more care and reached the top safely.

Now we were left with only nine mules and less gear. The march across the high mountain range took us northwards towards the well-known Gokteik

Gorge, which is about three hundred feet high. A bridge spans the gorge, linking two mountains and taking a railway line north. We passed many villages that had been burned and looted by the Chinese in their march to the northeast, thus robbing us of both supplies and of fresh food and shelter on our journey. From one village that had escaped the looters we learned that the Japanese had taken Maymyo and that they were also attacking Lashio on the Chinese border. This meant that we were at that moment right smack in the middle of the Japanese two-pronged attack.

Through the hours of daylight we saw plenty of air activity and it was mainly the enemy's. Our objective was to cross the Burma Road about fifty miles northeast of Maymyo, and we had to cross that road without being spotted by enemy aircraft and get across to the next range of hills that would take us into Mogok.

We descended the hills and tried to cut through the bottom of the gorge, which would bring us to Mogok. As we entered the beginning of the gorge with its high tree-covered walls rising up on either side, aircraft came over and began to bomb the bridge. We did not know whether they were friend or foe. The bombs that missed the target came cascading down into the gorge, causing the ground to shake with the explosions as they burst on the floor of the gorge, sending triple echoes up and down the narrow passage. The noise being flung from side to side made it deafening. Long after we had left the gorge behind and the planes had ceased their destruction, the echoing explosions could still be heard behind us.

Due to the Chinese looting and burning we were now running short of supplies. We had to use up rations that we had hoped to save, so these were now very low, but at Mogok we expected to be able to replenish our stock of food.

After some short breaks through the night we reached the Burma Road and managed to cross it just before dawn broke. It was not long before the sun was making it uncomfortable for us. By noon we reckoned we were about halfway to Mogok.

The sun was sinking in the western sky, and the air became cooler as we began to come down out of the mountains. Some distance away we could make out the black ribbon of the metal road winding its way around the lower hills that would take us into Mogok. We had been there before, to play the locals at soccer. On that occasion we were given VIP treatment. What sort of reception we would get this time, we wondered?

It was not quite dark when we trod onto the hard road about three miles from the town and came to an iron bridge with most of its planks removed by the Chinese, and Chinese sentries guarding it, armed with rifles and German-type stick grenades which they carried in crossed pouches on their chests. At first they tried to bar our way, but when we spoke to them in Mandarin they let us pass.

On reaching the town we found that the Chinese troops had taken over everything, including all the food and the main buildings. The place was also swarming with refugees, who were mostly Chinese. On seeing us they immediately gathered around, begging for food. It took a great deal to convince them that we had none for ourselves.

The colonel chose to make camp between two broken-down shacks occupied by refugees. When we had settled the mules down, he said, 'Go on lads, get what you can, and don't come back empty-handed.' He had a wide grin on his face as he said it. We paired off and went in search of anything that we could lay our hands on.

Morgan came with me down the main street. Two Chinese sentries were standing guard at the entrance to a large building. This was up on stilts, with the first floor about six feet from the ground. Under this and hanging from the beams were a number of legs of pork, while on the floor, stacked beneath, were hundreds of sacks of rice. Inside and squatting behind a Vickers machine gun loaded with belt and ready to fire were two Chinese soldiers. For a moment we both stood still, then I thought, nothing ventured, nothing gained. I said to Morgan, 'Come on!' We both strode to go inside, but the two sentries tried to stop us. Leading, I pushed past them and walked around the gun crew, Morgan following close behind. There were shouts from the sentries, and two more came running down the stairs from the room above, waving their arms and shouting. But they stopped in their tracks when I shouted, 'Boo–shaw–wha! Whor–mun–ying–gwor–bing, whor–mun–yow–chur–fan.' ('Shut up! We are English soldiers, we want food.') Without another word, Morgan with two sacks of rice and I with one sack and a large leg of pork marched out and back to where the rest had made a fire and were cooking something already. Between us we had not done too badly. Someone had got hold of five live chickens, about twenty eggs and a bag of sweet potatoes. We made quite a good meal and even had some left over.

While we had been cooking and preparing the meal, quite a large crowd had gathered around, among them young girls. We knew that had we wished we could have bought any one of them for the slightest morsel of food. When we had had our fill we tried to share it out among the very young and the very old who we thought could not fend for themselves, but even that almost caused a riot.

After our meal was cleared away we gathered around the colonel, who was outlining our next objective, a town called Mong Mit. We had a good fire going, as the night had gone quite cool, and were listening to what the colonel was saying when out of the darkness there came shouts and rifle shots. The refugees who had gathered close to our fire for warmth and for any more scraps of food began screaming and running about in panic. We reached for our weapons and turned towards where the shouts and shooting had come from. A Chinese officer came running towards us. He was shouting, almost screaming, 'Ying-gwor! Ying-gwor!' As he got near to us another shot rang out and he fell flat on his face close to Sharp. I rushed over, and Sharp and I turned him over. He was still alive and blood began to trickle from the side of his mouth. His lips moved and he tried to mutter in broken English, 'They not listen, they not listen!' and soon after, he died.

When we told the colonel, he wasted no time in ordering us to get the mules loaded as soon as we could. 'Let's get out of here and be on our way,' he said. 'We don't want to be involved in their domestic quarrels.'

We moved off just after midnight, and behind us followed streams of refugees. They must have thought it safer to be with us than with the Chinese soldiers. We had forty miles between us and Mong Mit, and had been marching for about two hours when the heavens opened. The rain came down in torrents. Luckily the track we were following was not so bad and we could keep going, but we had to cross quite a number of small rivers, sometimes up to our waists as we waded across them. As dawn came we began to climb the hills again. Here the villages were few and far between. No one grumbled or made excuses for rests. How could they? The colonel was twice most of our ages, yet he led the way except when he stopped to give encouragement, and set us all an example. He was a true officer and a gentleman, and gave his orders in a manner that was really like he was asking and could hardly be refused.

Mong Mit was a very small town, little more than a village. We rested for a short time there, cooked a meal and pushed on in a northeasterly direction towards a village called Molo, about thirty hours march away on the banks of the Shweli River, which rises in China and flows southwest for about a hundred miles inside the Burma border then does a sharp bend and turns west-northwest for two hundred miles before running into the Irrawaddy. The colonel's plan was to get to the Shweli, build rafts and let the river take us most of the two hundred miles west-northwest, then leave it and go across country to where we might be able to get a ferry across the Irrawaddy and thus join up with our forces on the western, far side of that river. What we had to do was beat the Japanese drive northwards on the west bank.

We came out of the mountains onto the sun-baked plains. The rain had stopped but the sun was taking it out of us, the sweat drying as fast as we made it. We reached Molo in the middle of the morning and there had some good luck. The colonel was able to swap the mules for three large rafts, which saved us the time of making them. We were also able to get a good supply of fresh food.

After a good night's sleep in the village, with the coming of daylight we set off on our new form of transport. By day we made very good progress, as we could see objects or sandbanks ahead, but at night it was a very different story. We ran into all sorts of trouble, hitting things that sent us spinning around out of control, and running onto sandbanks. When we ran onto a sandbank, hearing the water swirling around us you would have thought it was at least knee deep, but when we jumped in to free the raft it only just came over our boots. We then had to manhandle the raft to deeper water and scramble on board again before it got taken away in the fast flowing current.

For two days and two nights we managed on the rafts, but lost some of our food overboard during one of our many mishaps and were forced to stop at another village along the river. Here the colonel made another swap. This time he exchanged the rafts for eight dugout canoes. With some money we also replenished our supply of food. And remarkable as it may sound, two of the men found a large case of local beer. Each canoe had a share of the bottles. We had spent the best part of seven days on the river, and it seemed that our journey had been worth it. But we could get very little information about the Japanese. What we did know was that we were slightly ahead of their forward troops.

We did much better with the canoes and made better time, as they were easier to handle than the rafts and we had far fewer mishaps. When we came to the point where we had to leave the river, at a given signal we made for the bank and carried the canoes into the jungle. Disposing of all unneeded kit, we were down to the bare essentials: rifles, two bandoliers of ammo and a water bottle each, and nothing else.

The colonel told us in a low voice that we were going to make a forced march to a place on the banks of the Irrawaddy called Shwegu. 'It is sixty miles. We shall only stop for food and water and we shall be going towards enemy forward troops. Here ...' He paused. 'Here ... I am asking for a little marching discipline. When we come to a village that we cannot go around, I will use scouts before we go in. Is that understood?'

We all answered, 'Yes, sir!'

'Right, let's go!' He led the way, followed by the two captains, two sergeants and thirty men.

The time we had spent on the river had softened us a little, for after a while we were all saying how stiff we felt. To make it worse on our legs we had begun to climb the first of two ranges of hills that we must cross to bring us within sight of the Irrawaddy valley. As we topped the rise and struck off slightly to the west the sky began to blacken. Although night was coming on we could see that a storm was also coming, and if we did not find shelter we were in for a right soaking. In front of us lightning flashed across the sky, showing up the distant hills, followed by a clap of thunder. As we marched towards the oncoming storm the lightning seemed to be running along the top of the near hills, and in no time at all we were soaked to the skin as the rain came down in sheets. Still, we kept on going with our heads bowed against the rain. After all, where else could we go? Then someone shouted, 'Look, a light!' Two or three began to run. We all followed, and as we got nearer the dark shape of a building loomed up, one standing on stilts as is usual in Burma. We kept running until we got near, then quietly crawled beneath the raised floor of the house.

We all heaved a sigh of relief to be out of the lashing rain. The thunder and lightning seemed to have intensified, and the noise seemed to have covered our approach to our hiding place, for no one came to investigate, though we could hear people talking and moving across the wooden floor in the rooms above us. After some time the colonel decided to try his luck, so he and Sergeant McAteer went back out into the rain. Nerves were taut as we heard the heavy rap on the door. For a moment there was silence, and then we heard soft footsteps across the floor. We heard voices above the noise of the storm, then the heavy tread of boots, and after a while the sergeant shouted, 'Come inside!' The house was split into four large rooms, with a hall running the full length between them. Most of us sat down in the hall and stripped off our wet clothes. The occupants were a young Burmese woman and an elderly couple. The young woman told us that the elderly couple were her in-laws and that her husband was an officer in the Burma Rifles. She said that she had not heard from him for some months, and asked if we could tell her anything. We all fell silent, as it was well known that most of the Burma Rifles had gone over to the Japanese, and the colonel put her off by saying that he had probably made it safely to India. She made us a meal and some tea.

Before setting out the next morning, the colonel offered the family some money for the food and shelter, but they refused it. They did, however, warn us of the danger of going into villages on the plains, as many of the headmen had gone over to the Japanese. They also told us that it was about thirty miles to Shwegu and the banks of the Irrawaddy, and to go easy on our drinking water as it would be very scarce on the plains.

It was around midday when we reached the plains. We were all soon dragging our feet. The hard fast climb the day before, plus having had only one meal in well over thirty hours, was beginning to take its toll on our energy. The hot sun beat down upon our weary bodies, drying the sweat into white patches on our clothes as fast as it oozed from our backs.

The colonel set a raring pace. Some of the men said, 'He'll kill himself to save us at this rate.' Others said, 'He'll collapse at the river, so long as we are safe.'

Whether he heard or not, he kept up the same rate until at about five in the evening he called a fifteen-minute halt, during which he decided that we must risk going into a village to get food. 'But,' he said, 'we shall have to wait until dark to get the advantage of surprise, should there be any enemy in there.'

On restarting, the pace slowed a little, partly from caution, and partly because the rest seemed to have done us more harm than good, stiffening us up.

Dusk was falling when the colonel called us to stop and listen. We all stood motionless for a while. Then the sound came to us: the thud-thud-thud of someone pounding rice in a village not very far away and to the north. We went forward very quietly for about two hundred yards, stopped again and stood listening. Now the pounding had stopped. The colonel whispered to Sergeant McAteer, who in turn came to Jock Johnson and me. He told us to go forward and scout around the village. 'We will follow slowly behind you,' he said. 'We shall wait for you to give us the all clear before we come in.'

As we passed the colonel, he said in a low voice, 'Go careful, lads. We don't want anyone hurt.'

I led the way up the track with Jock following close behind. After about a hundred yards I called Jock to come closer, and whispered in his ear that I was going to cut into the jungle, go in a half circle and come out on the north side of the village. Should anyone be waiting for us they would expect us to come in from the south. Every ten yards I allowed Jock to get close to me. We both squatted and listened for any noise, but there was dead silence. Even the birds and insects seemed to have gone silent. I moved forward in the almost total darkness, dodging the ferns and twigs so as not to give ourselves away. The fallen leaves beneath my boots seemed to sound like breaking glass as I trod on them. When I thought that I had gone far enough I turned south towards where we thought the village was. I went as cautiously as I could, making out the huts of the village through the trees. Jock came and knelt beside me. I signalled that I was going to get behind one of the huts. He nodded and patted his Thompson submachine gun, telling me that he would cover me.

Together we moved quietly towards the edge of the jungle. I saw Jock nod his head, to mean that he was ready. In three or four strides I was behind the nearest hut. I waited a little, kneeling down on one knee, then moved to the end of the bamboo hut, peering around the corner. But all was quiet and there was no one in sight. I could see the hut opposite. This had a fire burning in front of it, and around the fire were a number of cooking utensils. The smell of cooked rice came to my nostrils and I realised how hungry I was. It seemed that the people of the village had been preparing the evening meal. I moved further round and could see right into the village. There was not a living soul. Taking boldness in both hands I walked into the middle of the village, had a good look around then signalled to Jock to call in the others. In front of most of the huts there were cooking pots. The villagers must have heard us coming and, thinking that we were either Japanese or Chinese troops, fled into the jungle. We were most probably being watched at that very moment.

It was during the issue of the food, when we got into sections, that we found we were one man missing.

Chapter Seven

The Separation

Immediately the colonel asked who it was. It was a man called Lacey. A search around the village came to nothing. It was then thought that perhaps we had left him where we first heard the rice-pounder. The colonel asked who had finished eating. Jock, Morgan, Ginger Hancock and I went over to him. 'Look, lads,' he said in that manner of his, 'I know he doesn't deserve it, but I cannot leave a man behind. We haven't lost anyone yet. Will you please go and look for him?'

Jock and Morgan led the way with Ginger and me following. We went straight to a fork in the track that Jock and I had seen about three hundred yards from the village and had a good look around, beating the sides of the brush with our rifles and calling out Lacey's name, but there was no sign of him. 'He could be miles back,' said Ginger. So we split up, Jock and Morgan going down one fork, Ginger and I the other. Later we all met back at the single track, with no sign of Lacey.

Jock led the way back to the village and reported to the colonel. The rest of the men were saying what they would do to Lacey if ever they caught up with him again, as they all had one thought in their minds: that he had fallen asleep somewhere. 'You four lads go and get your heads down,' the colonel said. 'We will give Lacey until four o'clock to show up, and then we move off.'

At the given time to go, we were all grumbling about the time we had lost through that 'bastard Lacey,' and saying again out loud how we would deal with him if he ever crossed our paths again. We had lost six precious hours, hours we could ill afford to lose. All the hard going that we had endured in the last few weeks was almost certainly now wasted because of one man. We still had a chance, but only a very slender one now.

Without even a glance down the track to see if he was coming we set off on what would be the last leg of our long and arduous march. We avoided villages, making slight detours. We crossed rivers by either wading or swimming, after which we took only very short rests and then pushed on again. The colonel was setting a really fast pace now, and we followed him. We were almost running by the time we reached one last river – a river full of leeches, which we had to burn off our feet and legs with cigarettes.

Meanwhile, the noise of gunfire and light automatic machine gun fire to the north of us reached our ears. The colonel was first to his feet. 'Come on lads,' he encouraged us, 'let's get on.' As we went on, the noise of the gunfire came closer. We glanced at each other, wondering whether we had already lost the race.

At about one o'clock in the afternoon we reached the village of Shwegu, about three hundred yards from the banks of the Irrawaddy and to our west. As we approached, a large stout man dressed in a white shirt and blue cotton trousers came towards us and said that the Japanese had passed by earlier that morning. All of us cursed and swore. 'It was that bastard Lacey's fault,' we all said.

The colonel decided to move away from the village and go to a large bamboo copse nearer to the river to work out our next move. In the meantime he sent Captain Brown, Sergeant Friend and two other men to make a reconnaissance near to the river to see what they could find out. While they were gone we were alerted to assume firing positions because someone was seen coming towards us. Through the long grass we could make out the cone shapes of Indian sepoy turbans.

When we challenged them they answered that they were British Indian. They were Rajputana riflemen, and said that the man at the village had told them to go to us. 'Damn!' the Colonel cursed. 'I hope he doesn't tell everyone we are here. Tell them to come quickly and get under cover.' This we did, and put them immediately on look-out duty.

The reconnaissance party returned and reported that they had seen plenty of Japanese infantry moving up on the other bank and also artillery being moved into position, but on this side of the river all seemed quiet.

After a short conference with his two officers the colonel gathered us all together. 'In view of the situation,' he said, 'I think ...' He paused as he picked his words. '... that it would be best if we split up into small parties and went in different directions. But ...' He paused again. '... I will put it to the vote. Who is in favour of going on as we are?' he asked, and looked around at all our faces. Only one arm was raised: that of Sergeant Friend.

Owing to the noise of the gunfire coming across the river, the colonel was forced to raise his voice to ask the sergeant why he wanted to stay as one unit. 'Well, sir, we have come this far together. I think we ought to carry on this way,' he answered.

'Look at it this way, Sergeant,' the colonel said after thinking for a moment. 'If we stayed together, we need food and water for over thirty, plus the fact that if we do run into trouble, we are all in it. Anyway, you are completely outvoted and that decision stands!'

'Right, men, we go in separate parties,' he rose to his feet and said, 'sort yourselves out into four parties. Sergeant Friend, you can take one. Sergeant McAteer, you can take another.' Captain Brown took another, and the Colonel with Captain Lancaster was going in the final party.

Sergeant Friend was given the first choice of whom he wanted and picked Jock Johnson, Ginger Hancock, Bill Bland, Smith, Ballantyne and me. The rest of the men he asked for refused, saying that they would go with any of the other three parties. No one was forced to go when picked. I had no objection because Jock, Ginger, Bland and Smith had all become my close companions. I did think that Morgan would have come with us as he had been with us a lot, but he elected to go with the colonel.

'Now, who will take the Indians?' the colonel asked.

'I will, sir,' Sergeant Friend shouted. 'They will come in handy with the language difficulty,' he added. The colonel glanced in my direction and gave me a sly wink.

The colonel and his party decided to try to cross the river, as did Sergeant McAteer and his party. Captain Brown's party and our party both decided to take the long route, by going northeast into China, striking back into Burma above Myitkyina and heading west to the Brahmaputra River and into India, a round trip of about three thousand miles – and all on foot.

There were four compasses and three maps. Captain Lancaster handed his compass to Sergeant Friend, saying, 'Look after it, it's a good one.'

The colonel gathered us around him for his final talk. 'Firstly we are here,' he said, 'because of one man. We cannot really blame him as we do not know what has actually happened to him.' He paused and looked at each one of us as if he was looking at us for the last time. Then he continued. 'If any of you should meet up with him, and well you may, if he has no good explanation to offer …'– the colonel's face had now turned sterner than we had ever seen before – '… then I say to you, deal with him as you see fit.'

We all knew that the colonel had the same idea why Lacey was not here.

He continued his talk, and said, 'I don't want that to happen again, so I am going to ask you all to make an agreement that should any man jeopardise the rest, then he is to be given twenty-four hours grace, and then left behind. Do you all agree?' We all agreed. 'One more piece of advice,' he went on. 'Do not get mixed up with any rabble, and fight only if you are cornered. Good luck to you all and I hope we meet in India.' His voice seemed to crack with emotion as he turned away.

Sergeant McAteer was the first to lead his party off. They went back the way we had come with the hope of crossing the river further down. We watched as they made their way through the long grass. They turned and waved and then went out of sight.

After about ten minutes Sergeant Friend led us away. The time was about five thirty in the evening. Jock was behind the sergeant, followed by Smith, Ballantyne, Bland and Ginger. The two Indians and I were in the rear. We headed in a northeasterly direction to make for the distant hills. Like the first party, we turned and waved until we could no longer see the others.

We kept off the tracks as much as possible to avoid any Japanese patrols that might have been skirmishing about. Darkness had fallen, and we were picking our way through the jungle as best as we could.

Our attention was drawn to a red glow in the sky, above the distant trees to our front. We came upon a track that led towards the glow. We estimated that it could be a village burning, about a quarter of a mile away. The sergeant called Jock and me to go forward and have a scout around to see what was happening and to see if we should steer clear of it.

I led the way up the track with Jock following some ten paces behind. As we got nearer we could see a village, but it was not on fire for we could not see any flames coming above the trees. We thought that the villagers could be entertaining guests, possibly Japanese soldiers, at dinner, so we had to move more carefully.

As we got nearer we could see the outline of the huts. We could also hear the crackle of burning wood, which I should think helped us both to get so near without being heard.

Leaving the track, I moved to the side nearest to the village and into the trees. I had quite a good view of what was going on.

A number of large fires were burning down the middle and between two rows of huts. Men were sitting around, waving their arms and talking frantically, while women and younger girls were squatting, tending food pots on the edge of the fires. Others came and went into the huts.

Jock joined me at my vantage point and whispered into my ear, 'What are you going to do, Fred?'

Gripping him by the shirt sleeve, I crept with him to the other side of the track. There, in comparative safety, I whispered, 'You go back and tell the others to wait until I give the signal before they come anywhere near. I'll wait until you come back before I go in.' Jock nodded his head, turned and left me.

While squatting there in the darkness alone, I thought how I would go about the task that lay before me. It seemed no time at all before Jock was at my side.

'At the very first sign of any danger, I will fire a shot. Then you belt off back to the others and get away from here,' I whispered. 'I'm going around the village and come in from the north side. This might confuse any who are not friendly and distract them from the rest.'

Jock nodded and whispered, 'I'll back you up,' tapping his Thompson submachine gun.

I got around to almost the opposite of where I thought Jock was. Creeping between the trees, I hid behind one of the larger huts. Then, stepping very carefully, I moved to the corner where I could see right down the middle of the village. The thing that I was looking for was men in uniform, and there were none. Everyone was busy eating, drinking and talking.

I waited a few moments just to make sure, and then with my rifle at the ready I walked as boldly as I could down the middle of the village. Everyone stopped talking and eating and stared at me in amazement. For a moment they all seemed too stunned to move. Then some of the women let out a yell and dashed off into the trees behind the huts.

I stopped at the first fire, dropped onto one knee and in Urdu asked the nearest man for food. At the same time I made a sign that I wanted food, just in case I was not understood.

A young man approached me and in broken English told me to take one of the large leaves that lay by the pots of food and to help myself. I loaded a leaf with food and at the same time kept a keen lookout for anything that might look like treachery.

I began questioning them why they were eating so late. The young man told me in a very excited manner how they had seen both Japanese and Chinese troops earlier that day and had left the village in case there had been a battle between them and had only just returned for their second meal of the day. This, then, was why they were now just eating.

I was beginning to feel a little safer when all of a sudden all eyes were staring at something behind me. My blood ran cold. I dropped my food, grabbed my rifle and, at the same time, spun around into the kneeling position. I heaved a sigh of relief, but cursed in the next. I was really angry. It was the sergeant marching the rest of the men into the village.

He marched straight up to me and said as I rose to my feet, 'What the bloody hell are you playing at?' Before I could answer, he raved on, 'Stuffing your guts and keeping us waiting out there, wasting time.'

My blood began to boil but, keeping as cool as I could, I said in a somewhat subdued voice, 'Sergeant, if you think that by making sure I have been wasting time, then I am guilty.' With that I walked away. I sat at the entrance to one of the huts. Jock, Ginger and Bland came over and sat by me. All had a large leaf of food. Each one in turn voiced their opinion that I had done the right thing in making sure it was safe and that the sergeant was in error. Jock said that he was sorry, and that he had told the sergeant to wait for the 'all clear' signal.

Using the Indians as interpreters, the sergeant persuaded the headman of the village to provide a guide through the jungle that would bring us close to the range of mountains that we had to cross. The guide stayed with us the whole night. We had short rests, and at dawn reached a high ridge overlooking a large grassy plain. Here the guide left us, telling us that if we followed the single track that ran across it, it would bring us to the foot of the mountains that were visible in the distance. 'Follow the path upward, and it will bring you to a friendly village that would give you food and shelter. You should reach it by the afternoon of the next day,' he informed us.

As we began our march downward the sergeant sent the two Indians forward as scouts, to give us some warning of any danger. After about half an hour Jock drew my attention to the way in which the two Indians were supposedly keeping a lookout. They were actually walking with an arm over each other's shoulders. Jock said, 'You would think that they were going to the local cinema in Calcutta, instead of being in enemy territory, wouldn't you?'

I agreed with him and said that we could easily run into trouble without any warning. 'Why don't you tell Friend?' I said. 'After all, you are second in command!'

'What! After what happened last night?' Jock burst out. 'Not me!' he said shaking his head. After a slight pause, he added, 'You try your luck with him. Perhaps he'll listen to you.'

'Alright,' I said, 'I will ask him.' I lengthened my stride and came level with the sergeant. 'Sarge,' I said, trying to be polite, 'I hope you don't mind me saying, but don't you think those two Indians should open up a little and keep their eyes open a bit more than they are?'

The sergeant half turned to me and in a 'couldn't care less' attitude said, 'They are alright. I only sent them up front because they can't speak our lingo. Anyway, it's none of your business!'

I stopped dead in my tracks and allowed everyone to pass me until Jock came level with me. 'Well, what did he say?' Jock asked.

'Oh, he told me to mind my own business,' I answered, looking straight ahead.

'Well, he can't say that he wasn't warned,' the little Scot retorted.

We both fell silent. I kept a sharp ear for anything and I am sure that my companion walking by my side did so, too.

We reached the plain at about three in the afternoon. Three hours later we were at the foot of the range of hills. The march across the parched and dry plain had made us use up most of our water. The sun had, it seemed, sent even hotter rays just to make the march harder. It was with some relief that we gained some shelter from the scorching orb as it began to sink down in the west.

The setting sun was now causing a semi-darkness to fall about us. The trees were getting denser as we climbed. After a while the sergeant called a halt. We had been marching for two hours since leaving the plain. While resting, the sergeant called us together and said, 'To make the journey to the village shorter we will go across country, not follow the track. I have decided to march by the compass.'

There was a murmur from everyone except the two Indians. Ginger could not hold back from saying loudly, 'What, in the dark!?'

The sergeant did not answer but got to his feet and led the way, leaving the track and going through the trees. It seemed that the further we went, the thicker the undergrowth seemed to get. At times we were having to crawl on hands and knees to get through the dense jungle in the darkness that had now completely engulfed us. We reckoned we had been on the go for at least two hours and had made very little progress. Some of the men were grumbling because they had stumbled into trees and given themselves knocks.

Tired, thirsty and hungry, the first light of dawn began to filter through the trees. We found that we were in a small clearing surrounded by thick impenetrable jungle. We all searched around for somewhere we could get through. There was a shout from someone that they could see a dried-up riverbed through the thick foliage. By getting down on our stomachs we crawled beneath the thick and wild shrub and managed to drop into the trench-like riverbed. Keeping down we managed to scramble along in that manner for some distance. The sergeant thought that this would eventually lead us to a village.

All of us were by this time grumbling aloud. After a while the sergeant changed direction, left the trench and headed back into the thick jungle again. One of the men lost his temper and shouted, 'Where the bleeding hell are you taking us now?'

The sergeant stopped, waiting for us all to get up to him. Then with an agitated look upon his face, as though he was at his wits' end at what to do next, he stammered, 'I think that we shall be alright if we follow those elephant droppings.' He pointed to two or three mounds of dried manure. Turning, he led the way once more. The men glanced from one to the other and shook their heads in disgust.

I held Jock by the arm, bent down and plunged my fist into one of the mounds, gripping a handful. I showed it to Jock. It crumbled to dust in my fingers. 'This,' I said, 'could be weeks old, and doesn't he know that there are wild elephants in this country?'

Jock shook his head and said, 'Come on, Fred, let's go.' Darkness was once more upon us. Had we stayed on the track as the guide had told us, we would have been at the village in the afternoon. There was still no sight or sound of any human habitation. Some of us were sure that we had gone in a full circle. Our water bottles were by this time empty. Throats were beginning to dry, talking became less, but mumbling got more and louder. Hunger was running a close second to thirst, for it had been two days since we had eaten.

A halt was called and we all just dropped in a circle. 'I think we are lost,' Ginger said, leaning his back against a tree.

'What do you say, Jock?' asked Ginger.

Jock would not commit himself. 'I don't think we are lost,' he said, 'maybe a little off course, that's all.'

'Boy!' Ginger blurted, 'I couldn't half go a plate of tripe and onions just now.'

'Just give me a paper-full of fish and chips,' said Bland.

'And a nice cold pint,' cut in Ginger.

'I'd be quite happy with a couple of slices of bread and dripping and a mug of tea,' said Smith in a low sad voice.

Our eyes had become accustomed to the dark. Sergeant Friend, who had all this time been sitting alone and silent, got to his feet and laid the compass down on the ground in the middle of the clearing. 'Look at this!' he shouted. 'That is the North Star up there, isn't it?' he asked, pointing to the night sky and in the direction of the Pole Star.

'Yes!' a couple of the men answered. 'Why? What's up?' they asked, going to him.

'Well,' the sergeant began as we all gathered around him, 'if that's the North Star,' he indicated with his finger, pointing to the Pole Star, 'then this compass is wrong!' He almost shouted. He stood up holding the instrument in his hand for all of us to look.

'Can I have a closer look, Sergeant?' I asked, holding out my hand.

'And I suppose you will say that it's me that's wrong!' he snapped as he put the compass into my palm.

'Not until I'm sure, I won't, Sergeant!' I snapped back.

First I faced the North Star, put the luminous 'N' in line with it, pushed up the small aperture and put it to my eyes. I waited until the needle had stopped swinging. At the same time I remembered that in this country the magnetic variation was 12½ degrees west of true North, thus the pointer would be swinging that much further over. We had, therefore, been going in a more westerly direction than we should have been. There was nothing wrong with the compass. Sergeant Friend had just forgotten to make the twelve-and-a-half-degree allowance.

Without a word I handed the instrument back. The sergeant looked at me with an inquiring glare and asked, 'Well, what's your opinion then?'

'How long have we been marching on the compass?' I asked.

'Oh, not very long,' he stammered, unsure of himself.

'Have you had the pointer at 'N' all the time?' I asked him.

'Of course I have!' he shouted. He was obviously losing his temper with the questions. I did not wish to show him up in front of the rest of the men who were listening to all that was being said. I was in a roundabout way attempting to show him that he was wrong and not the compass, but after the outburst, I turned and walked away.

He came after me and gripped me by the shoulder. He turned me around to face him. 'It is wrong, isn't it?' He almost demanded me to say that it was. His temper had really got the better of him by this time. I faced him squarely. He was slightly smaller than me. I was about five foot ten, he was about five seven or eight. I looked at his now twitching face in the gloom. His eyes were glaring at me. The rest of the party had gathered around us, waiting for me to reply.

We two stood in a rough circle of men. My temper, too, was beginning to boil. For a moment we stood face to face in dead silence. Even the general noises of the jungle seemed to be quiet, waiting for me to speak. I could no longer hold back what I had tried to avoid saying before. 'No, Sergeant!' I said through gritted teeth, then pointed at him. 'You are wrong, not the compass!'

'How can I be wrong? The needle isn't pointing north when I face north,' he raved, waving his arms.

'That is just it!' I said, trying to compose myself. 'I am sorry that it is me who has to tell you, but I think that you have forgotten something of great importance.'

'Oh, and what the bloody hell is that, know-all?' he sneered.

'You have forgotten, Sergeant,' I sneered back, 'to allow for the magnetic variation, which in this country is twelve-and-a-half degrees west!'

'No bleeding wonder we haven't reached that village,' grumbled Ginger.

'You know it all, don't you, Goode!' the sergeant snapped.

'No Sergeant, I don't!' I snapped back, 'I only remember what I have been taught. It does help sometimes.'

'Alright, what do you suggest?' His tone had cooled a little.

'I suggest we stay put until it gets light,' I replied, 'then strike due east until we come to a track and follow it. Try to go as much east as we can for about four or five hours.'

Everyone, including the sergeant, agreed that this was the best plan to adopt for the present.

It was in the middle of the morning after battling our way through the thick jungle that we came upon a track that led us upward into the hills. We were not sure if it was the track which we had left two nights ago, but at least we could get along with some ease. Slowly the track began to widen and we were then sure that we were coming near to a village.

The sergeant called a halt. He called me and asked me to go forward and scout to see what we were heading for. Jock came with me, but the sergeant called him back and said, 'There is no need for two of you to go. He'll be alright.' I turned to Jock, smiled and gave a wink. It was too obvious that the sergeant meant to get his own back on me somehow.

I soon brushed the thought from my mind as I made my way carefully through the trees, keeping my ears and eyes open. I had gone about fifty yards uphill when through the trees I could make out a number of small bamboo huts perched on the top of the hill. I got close enough to observe that there was no one moving about. The place looked deserted. I waited for some time, keeping the huts in sight and watching to see whether anyone came or went from them. After a while I decided to return, which I did not like, for one ought to keep the object in view at all times. Anything could happen as soon as I had left, but then, I thought, I was not in charge.

I returned to the party and reported what I had seen. I suggested that I return with the two Indians and give the village a good look-over. To this, the sergeant readily agreed.

We approached the village very cautiously. I led the way. At the entrance I signalled the two Indians to go one on each side of the path. We waited for a short time and then I waved them to go in.

There were only about six small huts. I stood in the centre of them while the Indians searched each one. In the third hut they shouted, and dragged out a dirty ragged young man they had found sitting in the corner. While one Indian questioned him, I sent the other back for the rest of the party to join us.

The young Kachin was the only one left in the village. Everyone else had gone into the jungle and hidden. He seemed to be the village simpleton. However, we managed to make him understand that our greatest need was food which he began to prepare for us all.

In no time he had a huge cauldron of rice going on one fire, while on another he had a pig cut up and boiling in a large black pot. When we had made some tea and were all sitting around for the meal to be cooked, the young Kachin alerted us that someone else was coming up the track. We all made a hasty withdrawal to the edge of the village and got down in firing positions. The word went around not to open fire until all of them were inside.

Jock and I had dropped down behind a fallen tree on the fringe of the jungle and the edge of the village. I had a clear view of the track up which 'they', whoever it was, would come. I am sure that Jock had the same view.

'I hope no one lets go before they are right inside,' I whispered to him.

'Aye, me too,' he replied.

The noise of marching feet grew louder. My rifle was trained right in the middle of where the track disappeared over the rise. I closed my left eye and squeezed the first pressure of the trigger.

Chapter Eight

The Return of Lacey

A head and shoulders rose above the dirt track. The head had a British bush hat on it. I released the trigger and lowered my rifle. It was Captain Brown with the other party.

After the general hellos and greetings we invited them to share our meal. The two Indians sat apart, as they were Muslims and could not go near the pork that was by this time well and truly cooked.

After exchanging stories of how things had fared for us, it was found that in the panic to get into firing positions Bland had knocked against the large pot in which the pork was boiling. The fat had spilled over and into his boot, scalding him. We removed his boot to see what injury he had. To everyone's amazement a large blister was beginning to form on the heel of his foot. This was burst and dressed, and the boot replaced.

While the injured foot was being seen to, talk had gone on between our party and that of Captain Brown about the row between the sergeant and me the day before.

Captain Brown called me to one side and asked, 'Are you quite happy with Sergeant Friend as your leader?'

I did not want to be labelled a rebel or mutineer, so I dodged the question. 'Why do you ask that, Sir?'

'Well, we have been here less than an hour, and all I have heard is how you got them out of a mess.' He stood squarely in front of me with his hands on his hips, looking straight into my eyes. 'Is that true?' he asked. I was at a loss for words. I dropped my gaze to the ground to avoid his stare. 'Don't be afraid to speak up,' he prompted. 'I myself have had doubts about his ability for some time. All that you will do is to convince me.'

'Well, Sir,' I began, raising my face to look at him, 'Neither I nor Corporal Johnson are entirely in agreement with what Sergeant Friend does or has been doing.' I was gaining more confidence as I went on. 'Some of the men don't think that he knows what he is doing half of the time,' I said, faltering slightly. 'After all, Sir,' I went on, 'we are surrounded by the enemy and every step can be a danger.'

'Well, Corporal,' the Captain came back, dropping his gaze to the ground as if apologising, 'I cannot take the leadership away from him, but I can ask you if you would prefer to join my party.'

I stood quite still for a while, thinking over what the officer had asked, but I answered, 'Thanks kindly, Sir, but I think I will stick it out.'

The captain and the sergeant had been together in a talk and had decided that we should all travel together. Some of the captain's party disagreed with this. Some of our party said that we were doing what the colonel had been against, which was travelling in a large party. A vote was taken and the majority said we should travel together, so we all set off as one party under Captain Brown. After all, we were both going in the same direction, making for Sadon, about fifty miles north of Myitkyina.

For two days our party went along together, but there were complaints from the others that Bland's injury was holding us up. We all took turns in helping him along. Bland never once complained, but it was becoming obvious that the walking only aggravated the injury more. We all took turns to carry his rifle and ammo.

Our route led us over a range of hills and a small river. As we approached these we could see that our path lay across the river up a steep bank, across a metal road and again up another steep bank. The road we have to cross, we thought, must be the main Burma Road running northeast to southwest.

Keeping under cover, as it was around midday, the question arose how best to get over the road without being seen. To our right, about a quarter of a mile away, we could see some well-built bungalows. They looked like a transit camp. The Japanese would certainly use this road for any heavy transport, both to supply forward troops and also bring back any from their frontal points.

Some of the men said that it would be best to wait until darkness before making the dash across the road and the river, but it was argued that we could not afford to waste about seven hours of marching time. So it was decided that we make the move right away. We formed up in extended line, swept down the hill and waded across the river, which in some parts was knee deep and in other parts came up to the chin. We scrambled up the steep grassy bank and across the road. Without looking either left or right we dashed up the steep bank above the road, gripping the long grass to help pull ourselves up. When we thought we had gone far enough, we lay flat on our bellies, completely exhausted.

As we lay there gathering our breath, the sound of motor transport came to our ears from the north, to our left. It was too late to move further up the bank, as we might have been seen by the driver of the leading vehicle, so we all lay quite still, pressing our bodies as close to the ground as we could. My heart missed a beat as the leading lorry stopped directly beneath us. Had they seen our wet footprints on the road? We heard the cab door open, some footsteps and then shouts of what we knew was Japanese. Other doors opened and shut, and there was laughter and shouting between drivers and passengers. Then after some time the engines restarted and the lorries slowly drove away on up the incline and around the bend of the road.

Quickly we rose to our feet and made our way up to the trees that covered the skyline. There we stood and watched as the lorries came back into view and turned towards the huts. There were five of them, and we thought how lucky we had been not to be seen. 'We ought to have asked them for a lift,' joked Sharp.

Bland's foot was becoming so bad that we had to take turns carrying him. Captain Brown's party was by now really grumbling, saying that it was not their responsibility. It was very hard to realise that these were the same men we had trained with, drunk with, played all sorts of sports with, who now wanted to ditch one of their friends because of an accident.

We were all resting and waiting for Sharp to come up. He was carrying Bland on his back, while Jock and I had carried both their rifles and ammo. The captain had called the rest of his party together, and they had voted to leave us and go on ahead and for us to look after Bland ourselves. Sergeant Friend changed almost immediately from the 'happy-go-lucky' man he had been since we joined Captain Brown's party to almost a nervous wreck. His face had begun to twitch on one side and his mouth had drooped at the corners.

'Look at Friend's face, Fred!' Ginger leaned over and whispered to me.

I had already noticed it and nodded my head. 'He's either dead scared, or he doesn't want the responsibility,' I whispered back.

The arrival of Sharp and Bland took my mind from the sergeant. Sharp staggered to where we were sitting, let Bland slide to the ground and said, 'I joined the army as a cavalryman and I finish up being a horse!' No one thought that it was funny. All the faces showed what was in their minds.

Before the goodbyes were said, Captain Brown took me aside and said, 'If you have any more nonsense with Sergeant Friend, there is nothing stopping you from going it alone. Do you understand?'

'Yes Sir!' I answered.

He held out his hand and added, 'Good luck!'

'Good luck to you, too, Sir!' I said, taking his hand. 'Thanks again!'

After the other party had forged on ahead of us, I decided to keep out of the sergeant's way as much as I could and took the rear guard position with Jock just in front. We had been going along quite steadily, helping Bland as much as we could, except for the two Indians who never offered to give him any assistance.

After a few days on our own again, at about eleven in the morning we came out of the jungle into some thinner shrubbery. Directly in front was a wide dusty track. The sergeant asked Jock and me to go forward and have a look to see if it was safe to cross. On closer inspection we found that a barbed wire fence of five strands ran parallel with the road on the opposite side. The trees on that side of the fence were set out in long lines, with uniform gaps in between. This told us that it was a plantation of rubber trees. The top strand of the fence was about five feet from the ground, while the bottom strand was about one foot from the ground. Jock went back and reported while I kept watch. He returned with the sergeant and they dropped down on each side of me.

'Is it all clear?' Friend asked.

'Yes, so far,' I answered, 'but what about that?' I pointed at the fence.

'Can you and Jock get across and hold it up for the rest of us?' the sergeant asked, looking at me.

'I suppose so,' I replied, glancing at Jock.

'Are you ready, Fred?' asked Jock, and I nodded. We darted across the road and rolled over on our backs. With a gap wide enough for a man to pass between us we lay with the wire over and across our chests. When the first man came we forced the wire up, me with my rifle and Jock with his Thompson machine gun. When all had gone under the wire I held up the bottom strand while Jock wriggled away. Jock then held the wire while I wriggled myself free. We were in the rubber plantation. The party had moved away from the fence and were hidden behind the trees.

We were getting ready to move off when someone said, 'Where's Bland?'

'Did he get under the wire?' the sergeant asked Jock.

'Can't say I noticed him,' Jock replied. 'Did you, Fred?'

'No, I can't say I do remember him going through,' I answered, looking around to make sure. 'I'll pop back and have a look for him.'

I made my way back in between the trees to the fence. There sitting on the other side of the fence and facing the road was Bland. He had taken his boot and sock off the injured foot. 'You stupid bleeding idiot!' I shouted at him in anger. 'Haven't you got any more sense than that?' I took off my hat, laid down my rifle and worked my way beneath the wire again. Then, getting up on my feet, I ran to Bland, shouting, 'Bill, you bleeding fool …' My anger died there, as I glanced at the injured foot. It was swollen to twice its normal size, and the heel, where the boot had rubbed, was a red open sore as big as the top of a teacup. It must have been absolute torture to even get a boot on, let alone walk any distance with it. I felt real pity for the man. 'Come on, Bill,' I said, 'let's get you over the other side of this wire and out of sight.' I had hardly finished when in the far distance I could hear the sound of some kind of vehicle. 'Quick, Bill!' I shouted. 'Stand up with your feet apart.' I bent almost double and put my head between his legs and hoisted him up. 'Get your feet onto the top wire,' I shouted to him, 'and jump!' I helped him with a slight push, and he dropped safely to the other side. I pushed his rifle and boot and sock under towards him. 'Move away under cover,' I shouted as the noise of the vehicle grew louder.

I dropped to the ground, rolled over on my back and, digging my heels into the ground, began to force my body beneath the wire, at the same time trying to hold it away from my clothes. When I raised my knees to get an extra push my shorts got caught, and in my haste to free them one leg tore down, splitting them, but at least I was free. I could now see a cloud of dust rising above the trees, and the noise of the vehicle was almost upon me as it came along the hard road. I cursed and swore as I continued to wriggle the rest of the way beneath the wire. Free, I grabbed my rifle and hat and crawled along the fence until I was hidden from the road by a bush. I saw a truck, a three-tonner, as it came around the bend in the road about thirty yards away. Two Japanese sat in the cab. The one in the passenger seat wore a white shirt – an officer. There were two more behind the cab with a light machine gun between them.

I had raised my rifle to shoot, but I didn't know whether to try to shoot the driver or aim at one of the tyres to cause a wreck. But then I thought of what the colonel had said. 'Don't fight unless you are cornered.' In those split seconds, I also considered that if I missed or did not cause a wreck, or if there were other trucks following behind, then the hunt would be on for us and anyone else who happened to be coming behind us following the same route.

The lorry was abreast of me. I kept perfectly still, and it went by, sending up a cloud of dust that almost choked me as it billowed in my direction. Through the dust I could see that there were more men in the back and it was towing what looked like a water container.

I waited until the vehicle was well out of sight before I moved. On my way I found Bland crouching behind a tree. I picked up his rifle and together we made our way back to the others who were spread out among the trees some two hundred yards back.

The sergeant's voice bellowed from behind one of the trees. 'Where the bloody hell have you been?' He came from behind the tree as he spoke.

'Sorry, Sergeant,' I said sarcastically, 'I got held up a little.'

'You're getting too bloody clever,' he rasped back. 'You might have given us all away stopping there.'

'How did you come to rip your shorts, Fred?' Ginger cut in.

'Oh, I caught them on the wire as I got back under,' I answered, as if it was of no importance.

'Yes!' Bland put in, limping towards the sergeant so that he heard what he said, 'He did it getting me over that fence and he had to sit tight while the Japs went past.'

All but the two Indians were now gathered around in a circle looking at the sergeant. I spoke loudly. 'We shall certainly have to be on the alert. They seemed to be going somewhere to search out.'

'Oh, and what gives you that idea?' said the sergeant.

'Well, for a start,' I began, 'they are carrying their own water and don't need rivers or villages and they have got transport that will take them anywhere fast.' I ended by walking away.

Bland kept getting left behind. We would have to wait for him to hobble up to us and by the time he had reached us it was time to move on once more, so that in fact he was not getting any rest at all.

It had begun to rain very hard. We could see some bamboo huts of a village through the falling rain, and we were soon drenched to the skin. Some of the men in front had started to run to get out of the torrential downpour. Jock and I were bringing up the rear, and behind was Bland somewhere way back. We, too, began to run, but then, looking at each other from beneath our dripping bush hats, we stopped, turned and walked back. Jock said, 'What's the use. We're soaking now anyway.' I looked at him, grinned and bent my head down against the driving rain.

We made a chair of two rifles while Bland slung Jock's Tommy-gun over his back, and between us we got him to the village. The rain by this time had stopped. The others got a fire going and had been given some dry clothes to put on by the villagers.

During the evening the headman of the village came to the hut and spoke to the two Indians. They talked in Urdu, while the sergeant stood by listening. I, too, listened, and from their conversation I gathered that the headman was expecting a visit from the Japanese at any time in the next day or two. The headman was very frightened and pleaded with the two Indians to get us to leave the village as soon as possible.

The sergeant, the two Indians and the headman went outside the hut, leaving us to go to sleep. After breakfast the next morning the sergeant called us to pay attention. Standing with his back to the door, he said, 'Look men! We must get going and we must go fast.' Turning to Bland, who was sitting in the corner of the hut, he said, 'I'm afraid we shall have to leave you behind.' He paused. 'But I shall take a vote on who wishes to go on and leave you. Is that understood?'

I looked first at the sergeant and then at Bland. It was pitiful. I felt nothing but sorrow for the poor man. The sergeant turned first to the two Indians who were sitting on his right and said to them, 'Tomorrow we go on, yes?' I don't know whether they understood what was being asked of them, but they both looked at him and nodded their heads. The next was Smith. He said 'Yes.' Ballantyne was next. He, too, answered 'Yes.' Then it was Ginger's turn. He never glanced at Bland and he surprised me when he said yes, because he was Bland's real mate. Next came Jock. He will not say yes, I thought. He looked at Bland then dropped his head and said in a quiet voice, 'Yes.'

I was completely shaken by the thoughtlessness of these men who were supposed to have been the very friends of this man, and yet here they were, going to leave him alone in a jungle village. Had it been me I could have understood it, for I was really the odd man out among them. I had only got to be acquainted with them at the Bush Warfare School. The sergeant and Smith had been in the same unit in North Africa, and so had Jock, Ballantyne, Ginger and Bland.

The sergeant was asking me. I glanced around at all of them except the Indians. 'I'll stay with him and take a chance,' I answered.

For a moment there was complete silence, and then all of them, except Sergeant Friend and the two Indians, crowded around me and patted my back, saying how good I was. When the backslapping had ceased, the sergeant said, 'You really want it this way, don't you, Goode?' He seemed to be probing why I had decided to stay.

'No, Sergeant,' I answered quickly. 'It was the last thing that I thought would happen, but you go on and don't let it worry you.'

At a little before dawn the next morning, all were ready to move off. Sergeant Friend came to me and said, 'I'll leave messages for you as often as I can with any headman we come across in case we alter our plans and try to warn you of any danger, if there is any.'

I thanked him and said, 'Don't forget to mark the tracks at any junctions with the usual signs. Remember we have got no compass or map,' I reminded him.

They were about to move off when I called to them, 'Just a minute!' They turned towards me and waited for me to speak. I stood in the doorway of the hut with Bland close behind me. I began in a slow clear voice. 'This journey that we are attempting is a very long and hard one.' They all looked a little bewildered. 'We have gone barely a quarter of it,' I continued, raising my voice slightly. 'If it so happens that Bill and I do catch up with you again ...' – I pointed my finger at each one of them – 'and if any of you or all of you fall to the fate that has fallen to Bland, don't ...' – I repeated the word more loudly – 'don't expect any sympathy from me or Bill.'

For a moment they all stood there staring at me. No one said a word. Then, slowly, one after another they shook their heads and meekly said, 'Oh, no, that was the agreement we all made.'

I think my little speech had touched their consciences. They came to me one at a time and shook my hand, saying, 'Hurry up and catch us, Fred!' The sergeant was the last. He shook hands, and said, 'I promise to give you all the help I can.'

As they walked away Jock turned, stood for a moment as if undecided whether to stay or go, then raised his arm in a last salute, turned and was gone.

Our planned route would take us into the Yunnan province of western China that borders on to Burma. Two frontiers meet in a valley between a range of mountains. These went as high as twelve thousand feet or more, but they were about another six hundred miles away.

The headman of the village was eager for us to leave and brought all sorts of herbs and other concoctions to put on Bland's foot, all to no good. He even brought an old woman from somewhere to say some kind of incantations over the injured foot and lay on some dung mixed with other herbs. Immediately after she had gone from the hut I ripped off the dung dressing, washed the places that were dirty and placed on our own clean dressing.

We had been on our own in the village for four days. In the middle of the morning of the fifth day a young boy came dashing into the hut to tell us that some soldiers were coming. I quickly got Bland over my shoulder and carried him away from the hut and into the jungle. After dropping him down in high grass hidden by a thick cluster of bamboo and teak trees, I returned to the hut to fetch all our gear, making two trips, then hid myself next to Bland.

It was not long before we could hear the jingle of a number of bridles and other mounted equipment. I looked at Bland, who had turned his face in my direction. Leaning over, I said in a whisper, 'If it comes to the worst, make a dash for it. You go that way and I'll go this way.' I pointed in two opposite directions deeper into the jungle.

The noise of the horses was very plain to hear, when the young boy who had told us of the soldiers came running towards where we lay and shouted, 'Ingris, Ingris!' The little bastard had given us away, I thought. Then, rising up so that I could see better, I saw that the men on the horses were British officers. Heaving a big sigh of relief, I helped Bland to his feet. With him hobbling along we made our way towards what we could now see was a platoon of Gurkhas with three British officers in charge.

We recognised each other straight away. They were the same officers who had come along in the car on the night we had caught the fire-raiser. After all the greetings and what-are-you-doing-heres were sorted out, Captain Thompson, who was the senior, said, 'We have got a friend of yours with us.' He turned and pointed back down the track.

'A friend of ours, Sir?' I asked in bewilderment.

'Yes, his name is Lacey.' He smiled as he said the name.

'Lacey!' I shouted in anger at the mere sound of the name. 'I don't want to see that lousy bastard. I'll shoot him as soon as I look at him,' I said between gnashed teeth.

'Now, hold on a moment, Corporal,' the officer said, coming closer and putting his hand on my shoulder.

'But Sir!' I blurted out. 'Do you realise what he has done to about fifty decent men?' I asked, half pulling myself away from the officer's friendly arm.

'No, Corporal, I do not know, but what I do know is that he will be an extra rifle to you should you get into any trouble. You may need that somewhere along the line.'

I knew that the officer was talking sense, but I still had to have my say. 'He's no good sir, no good to anyone.'

'Now, Corporal, you cannot be both judge and jury,' the captain said, trying to soothe me. 'We don't know what happened. Do you?'

'Not really sir,' I answered, 'but I do know what happened because of it. We got bloody well cut off and I shall not forget that in a hurry.'

'Well, let's hear what your other half has to say on the matter.' The captain nodded to where Bland had been standing silently on his good foot. 'What do you say?' he asked Bland.

'Well, I know how Fred feels about Lacey, and I feel the same.' He stopped for a minute as he tried to ease his injured foot, then went on, 'But you are right, sir. He could be a help to us, so I say that we should have him with us.'

'There you are, Corporal,' the Captain said, smiling and once again putting his arm on my shoulder.

Just then Lacey came into sight. He walked straight to where we were standing and his face broke into a wide grin, his black bearded face making his teeth show up white. He was a bit taller than me and a lot heavier and much thicker built than both Bland and me. 'Hello, Fred!' He put out his hand for me to shake.

Not taking it, I stared hard at him and asked, 'And what happened to you?'

He must have seen the hatred in my face, for he said, 'I'm sorry, Fred, I fell asleep. I was tired, really tired.' He almost cried as he said this.

If he was expecting any sympathy, he never got any. 'We were all tired,' I almost shouted at him, leaning forward, pushing my face so close to his that he backed away. 'We were all really very tired. Do you realise what you might have done to all of us? Do you?' I waited for him to answer.

'No Fred, what have I done? Tell me,' he almost whispered, 'what have I done?'

'You, you lousy black-bearded bastard, have probably caused the deaths of every man jack of us.' I stepped forward and raised my hands to get him by the throat, but two of the officers got between us.

Captain Thompson walked me away while the other officer took Lacey to one side. It took some time before my temper would allow me to go near the hut where Lacey and Bland were sitting near the fire.

One of the officers gave me a small packet of permanganate of potash to bathe Bland's foot, telling me to add a few of the crystals in warm water and bathe the injury three times a day.

The three officers left later in the day. They wished us well. They pulled me aside and said that they understood how I felt about Lacey, but for the time being let things lie and perhaps it would not end as badly as I thought it would.

I had spoken very briefly to Lacey, telling him that if he caused any mishap between us three I would not hesitate to shoot him.

He never answered me but dropped his gaze and would not look me in the face. I had but to ask him to do something and he would do it without question.

We followed the officer's instruction to bathe Bland's injured foot and it was about five days later that Bland was able, with some difficulty, to at least get his boot on. He was still not able to walk, though, and the headman was really getting agitated about us being in the village so long. I approached him about the sale of a quiet pony and we struck a bargain of one hundred rupees with food enough to last us for a journey of three days, which was the distance to the next safe village.

At dawn and with the young son of the headman as a guide to show us the right track to take after we had left the village, we set off with Bland sitting astride the pony on a rough saddle made from old sacks, with all the food, his rifle and ammunition slung across his back.

It was a very happy and smiling headman that waved us goodbye in the early morning mist. I led the way with the rope of the pony while Lacey brought up the rear. It was in this way that we travelled, stopping only now and then for rests and allowing Bland to ease his backside. We rested at night and kept to the cover of the jungle trails by day.

We were, I reckoned, almost ten days behind Sergeant Friend and our party. So it was no use hurrying to catch them up. I thought that if we went at a steady pace and kept our eyes and ears alert we would avoid trouble and maintain a steady four miles an hour. From dawn to dusk, with the minimum of rest, we could cover an average of thirty to forty miles a day.

We were still bathing the injured foot by warming some water. The swelling had gone and the sore was beginning to heal. Bland made one or two attempts at walking, but I had warned him not to do too much as he could undo all the good we had done.

We had used up the three days food we had bought, for we were now in the fourth day. It was getting well into the afternoon, and we were following a trail that took us up the side of a huge mountain. Above us we could make out the rhythmic sounds of a rice-pounder, which told us that we were coming to a village. This could be the village that we had been told to go to. We were a little late in our estimate. Still, it was better late than never.

A young woman carrying a baby greeted us as we reached the village. She took us to the hut of the headman who invited us in, while the woman prepared some food.

We all sat around the fire in the centre of the hut after we had eaten our meal and I tried to hold a conversation with the headman. First I tried Urdu but, grinning and showing a row of black tobacco-stained teeth, he shook his head and waggled his fingers, a sign we knew meant that he did not understand. I tried Chinese next, and once again I got the same grin and hand sign.

Bland and Lacey had by this time made themselves comfortable lying on the floor near the fire, leaving me and the headman to sort it all out.

Next I tried sign language. My patience was becoming exhausted. After about a quarter of an hour of trying to make him understand, the man sat upright. The grin left his face and, mumbling in his native tongue, he began fumbling at his waist and produced a small piece of paper which was carefully folded. Now it was my turn to grin, and I slapped him on the shoulder. The message on the paper read, 'Sinlum, two days march, J.F.'

Leaving the village at dawn we made a descent into a small valley and then climbed another small range of hills covered with bamboo and tall teak woods. It was well into the afternoon when we again began to descend. Through the trees we could see before us a long wide plain, across which the track ran and disappeared into the distant hills. I called a halt while we were still in plenty of cover.

'How far away do you think those hills are?' I asked.

Bland answered first. 'I would say ten to twelve miles.'

Lacey hesitated. 'Well, I would say they are a little further than that,' he said looking at me. 'About fifteen miles. Don't forget that the sun is shining on them, making them clearer and nearer.'

'Yes, I think you are right!' Bland agreed with him.

I said nothing, but tied the pony to a tree and sat down near my two companions. 'We'll wait here until it is dark,' I said, 'then cross that plain. The track is quite visible to see,' I pointed out. 'If there are any Japs in those hills, they will not see us crossing that wide open space in the dark. Do you agree?'

Both men agreed with my plan. 'How long do you think it will take us to cross?' Bland asked.

'Well, if we go at a steady pace at three miles an hour, and they are fifteen miles away, we should be into those hills and out of sight by daylight,' I said.

Between catnaps we watched as the sun sank behind us and the mountains to our rear. We got started while there was still a little light and made our way down the side of the hill. Darkness had fallen completely when we reached the flat dusty plain.

Chapter Nine

Father McGovern

No sooner had the sun sank and darkness had fallen over the plain than red glows began to show in the hills, dotted here and there.

'I wonder what they are?' asked Lacey, speaking more to Bland than me.

'Dunno! Could be villages,' answered Bland.

'They are too close together,' I butted in. 'More like a Jap column settled down for the night. After all, they have got nothing to worry about who sees them?'

'S'pose you are right, Fred,' Bland replied.

I was leading the pony by the lead rope. Bland was sitting astride the animal. Suddenly there was a piercing howl to our right front. Coming out of the darkness it made me jump, and the pony shot up its head and began to gallop. The rope was out of my hand and I could see Bland crouched over the animal's neck, holding on for all he was worth. In a few seconds I gathered my wits and gave chase, managing to keep the dark shape in view. As the howl seemed to die, so another began in an even higher pitch. This caused the pony to stop for just long enough for me to get up to it. Its nostrils were blowing two large comets of steam into the cool night air. I grabbed the rough bridle that we had made and began to soothe the animal. Once again another screeching howl was sent up into the night, but this time from a different direction, then another close on the last, and then another. It seemed that we were completely surrounded. In the meantime Bland had dropped from the back of the pony and was standing beside me, while Lacey had come up panting.

'Fred, they're all around us,' he half whispered, hardly able to get his breath.

'What're they?' both men asked at the same time with a worried sound in their voices.

'Could be jackals,' I told them. 'You two, get on each side of the pony. I will keep close to his head and lead him. Bill,' I addressed Bland, 'I am afraid you are going to have to walk, but whatever you do, just keep on the move and don't stop for anything. We cannot afford to fire on them to frighten them off. One shot will echo all across the plain. So just keep swinging your rifles if anything comes near you and don't be afraid to clobber them with your rifle. We must keep them away from the pony's legs. They will try to bring him down and have a go at us.'

I was leading the pony on a short rope and swinging my rifle from side to side. As I looked from one side to the other I could see the dog-like shape of the animals as they slinked from one side of the path to the other, obviously waiting for the opportunity to attack.

'How are you two back there?' I asked without turning my head away from the front and peering into the darkness.

'We're not doing too bad,' Bland answered, 'but I don't think I can run very far.'

I tried to reassure him and Lacey by saying, 'If they don't come at us in the first half hour, I doubt if they will come at us at all.'

We had been walking at a steady pace for about two hours. The howling had died down somewhat, but the dark shapes were still slinking about, though not coming too close. I thought that we were slowly getting rid of them when dead in front of me and right in the middle of the track was a large animal, like a wolf. It was sitting on its back legs as if waiting in defiance for us to approach. As I got near, it bared its teeth and snarled. Gripping my rifle by the barrel I swung the butt fiercer. I did not slow down or alter my step but just kept going forward, looking at the animal in front of me. I must have been but a few paces from it when, with a snarl and show of its fangs, it got up onto its legs and slinked off to the left of the track, looking back at us and showing its fangs again. That was the end of them.

Dawn was breaking as we began to climb the hills. The early rays of the sun were coming up into the sky in front of us. Behind us, as we looked back, the plain was covered in a sea of mist. It was cold and damp as we made the climb. The trees were clouded here and there in white grey fog. I called a halt and tied the pony to a tree. Then we turned and looked back. It looked like a great white lake, moving very slowly as the rays of sun caught it and sent it skywards. The pony was munching at the grass that was soaked with the early morning dew. His head shot up and his ears went first forward and then back as if he had heard something higher up the hill.

'I wonder what he heard?' asked Lacey. 'Probably an animal,' he ventured to add.

'Not more bloody jackals, I hope,' said Bland.

'Come on, let's move,' I said, 'I'm getting cold in this mist.'

'Yes, and in a couple of hours we'll be sweating our cobs off,' Lacey grumbled.

About ten minutes later we had to cross a stream which cut across our path. Here we filled our water bottles and splashed the cold water over our faces and allowed the pony to drink. Further up the hill we came to another path running across ours but parallel to the stream lower down, going in a north to south direction.

'Hey, Fred, look at this!' said Bland in a half whisper, pointing at some fresh horse droppings which were still steaming.

'Quick! Let's move!' I said as I glanced and saw boot marks in the wet mud. 'We could be in the middle of a Jap column.'

We moved fast up the hill, not stopping until we were on the other side.

We spent the night in the thick jungle. We had no way of telling the time except by the sun during the day, so we had to guess when it was time to take over sentry duty between us.

At the crack of dawn we set off again, walking at our usual steady pace. Bland had now recovered from his injury and was walking without any pain. It was about nine in the morning when we came to a thickly covered valley. After about another half hour we came to a fork in the path. We searched around for a sign from Friend to tell us which track to take, but there was none. We generally left a broken twig or a loose branch near the track not to take, but there was nothing.

'Perhaps they forgot to leave a sign,' said Bland.

'Perhaps they have forgotten us altogether,' I said, cursing. 'Well, which one do we take?' I asked, looking at both of them.

'We'll leave it to you, Fred,' they said together.

'Alright, but don't blame me if it's the wrong one,' I said.

I led the way up the left-hand fork. After a while the vista opened up. On our right was thick wooded jungle, on our left a large stretch of paddy fields. A woman working in the fields near the track looked up and saw us. I stopped and asked her in Urdu, 'Sinlum-ooder-hai?' I pointed in the direction of some buildings perched on the hills to our left. She stood up and stared at our bearded faces and ragged clothes. 'We are English. We want to get to Sinlum,' I said again in Urdu. Without a word she gathered up her sari-like dress, ran towards me, grabbed the pony's rope from my hand and waved us to follow. She went off the track into the jungle on the right-hand side, and we followed her close behind.

'Where's she taking us?' Bland asked.

'Dunno,' I answered, 'but I think she's leading us out of danger.'

The woman picked her way through the trees and shrubs, and after what seemed a couple of miles she stopped at another track. Putting the lead rope back into my hand she turned, pointed to the way we had come from and said, 'Sinlum-Gagee Japani Hai.' Then, pointing up the track she had led us to, she said, 'Sinlum-Gabah, Teek-hai! Jow-Jaldee-jow.' Before we could thank her she had disappeared into the jungle.

We arrived at Sinlum-Gabah at around noon. There we were given a good meal and our first hot bath in months. We were also given some decent clothes. Bland and I had torn our shorts so badly that we were a disgrace. We were given a pair of the wide black cotton pantaloons that the Kachins and Karennis wear. You had to pull the waist band tight, tie a knot with it and tuck it in. It was the women of the village who showed us how to do this, so that the trousers would not fall down as we walked. We caused some laughter as we paraded around the village trusting that we had got it right but only to find that after a few strides we were standing there with the trousers around our ankles and showing everything.

The villagers told us that the sergeant and his party were about fourteen days in front of us. So we had gained no ground on them at all. As English was spoken well in the village, we had no difficulty in asking whether the sergeant had left any messages, but they shook their heads and said no. I also enquired if he had told them that we would be following, and again the answer was no, he had said nothing of other men. I then asked where the next friendly village was. They told me that if we marched fast we could reach it by nightfall, but that we had a high mountain to climb. They also told us that it was not safe to stay the night but to get on our way as soon as we could, which we did.

The mountain range that they had told us about was called the Karenni-Bum range stretching north to south. Once over it we were within striking distance of the China border.

Bland's foot had by this time completely healed. We were both pleased how it had got better despite having to keep on the move.

During one of the short rests, he said, 'Fred, I shall never be able to thank you enough for staying with me.'

'That's alright, Bill,' I replied, 'I wanted to get away from Johnny Friend anyway.' I felt a little embarrassed, yet I was grateful for him for saying it.

'If it ever comes about that you are in the same situation,' he went on, 'I shall not hesitate to stay with you.'

'Thanks, Bill, but I hope it never happens,' I replied.

We marched at a cracking pace, reaching the range of hills at about five thirty in the evening. This left us about two hours' full light to climb the mountain and reach the village before dark.

The track went up almost vertical, winding here and there. As we went higher the air became thinner, and we found it more difficult to breathe. The trees had changed from the tall teak and bamboo to the more familiar pine and maple. They were further apart and the path became more slippery.

It was a long hard climb. We had to rest more times than we really wanted, for time was not on our side. We did not want to spend the night on the side of a mountain at about ten thousand feet. The sun had already sunk down and the air was already getting chilly.

Then through the thinly dotted trees we saw our objective perched on a long flat plateau. The light was beginning to fade as we entered the village. A couple of young men and bare-chested girls came towards us together with a couple of barking dogs.

To a girl who was carrying a baby and wore a crucifix which hung between her bare breasts I asked, 'Burrah admi kidder hai?' in Urdu, but she surprised me by saying in English, 'The headman is in that hut. Come and I will take you.'

The headman was old and bearded, his face wrinkled with age. We used the girl as an interpreter, as he could speak neither English nor Urdu. She told us that the old man, who was her father, wanted us to leave the village as soon as it was light, as they were expecting the Japanese to visit later in the morning.

We readily agreed that they would see us on our way at first light. Then the girl said, 'Go with my father and he will show you where you can sleep.'

'Aren't we sleeping here by this lovely warm fire?' I asked, a little surprised and thinking it strange.

'Oh, no!' she replied. 'We have a place all prepared for you,' she said smiling, showing a perfect set of white teeth.

We followed the old man out into the darkness to a lone hut which was built high in the trees and standing on stilts. It must have been at least twenty feet from the ground. A bamboo ladder leaned against what seemed to be a kind of platform. The hut itself was perched over the side of the mountain with a vertical drop of some hundred feet. We followed the old man up the rickety ladder. Stepping onto the bamboo platform, he led the way to a door in the side of the hut, entered and lit an oil lamp. To our complete surprise, we found ourselves inside a church. At one end was an altar with candlesticks and all the other trappings, such as a chalice, plate and other things needed for Holy Communion services.

The old man signalled to us that here we would sleep. While we were still looking around to see where we could best do this, he left and closed the door behind him.

We chose a place to lie down and had hardly been asleep when the wind began to get up, screaming through the slats of the floor and making the whole place rock and sway as if trying to tear it from its stilts.

'Come on,' I shouted above the noise of the wind, 'I'm going down to get some shelter among the trees. I think we shall be warmer down there than stuck up here.' We all moved over to the door. I tried to open it, but it was secured somehow. 'Come on, one of you have a try,' I shouted. 'I'll try to find some other way out of here.'

I searched around but could find no other opening. I then thought of going through the floor. Lying flat on my belly I peered through the slats but could not see the ladder. I asked one of the others to have a look, to make sure. 'No Fred, the ladder has been taken away,' Lacey said.

So, that's it, I thought, we have been lured here like rats into a trap until the Japs come the next day. We sat huddled together and talked of what we could do. We had made a hole in the floor but we would have to wait for a little light or we could cripple ourselves if we jumped in the dark. As the stilts of the hut were half over the edge of the mountain, we kept on peering below to see whether anyone was on guard or not, but we could see no one.

As the night wore on the wind died down and one by one we dropped off to sleep. It seemed that I had been to sleep for no more than a couple of minutes when in the semi-darkness I was being shaken. I started up and grabbed my rifle, pointing it at the old man. He stood wide-eyed and afraid. His hands open and in front of him, he shook his head from side to side saying, 'Nay, Nay.' I woke the other two with a shout. Then the old man waved his hands towards the door. Us going down first, and the old man bringing up the rear, we went down the ladder.

There was a quick meal of rice and green sweet tea waiting for us in the old man's hut. Our fears of the night had been for nothing. Our pony was brought to us and once more we were on our way.

The path took us down the mountain and into the hot sunlight and with it came a weakness and tiredness that made my whole body ache. I noticed that the other two were in a similar state. I, as usual, was leading the pony. Stopping now and then, through aching eyes which I could barely keep open I could see that both Bland and Lacey were staggering about as if they were drunk.

I stopped and asked if they wanted a rest, and immediately they sank down where they had stopped and I did the same. Half conscious and in a kind of stupor, I knew that we could not stop anywhere too long, so I got up with some difficulty, staggered over to the other two and roused them. I told them through half-closed eyes that we must go on. For how far we went I have no idea. The next time I came to any sort of sense, Bland was shaking me and asking me to get up and move on.

We had no knowledge of where we were or where we were going. Darkness fell and daylight came. My throat was parched and I could not move. I just lay on my back on the ground and looked at the sky. I could hear voices that seemed miles away. Then, turning my head I saw Lacey and Bland lying on the ground as I was. Nearby was the pony munching grass. I did not want to move, for my whole body ached. I just closed my eyes and slept. Once more when I returned from the blackness I was astride the pony, my head resting on the heaving long neck. I was aware that I still had my rifle for I could feel it bumping on my back. This seemed to give me some little satisfaction. Lacey was leading the pony with Bland walking slowly by his side with linked arms. They too had their rifles. Once more I slipped down into that peaceful blackness.

The sound of voices, many voices, brought me back once again to my senses. I opened my eyes to look up into a ring of strange faces. I allowed my eyes to slowly move around so that I could take in what and who were gazing down at me. They were weird-looking people, the like I had never seen before. Their dress was of a strange nature. All this was being taken in by my brain that was only half awake and still wanted to fall back into the inky blackness. I felt my head being lifted and water being passed between my lips. It was so cold and so lovely that I wanted to drink and drink and drink. I was picked up by what seemed a number of strong arms and carried out of the sunlight and into the cool dimness of what I found to be a small bamboo hut when I opened my eyes again. Once again I fell into the blackness of unconsciousness. It was pitch black when I opened my eyes again. I did not attempt to move, for in my mind I did not wish to. I felt that weak, so weak that I went back to sleep again.

It was daylight when I was carried from the hut. Still in a stupor and placed upon the pony's back, I saw Lacey and Bland staggering out of a hut helped by two men. The two men were carrying our rifles and ammunition between them. One of them took the lead rope of the pony and we moved out of the village. The movement of the animal sent me off into another deep slumber. It seemed too much trouble for me to keep my eyes open longer than I needed.

I was in a dream, I was falling and falling. The swaying had stopped and I was out in space. I was again falling, then bump! I had hit the ground. My eyes were open. I looked around. Lacey was half lying and half sitting against a tree, and Bland was lying face down upon the ground, but they were about ten yards away from me. Of the two men and our rifles and ammo there was no sign.

Too weak to stand, I crawled over to Bland who was the nearest. 'Bill! Bill!' I shouted, shaking him, 'They've gone and taken our rifles! Lacey!' I shouted at the top of my voice, 'Lacey! Our rifles have gone!'

Lacey raised his head and said, 'Yes, I know. Those two men took them.' His head dropped back down onto his chest again.

'Did you see them go?' I asked.

'Yes,' he answered, closing his eyes as if to go back to sleep.

I gripped his shirt and pulled myself up into a kneeling position in front of him. Holding him with both hands, I shook him. 'Why the bloody hell didn't you stop them?' I raved at him.

Putting his hands over mine to stop me shaking him, he said in a weak voice, 'I didn't see them until they were almost out of sight.'

I fell back onto my hands first, then in sheer weakness flat on my back. I lay there not moving a finger. I was too weak to even move my eyes or head.

It was some time before Bland and Lacey got me to my feet and tried to walk me about, for I was too weak to stand. After wandering around for some time in the thick jungle where we had been left, we all three finished up lying upon the ground where we had fallen.

For how long we lay there, I have no idea, but I became aware of voices. I watched as Bland and Lacey rose to their feet and staggered away in the direction of the sound. Sometime later they returned with some other men. The strangers bent over and looked at me. Then one gathered me up in his arms and carried me like a child.

It was getting dark when I opened my eyes to see that we were entering a village. I was carried into the hut of a man dressed in the uniform of the Indian Army. I heard him tell my two companions that he was a lieutenant and, like us, had been cut off.

I was offered food. Although I had not eaten for almost three days I had no appetite. In the semi-darkness before dawn I was placed upon a bamboo chair-like structure with poles attached for carrying. Four men hoisted the structure with me in it up onto their shoulders. Before setting off, the lieutenant said, 'I am sending you to someone who will get you well again.' I thanked him as best I could and sank back into the darkness that had been so common to me in the last few days.

The next time I opened my eyes it was again dark. The chair was lowered to the ground, and strong arms carried me up a flight of stairs. I barely opened my eyes as I felt my clothes being stripped from my body, and then blackness overcame me once more.

I opened my eyes. Everything was white: the walls, the ceiling. Around the walls were pictures of Jesus in different phases of the New Testament and the Stations of the Cross. I then glanced down. I was lying in a bed, covered with thick blankets and white sheets. A movement in the room made me turn my head.

There stood a well-built man with his back to me. He was dressed in what looked like a white cassock with a black cord tied about his thick waist. He turned and faced me as if expecting me to be awake. His head was shaven. His face was pink, round and jovial. The lower half of his happy face was covered by a King George V beard. His smile showed a good row of white teeth. The moustache and beard had a reddish brown tinge to it, giving a kind of holy halo to the whole of his beaming face. As he came towards me, he asked, 'How do you feel?' in such a soft voice that I could hardly believe he had asked the question.

'I feel a little better, thank you,' I answered weakly.

'Could you drink a cup of tea?' he asked in his soft voice, and went on, 'Would you like to try and eat a little something?'

'I'll try,' I answered, returning his smile. The man turned and left the room.

I began then to try to puzzle out who this man was, where I was and what had happened to Bland and Lacey. No, I thought, I am dreaming, and in a moment I shall drop off into one of those black deep sleeps again and wake up somewhere out in the jungle.

But my dream never faded and the man returned with a steaming cup and saucer in one hand while he held a plate in the other. He put them down and arranged my pillows so that I could sit up. While he did this I slid my hand down to my bare leg and gave myself a good hard pinch, for I could not believe my eyes. On the plate was white bread spread with butter and red jam. The tea also had both milk and sugar in it.

For the next four days I was fed nothing but goat's milk and raw eggs. After that I was allowed to get up and walk a few yards.

Bland and Lacey recovered after two days. They came and visited me while I was still in bed. They informed me that our saviour and benefactor was a priest named Father McGovern. He lived alone in this Mission with two helpers. One of them was named Samantebo, but we called him Sam. He came from a village about six miles away. The priest was an Irish Catholic and he visited quite a number of villages in the area, converting the villagers to the faith.

Father McGovern told us that John Friend and the others had passed this way, staying one night only. We enquired if any message from Sergeant Friend had been left, but the priest said not. The sergeant had said to the priest that he had been forced to leave two men behind. 'But why are there three of you?' the priest asked. I explained the situation as best as I could. Lacey looked a little sheepish as I told him.

On the sixth day of our stay with Father McGovern I began to feel fitter. The strength came back into my legs as I went for short walks around the Mission. In the evening the priest invited us to listen to the news on his wireless, which he told us he rarely used, but for our benefit he would put it on.

We sat around waiting, and then it came. 'This is Radio Delhi!' After the preliminaries the newscaster said, 'All British Troops have now been evacuated from Burma.'

We looked at each other for a few moments, and our heads dropped. The priest broke the silence that had fallen. 'Cheer up, lads! It's not the end of everything,' he said smiling.

Later that evening Sam came in very agitated and told the Father that the Japanese were in a neighbouring village and intending to come to the Mission the following day.

The priest came to us as we sat talking among ourselves. He was almost in tears as he told us that we must go early the next morning. He sat on the edge of the bed with his head between his hands.

'Father,' I said, 'you have done more than enough for all of us.'

'But boys, you are not well enough to go out into the jungle,' he sobbed, unable to hold back the tears that streamed down the pink cheeks and mingled with the reddish hair on the lower part of his face. 'I meant you to stay until I was sure that no harm would come to you,' he went on, still sobbing. We three stood looking on as his shoulders shook with the sobs.

As I stood there I had a heavy feeling of guilt. Why should we bring so much sorrow to this happy isolated jovial man who had set himself apart from all the things of our outside greedy and selfish warring world?

Suddenly he stood erect. He wiped the tears from his eyes. 'I'm a fool,' he said, looking at us, 'a silly selfish fool!' Before we could say anything he was ushering us to our beds. 'Come on, lads, go to bed and get as much rest as you can. I will wake you up in time to get a good start. I'll draw you a rough map and get food ready for you. Now, to bed!'

Sam came and roused us. It was still dark. A meal was ready. As we ate, the priest explained the rough map that he had drawn. We were, he told us, about sixty miles from the Chinese border. From the border to a place called Man Ying it was about two hundred miles. To cross the frontier we would have to cross a river. Six miles after that we would come to another Mission where there was a Spanish priest and an Italian priest, and there we should get food and shelter. He continued to tell us that after that, about half way to Man Ying, there was a Mandarin's house where we should be well looked after, but after that we would have to fend for ourselves until we got to Man Ying and the Taiping River.

Before leaving, Father McGovern asked us all to kneel. First he blessed each one of us. This seemed strange to us three, for, let's face it, there was not a true believer amongst us, but it was the priest's wish. The prayer he finished off with was the 23rd Psalm, 'The Lord is my shepherd, I shall not want.' Further on it goes, 'Yea, though I walk through the valley of the shadow of death, I will fear no evil for thou art with me.'

We got to our feet, said our goodbyes and thanked our saintly friend again. Sam led the way down the hill to the track that we were to follow. Here I took the pony's lead rope and we said our goodbyes to him. He turned and ran back up the hill so as not to be away when the Japanese visitors came.

The track we were following had become very wide, more like a road than a track. It was also very dusty. The trees were much thinner. We all agreed that it appeared to be a well-used road. We had been going at a steady pace for over an hour when from behind came the sound of someone shouting. We stopped and tried to make out from which direction the shouts were coming. Then we heard it. 'Mister Fred! Mister Fred!' It was Sam running towards us. We pulled off the track as he came to us. He had come to warn us that the Japanese were coming this way on motorcycles and in a small car.

To reach us the lad had run the best part of twelve miles. There were, he said, seven Japanese. While talking he led us away through the sparse undergrowth. 'Father,' he said, gasping for breath, 'he make them drink much tea and eat plenty cakes. He say, Sam run quickly, tell Mister Fred, go other way, long way but better, and will come same place.'

'Sam,' I said, 'you are a wonderful lad, and as long as I live, I will never forget you.' The young boy led us through the jungle until we came to another track. Here we said goodbye again.

Chapter Ten

Attack by Bandits

After Sam had gone we went all day without seeing anyone or anything. The jungle had become thicker, giving us more cover. We ate the food the priest had given us. When it became dark we made camp but dared not light a fire, so instead snuggled together to keep warm and prevent the sickness, whatever it was. The only thing we could put it down to was that night on the mountain in the draughty hut.

Dawn came and once more we were on the move. We did not stop for any breaks, except, of course, when nature called. It was the best way, we all agreed.

It was on the third day out from Father McGovern's Mission that we caught sight of a river down below in the valley between the two mountains. That was the frontier between Burma and China. As we descended, we realised the river was further away than we thought, and it took another eight hours or so of marching before we even got another sight of it. We carried on in the dark, keeping our eyes and ears strained as we got nearer, and reached the bank at about three in the morning. Looking both right and left I led the pony and waded into the cold water with Bland and Lacey following. It was not a very fast river, perhaps because there had been no rain, and was only waist deep. The pony was a little reluctant at first, and my main concern was that it might make too much noise. Some rocks made us stumble, but we made it to the other side, scrambled up the bank and were away as fast we could go.

It was full daylight as we approached the Mission that Father McGovern had told us about. A young priest came running out to meet us, greeted us with a wide grin and shook our hands. He took us to a place where we could eat and sleep. He was the Spanish priest, and could speak very little English. We in turn knew no Spanish. So we conversed in Chinese as best as we could.

There was another priest, the Italian, who ignored us except to say, 'As a Christian, I will give you food and shelter for one night, then you must go.'

The Spanish priest told us that Captain Brown's party had passed through twelve days ahead of Sergeant Friend's, and that they had left the mission nearly three weeks ago. This meant that it was nigh impossible for us ever to catch up with them. Once again Bland and I felt that we had been let down and given up for lost or even dead, as no mention of us following was given to the priests.

At dawn we set off. We felt a lot more at ease and had a feeling of safety as we were outside the Japanese area of occupation and among friendly people in China. When we stopped, we had little to fear. We could now light fires and cook at leisure. We were in no hurry. There was plenty of water. Our main food became maize, which we burnt over the fire, wild cherries, peaches and plantains, and we dug down for the shoots of the large clumps of bamboo growing all around. There were also some different types of nuts to be had. We made much use of what we could gather in this way, for we knew that once we began to climb into the mountains again, food would be in very short supply.

The strange sickness that had attacked us all had now gone completely. What it was that brought us near to death, we still did not know.

Now and again we passed men going in the opposite direction, and nearly all were armed with some kind of weapon. We saw men carrying old-fashioned flintlock rifles that would have been welcomed in any museum. There were all types of rifles and in some cases they were carrying double-handed swords. Seeing these armed men made me wish that we still had our rifles. All that we had between us now were our Commando knives.

The next resting place for us to look for, according to Father McGovern, was about three days march. With the food we had collected we were not doing too badly. The thing that we were running short of most was tea, which between us we joked about: 'all the tea in China and we could get none.'

It was in the afternoon of the third day that we saw a large white building in the distance. It was quite flat country that we had to travel over, so we could keep the place in sight most of the time, although the path zigzagged somewhat. We must have been seen from some distance away, for as we approached a man came out to greet us, then led us through a kind of courtyard. In front of the large building another man stood on the steps and welcomed us. He was in European clothes and spoke almost perfect English. He told us to take our gear from the pony. This we did, then the animal was led away and we were ushered inside. A servant was in attendance and waved us to follow him. The man in European clothes then left us. The servant took us up some stairs and told us to make ourselves comfortable on the balcony. He then told us that we must not move around but stay put. Food was brought to us at about eight o'clock in the evening, and it was worth waiting for.

We slept well, and as was our usual custom were ready to move off just after dawn, but were told that we must not leave until the master of the house had eaten his breakfast. This we did not mind, but when it got to about ten o'clock in the morning we began to get a little impatient. Our main reason for wanting to get off was that we wanted to get as much marching time in each day so that we did not have to spend too many nights in the jungle. We had been told that if we reached a place like this with a wall around it, as most villages were, we would not be allowed in after a bell had been sounded to bring all the workers in from the fields just before dusk. After that the gates were locked for the night because of marauding bandits who swooped down on the villagers and robbed them. It was when we heard of this that we could understand why the men we had passed were armed.

When we did eventually get our breakfast, once again it was worth the wait. The next thing was to get our pony. Where it had been taken we had no idea. We searched everywhere. We asked for it, but no one seemed to know anything about it.

We were desperate and eager to get on the move. So, seeing ten or more ponies grazing, I said to Bland and Lacey, 'Get the gear ready. I'll take one of these ponies. It won't matter. It will be a straight swop.' All the ponies had lead lines hanging. I selected one and took it to where Bland and Lacey stood with the gear. 'Quick!' I shouted, 'Let's get going before anyone notices.'

Leading the pony we moved off in the direction I thought would take us out of the village. Instead we found ourselves in a dead-end. Quickly we turned around to make our way out when from all sides came a screaming angry mob, men, women and children, all waving their arms and surrounding us. In no time they had taken the lead line from my hand and pinned my arms behind my back and tied them. A noose was placed over my neck and I was forced down onto my knees.

I tried to shout to the men to explain, but my shouts were drowned by the noise of the crowd. I managed to glance across at my two companions. Their faces were ashen but they were still standing with their hands tied behind their backs. But it was I who had the lead line to the pony, so I suppose I was the culprit. The rope was tugged, and I was allowed to get to my feet. They marched us back to the Mandarin's house.

'What do you reckon they'll do to us?' Bland asked weakly.

'I don't know,' I replied, licking my dry lips.

'They won't hang us, will they?' Lacey asked in a shaky voice.

'I don't know, what's the penalty for horse stealing in China?' I said, trying to put on a brave face. 'They didn't teach us that in our Chinese lessons, did they?' I tried to joke.

The noise of the mob had been heard by the occupant of the big house, for as we came near, a number of well-dressed Chinese men were standing on the steps. One man stood out from the rest, the man we had seen the night before in Western dress. One word from him and the crowd went silent. He spoke to the crowd in Chinese. A few shouted back at him, pointed at me and said that I had stolen their pony. Looking straight at me, he asked in English if I had taken the pony. 'I am deeply sorry, sir,' – I was almost pleading with him – 'but I thought that it was our pony.'

The man repeated what I had said to the crowd, but it only brought more shouting. He quietened them again and asked me, 'What colour is your animal?' For the life of me I could not remember what the colour was, whether it was black and white or all black. I made a quick guess and said that it was black and white. 'But that animal is white and brown!' he pointed at the pony I had taken. I was stumped.

The crowd must have partly understood, for they began to shout for my blood and started jostling me and my two companions. The man holding the rope around my neck began tugging at it as if wanting to get it over with.

On the steps of the house there appeared another man. He, too, was in Western dress and his suit was immaculate. This man was much taller and slimmer. There were a few words spoken between the two men, then the newcomer began talking to the crowd in a very loud voice. The rope was taken from my neck and our hands were untied. The crowd began to disperse, with the exception of one or two who hung around to see what was going to happen to us.

The two men came down the steps and the man who had spoken to the crowd first said, 'You are very fortunate! Only one person could have saved you,' – he turned and motioned towards the tall thin man – 'and that was the Mandarin himself. A few minutes later he would have been gone. I will have your animal brought to you,' he continued, 'and I will instruct a guide to take you along a trail that will bring you much nearer to Man Ying than the ordinary route.' We all thanked him. I was much relieved, to say the least. Our guide then led us out of the gates of the village. Some of the villagers watched as we went, but caused us no further trouble.

The guide led us up into some red sandy hills. At the top he stopped, pointed down into the grass–covered plain dotted here and there with trees, turned and left us to find our own way from there.

Walking continuously from dawn to dusk and barely resting, we spent four nights on the plain. We did not see a single human being in all that time. We saw plenty of wild pigs, but having only our knives we stood very little chance of catching one. We did try making bows and arrows, but were so off target that we gave up. On the lower ground we managed to get plenty to eat from digging up sweet potato roots and bamboo shoots which we cooked together with maize, which was plentiful.

The first evidence of humans was when we saw the signs over the track of a Nat's, or spirit's, village. These signs were made with brown paper made from the bark of a tree. There were stars, triangle shapes and sometimes squares. On one side of the track near these signs was always a pole with a platform on it, on which was put food for the spirits. This indicated that we were not far from a village.

We stayed the night at the village. They were about to celebrate the birth of a child to the headman and they hoped that the spirits would smile upon the headman and give him a son. A large cockerel was prepared to be sacrificed to anoint the newborn with its blood.

We were pleasantly surprised to be told that Man Ying, the point where we were to turn north and go into the hills, was only ten more miles and downhill all the way. As we made our way down through the trees we could see now and then a wide river. This, we knew, was the Taiping, flowing north to south. To get to the hills we must cross this river. Here we would find the French priest that Father McGovern had told us about and it was here that we planned to stay for a few days' rest.

It gave us a great deal of satisfaction to know that we had made it this far with no map or compass and without any harm coming to us. I had to admit that we had been very fortunate in having help from many people.

We came down to a small river which was about four hundred yards from the Taiping. It was only six feet wide and not very deep, and we just walked through it. We were up to our knees when I looked down and saw thousands of leeches coming for us. I shouted and got out of the water as fast as I could, pulling the pony after me. Bland and Lacey quickly followed. On dry land we began to burn leeches from our legs by lighting cigarettes. The pony's legs were covered with them too. Some leeches were already dropping off on their own accord, as they were gorged to fullness with our blood. It took us about a half an hour to clear us and the pony of those dreadful blood-sucking creatures.

It was a short walk to get to the Taiping river. Man Ying was sprawled on the opposite bank. As usual it was a walled town. It was obvious that we must cross by the ferry, which was a dug-out canoe, but we had to wait our turn as we were not the only ones who wanted to get to the other side. Besides, there was only one canoe on the river. It was the first time that we had had to use money since buying the pony and we only possessed rupees. When it came to our turn to get on the canoe, the ferryman was very reluctant to accept rupees, but after a quiet chat in Chinese (how grateful I was for the Chinese lessons!) he said that he would take us across.

After getting to the other side I asked around for the French priest, but we were shown to a bamboo hut on a narrow street. Hanging over the door was the sign of the YMCA. This amazed us as we did not expect to find anything like that here.

I tied the pony to a post outside, and we went in. On the walls were pictures of Sun Yat-sen and groups of children as well as flags of the Allies. There were two rough bamboo tables, around which were a number of chairs. The floor had no covering; it was just a dirt floor.

Sometime later, a young Chinese came in. He spoke very good English, and when we asked him how we could get to the French priest he said, 'First, take some tea with me, and I will take you to him.'

After tea with the young man he led us through some very narrow cobbled streets. They seemed to be crowded with people, but that was only because of the narrowness. The young man stopped in front of two large wooden doors set into a high whitewashed wall. Reaching up, he tugged at a rope that was hanging near the side of the door, causing a large bell to ring high above us. After a short wait we heard footsteps, then a small wicket door set into one of the larger doors opened and a short bearded man stepped out. He was dressed in a white cassock and had pale and sharp features. His nose was long and pointed, and he had blue eyes. His face broke into a smile when he saw us. Speaking in Chinese he thanked the young man, and opening the larger door ushered us into a large courtyard, around three sides of which were buildings. The largest building was two stories high with a veranda running the full length of both upper and lower stories. On the left was a single-storey building which was a stable. Here the pony was taken. The priest then took us up a flight of stairs to a room with three beds in it. None of us spoke French, and the priest spoke no English, so we had to converse in Chinese, which he thought was very funny.

Over afternoon tea, for it was about five in the afternoon, we asked whether he had seen or heard of any others coming past this way. To our surprise he told us that Captain Brown and his party and also the three captains with their Gurkhas had passed, but not any English sergeant with four Englishmen and two Indians. This set us somewhat of a puzzle as to where the sergeant had gone.

'Perhaps the compass has gone wrong again,' Bland quipped.

'Well, I certainly don't wish them any harm, but where can they have gone?' I wondered.

From the priest we found out that up to the time of their leaving this Mission Captain Brown had suffered no casualties. I could tell that this came as some relief to Lacey as I glanced at his face.

The priest told us to go back to the young man at the YMCA and ask him to enquire about the sergeant and our party. As for myself I was not really interested now that we had come this far on our own. I was all for going on to make for Sadon in northern Burma and carry on with our original plan, as Captain Brown seemed to be doing.

I put this to the other two and they agreed, but Bland wanted to find out what had happened to the others first before leaving. I could not understand why. After all, they all voted to leave him behind. However, we said that we would take a week's rest here, and if nothing turned up by the end of the week we would move off on our own.

We went down into the town every day to see if there was any news of them. On the morning of the seventh day, with a guide who claimed to have been sent from the YMCA, we set off on our long journey that we hoped would take us back into Burma and across to India, a journey of some two thousand miles over some of the roughest countries in the world, and mountains that we would have to climb rising to fifteen or sixteen thousand feet.

Our first target was Tengchong, well up in the mountains. The priest advised us to try to make it to a village before nightfall and also to save any food that was given to us, as villages were very few and far between. He also told us that the country we were to pass through was very barren and could give us little in the way of vegetation to eat. The only satisfying thing about this part of our journey was that we had no worry of running into any Japanese, not for about one thousand miles anyway. We were also warned to watch out for bandits who roamed the hills and would attack travellers who they thought carried anything of value.

I thought it very odd that the YMCA had sent a guide and yet after a while I let it pass. He seemed alright and I allowed him to take the lead line of the pony. Once we had got outside the walls of the town we went up a steep path which began to wind itself up and around the mountain. All three of us stood and looked back at the small town with the river running down the one side.

The guide was making good progress and had got quite a way ahead. I had to call to the others to speed up their pace so that we could keep the guide in sight.

Tucked in a bag between the blankets that Father McGovern had given us was a bundle of three thousand rupees in ten-rupee notes that the colonel had issued between Bland and me. The blanket was tied to the pony. Lacey, not being at the split, had none. On my person in the pocket of an old jacket I had sixty rupees in ten notes and about forty in coins. Bland had about the same. Lacey, I knew, had none.

This was the reason I did not want the guide to get too far away from us. Frankly, I did not want a guide anyway. The further we went the more suspicious I became. I told the other two what I thought, but they poo-pooed it and said that I was imagining things, and was he not from the YMCA? But I began to notice that he made furtive glances both at us and at the higher country above us, as if he was looking for someone or something.

We must have put about five miles of hard climbing between us and Man Ying when the guide brought us to a small village of no more than three huts perched on the side of the mountain as it was getting dark. We were given food, and room was made for us to settle down for the night around a blazing fire.

I tried to keep within earshot of what was being said by our guide and our hosts, but every time I raised my head they fell silent. Being tired after the hard day's climb, I eventually fell asleep.

I woke to find that it was full daylight. I rose quickly and went outside. The pony was still there and so was the guide.

I got hold of the others and asked them again in a whisper, 'Do you think it wise to leave the money on the pony?'

Bland answered, 'Well, if it isn't, we can't bring it out now. They'll all see it. So, we might as well leave it where it is.'

I thought about it and had to agree with him that it would be fatal if we did remove the blanket, at the moment anyway.

We had been going about three hours, still climbing, when the guide called a halt to eat the rice wrapped in banana leaves that we had been given at the village. These packs of rice had to be eaten before a certain time or they would turn sour.

After the break we started our climb again and were getting a little strung out. I was just behind the guide with the pony, while Bland and Lacey were about twenty yards further back. The guide took the pony down into a deep ditch with a stream running through it and a rough bridge spanning it. I took a couple of steps onto the bridge and turned to see Bland and Lacey coming up the steep slope. Suddenly, as if from nowhere, a Chinese carrying a rifle stepped on to the bridge in front of me. He wore the traditional blue cotton jacket and black wide-legged trouser, and on his head the wide-brimmed straw hat that peasants wear. I greeted him in the usual manner as he came towards me, but instead of returning the greeting he pushed the rifle into my ribs and said, 'Wor-yow-chien!' ('I want money!') For a moment I was taken aback, then I turned to warn Bland and Lacey, but the man shoved the rifle harder into my ribs and said, 'Boo-dzor!' ('Don't do!'). I looked down into the ditch and saw another armed man with the guide and pony going up the bank. I half turned again and saw that neither Bland nor Lacey were aware of my predicament. Turning back to face the man, I noticed a movement in the bush opposite, so I knew that he had at least one accomplice.

All this had taken place in just a few seconds. Once more the man demanded money, at the same time watching for my two companions behind me. I rattled the coins in my jacket pocket and he nodded his head. I slid my hand into my right-hand pocket and pulled out some coins. These I showed him in my open right hand, while at the same time I slid my left hand to my knife which was on my left-side pocket. Being left-handed, I always kept it there.

I pushed my right hand further forward, inviting the man to take the coins. He let go of his rifle with his right hand, allowing the butt to drop, and stepped forward with his right hand outstretched to take the coins. As he did so I swung up with my knife in my left hand and brought it down between his neck and shoulder bone. It went in the full length of the blade, and his piercing scream shook the whole forest to life. I tried to get my knife out as the blood spurted over the hilt and over my hand. A thin spurt of blood gushed up underneath the wide hat, and the man's head flopped, trapping my knife. As he dropped the coins to the ground I let go of my knife and he fell to the planks. For a split second I stood looking down at him writhing there, then a shot rang out and something whistled past my head. I turned and ran towards Bland and Lacey, who by now were aware of what was happening. 'Run!' I shouted, 'Run!' They did not need to ask why, and turned and ran before me down the hill. We ran and ran, going in and out of the trees in case another shot should be fired.

Eventually, when we thought that we were safe, we gathered ourselves, and still out of breath asked each other what to do next. After that I told them both off for not watching and keeping their eyes on me. Still, I was as much to blame for not taking more care. After all, we had been warned!

What to do? That was the question. We could not go upwards, that was for sure, as the robbers might still be there. We did not know any other trail. We decided therefore that there was only one thing to do, to go back to Man Ying to see whether we could get help to get our goods and the pony back. We all doubted this very much, but as Bland said, 'What else could we do?'

Chapter Eleven

The Confrontation

We got to Man Ying just as the curfew bell was ringing. I was ahead of the other two and warned the gatekeeper that my two companions were coming. A few people gathered around and asked why I had returned. I did my best to tell them, and the news soon spread. I was then met by the priest and some notables. Among them was the young man from the YMCA.

The French priest took us all back to the Mission, where we occupied the same places that we had vacated previously. There was no doubt that the episode had shaken us all. I asked Bland how much money he still had. He answered that he only had a few rupee coins and that was all. Lacey had nothing. I had the sixty rupees rolled up in a piece of blue paper tucked in the inside pocket of my jacket.

We expected to hear some reports of the man that I had at least injured, but there were none. It was said that the local authorities had been out into the surrounding hills in search of our goods and pony, but nothing came of it and after a short time no mention of it was heard again.

We hung around the Mission. I was not feeling too well. I was hoping that I had not got a bout of malaria coming on. The priest advised me to stay in bed after he had taken my temperature. It was on the second day I was in bed that news came to us of a small number of British soldiers at a village called Tiu-Tien, two days' march away to the south. I told Bland and Lacey to try and find out more about them, so they both went to the YMCA, in whom I had little trust now. News must have travelled fast, for they brought back a message, written on rough paper: 'We are at Tiu-Tien. Come if you wish. J. Friend.'

I was at that moment not fit to walk down the road, let alone walk for two and a half days in the jungle. But Bland and Lacey said that they were going back into town to get more news. I paid no attention to this. After all, we had been here, sitting still for nearly a week. So, I just laid back and rested.

My fever had now begun to really get hold of me, and when my companions returned I could not keep a limb still. They told me that they were setting off early the next morning and that they had got someone to show them the way. I was a little shocked at this, and the words that Bland had said came back to me, about me not leaving him and that if I was ever in the same situation, he would stay with me. Well, was it not similar?

I just covered my head with the thick blankets that the priest had laid on me. I was now shaking from head to toe, but I tried to sleep. I dimly remember the two of them coming to me and drawing back the blankets and saying, 'Farewell, see you when you get better.'

I know that I was in no immediate danger and neither were they. So they, at least Bland, did not have to dash off. And what about Lacey? What sort of reception would he get from the others? This went over and over in my mind.

During the rest of the day, the priest brought me hot fluids, as that was all I could manage, plus some drops of medicine that he gave me at intervals.

I was awakened by a hand shaking me by the shoulder. It was dark, and I was standing at the doors in the courtyard of the Mission. A Chinese man and woman led me back to the priest. He in turn led me back to my bed. It seemed that I had woken in my feverish sleep and tried to go to my companions.

It was on the third day that the fever broke and I was able to get up and go for a short walk into town with the help of the French priest. There I had a talk with the young man at the YMCA. I did not trust him fully at first until I asked him what had become of his 'guide'. He was puzzled and informed me that neither he nor his colleagues had sent us a guide. When he told me this, I began to have some faith in him again. He told me that when I made up my mind to go he would see to it that no harm came to me on the journey to my friends.

Two days later I set off with two genuine guides to whom I was introduced at the YMCA. With the fever still in me I was feeling a little weak and found it difficult to keep up with them, and now and then they stopped and waited for me to catch up.

It was about five in the afternoon when we entered quite a large village. There the two men led me to a dingy-looking house. Through the door we entered a large room with cubicles arranged around the walls. In the cubicles were bunks in three. Upon these bunks men were either asleep or smoking opium pipes. The air was full of blue smoke as the half-drugged men on the bunks sucked on their pipes.

A large-built woman came forward as we entered and spoke to my two guides. I did not hear what was said, but she turned to me and said in what seemed a foreign tongue to follow her. She led me to a bunk that was not occupied, neither the upper or lower. I was in a cubicle on my own. Then she asked me in Mandarin, 'Do you want food?'

I answered 'Yes,' and thanked her.

'Do you want tea and a bed for the night also?' she asked.

'Yes,' I answered, thanking her again.

She returned after a short time with a steaming bowl of rice and a bowl of curried vegetables. 'Do you want spoon or chopsticks?' she asked.

'Wor you kuaizi,' I answered, meaning chopsticks. This made her raise her eyebrows. She went quickly to get them, and I had a small audience watch me eat until she made them move away.

No one bothered me. The woman came once and asked whether I wanted any more blankets to cover me. Of my two guides I saw nothing.

It was still dark when the woman awoke me with some hot green tea. An oil lamp on the wall burned. I asked her if I could wash, and she brought me a cloth and showed me to the well outside.

Before leaving, I thanked her and asked how much I owed her, but she refused any money and wished me a safe journey. I set off with my two guides, who soon began to leave me behind. This time they did not wait for me to catch up, so I was left on my own.

I did not hurry, but just strolled along in my own time at my own slow pace. I just kept following the Taiping River on my left hand side.

There were times when I lost sight of the river completely, when the track veered away and went into the thick jungle and ran alongside paddy fields. Here I asked the workers planting rice if I was on the right track for Tiu-Tien, and they assured me that I was.

Another track forked onto the one I was on and with it came a young Chinese youth of about fourteen. At first he walked behind me, keeping his distance and not trying to go past. After some time I waited and let him come abreast of me and asked if he was going to Tiu-Tien. He answered no. He was carrying a long bamboo pole across his shoulder, and from the end of it hung two large baskets, with a small pig in one basket and rice and vegetables in the other. He told me that he had been to a market in a village some ten miles away to buy the goods he was carrying, and was taking them back to his own village which was about three more hours walking.

After walking for some time the youth said that he would find me shelter for the night at his village. I had told him where I was heading and he said that I would not reach Tiu-Tien until the next day. I then let him take the lead and followed him. It was getting dark when we turned off the main track and took a fork which led us into quite a large built-up area. Once again we had to pass through a gate in the wall that surrounded the village. The youth then led me to a whitewashed house. This, too, had a wall around it. The youth knocked on a large door in the wall. After a short wait, the door was opened and a very tall woman dressed in royal blue and black costume came into view. On her head was a tall hat of the same colours, making her look even taller.

The youth went forward and spoke to her, leaving me standing away from the door. She peered at me and seemed to be measuring me up and down. She then bent down and said something to the youth who went inside. The door was closed behind him and the woman, leaving me standing alone.

After what seemed a long time the door opened again and the youth came out less his baskets, and told me to follow him. He led me through some trees to a Buddhist pagoda. Before entering, he motioned for me to take off my boots and socks, which were by this time well-worn and barely covered my feet. I left them on the steps and entered behind him.

Inside I could hardly believe my eyes. The floor was of very highly planed polished teakwood which would not have been out of place in any large dancehall in Britain. From the ceiling hung glass chandeliers lit by oil lamps that reflected the light ten thousand times over. Around the walls were different poses of the Buddha. At the far end and away from the door was a twelve-foot-high Buddha in the sitting position with legs crossed and the hands on the lap. This Buddha was covered with pure gold, and in the centre of the forehead was a large red stone that now and then caught the light of the chandeliers as they moved in the slight breeze, which also made the glass tinkle in an uncannily tuneful way.

I was taking in all this wonderment when the youth drew my attention to a Buddhist monk who seemed to have come from nowhere. He was dressed in the usual orange robe and had the usual shaven head. His eyes were slanted and dark, and he was slimly built and slightly shorter than me.

I had removed my hat on entering. I stood with my feet together, put my hands together and bowed slightly in the manner that we had been taught to greet people of the Orient. The monk returned my greeting in the same manner and motioned me to sit. We sat cross-legged facing each other. The youth left us alone.

The monk spoke to me in a strange language. I told him in Mandarin that I did not understand him. From his manner and the shaking of his head, I guess that he did not understand me either. So we tried sign language. He asked where I had come from, and I managed to make him understand that I had walked from Burma and was on my way to join my friends at Tiu-Tien.

The youth returned with a basket and a kettle which he gave to the monk. The youth spoke in the strange language to the monk and motioned towards me. He then turned to me and said in Mandarin, 'The Great Lady has sent you food and drink and she hopes that you will sleep well and have a good journey tomorrow.' He retreated to the door of the pagoda, bowed and said, 'Zaijian, Yinggelanren, Zaijian.' ('Goodbye, English, Goodbye.')

I bowed my head to him and answered, 'Zaijian,' before he turned and disappeared into the blackness outside.

The monk helped himself to the food first before offering me the basket. The kettle contained green tea, which the monk poured out into two small teacups that had no handles. The food was piping hot, so was the tea. I ate everything and drank all the remaining tea in the kettle.

After my meal, I rose and walked around, still amazed at the magnificent splendour of the interior of the pagoda. The monk brought me a mat and a blanket for my bed.

There was some kind of fear about sleeping in the pagoda, but at the same time I was very glad that I had not been forced to sleep out in the jungle that night. I awoke several times to have a look around, but all was silent and the lights were on all through the night. I arose when it was light outside, rolled up the mat and folded the blanket and sat waiting for the monk to appear.

I thanked the monk as best as I could, and then he walked to the steps to watch me as I put on my boots. He stood on the steps and pointed towards a path that went between the trees and said, 'Tiu-Tien.' Again I thanked him and turned towards the path. I looked back and he was still standing on the steps. I waved at him until the trees blocked the view.

It must have been about six thirty when I left the pagoda. I had been walking for about three hours and had not taken any rests as I did not know how far I had to go to reach my destination. I did not want to spend a night in the jungle. Being on my own, I was courting trouble and I did not like the look of the countryside anyway.

The path led me away from the river and up onto some high ground. I had just climbed a small hillock and was making my way down when I saw at the side of the track a small mound of earth with a rough cross at one end. Upon the cross hung a bush hat. The hat swung around and back in the slight breeze. For a moment I stood still, and then walked a few steps closer. I knew the hat. It was Jock Johnson's. I took the hat from the wooden cross and looked at the words that had been roughly cut out. It was Jock's name, rank and the abbreviation of our unit. There was no date. For a moment I was unable to move. I just stared down at the mound of earth. I replaced the hat and sat nearby. The last words that he had said to me before leaving came back to me. 'I'll see you in China.' The beer parties, football matches and dances that we had enjoyed together all went before my eyes as I sat there. I rose to my feet, took a last look at the mound of earth, and with a lump in my throat walked away.

I had been walking about another half an hour when, coming round a sharp bend and near the river bank, I met Lacey and a Chinese.

'Hello, Fred,' Lacey greeted me, 'I thought you would be about here.'

'Hello,' I greeted him, 'but how did you know I was coming?'

'Oh, we had two men come to us yesterday,' he replied, 'they told us that you were on your way here.'

He turned and walked with me. For a time we were both silent. The picture of Jock's grave was still in my mind and, of course, Lacey being the first person I saw did not help matters.

At last I broke the silence. 'How far is this place?'

'About four miles and it's terrible,' he replied quickly.

'Why? What's wrong with it?' I asked, puzzled.

'Well, in the first place,' he began, 'it's in the stinking swamps, and secondly they can't get any decent food there,' he said bitterly.

'Well, why have they gone there?' I asked, looking at him.

'They got ambushed by some bandits. The two Indians got killed and Friend got wounded,' he went on.

I stopped walking, and he stood facing me. 'Blimey!' I shouted, 'And what about the others?'

'Ginger and Ballantyne are down with the squirts,' he continued. 'They've caught a bug and also have something else wrong with them, and now Bland has gone down with the squirts as well.'

'Bloody hell!' I swore, 'Not already!'

As I began to walk again, I said, 'It sounds a grim place to me.'

Lacey fell in beside me as we went along the path. After a while, he said, 'Did you see Jock's grave?'

I turned my head sideways to look at him, but he was looking at the ground. When I answered, 'Yes, I saw it!' his head came up and turned to look at me. I looked him in the eyes and went on, 'That's one for you to carry on your back. One that we know of.'

We walked on in silence after that, until we came in sight of a wooden building through some mangrove trees that grew quite thickly. 'That's it there,' said Lacey, pointing his finger in the direction of some more buildings that had come into view.

The ground underfoot had become soggy, and the path wound in and out of the thickly growing trees. On each side of the track was dank green smelly water. We had to jump across this to make it to the path that led us to the buildings. As we neared the wooden double-tiered huts I could see that they were broken down and hardly fit to live in. Some of them had been half pulled down already. There were about six buildings in all.

I had to ask myself the question, why of all places had Friend come here? Surely, I thought, everyone would have been better off, both for food and health reasons, to make for higher ground. I had made this assessment even before I had got into the buildings.

Lacey led the way up a rickety flight of stairs to the second floor, turned to the right and entered a long room. In the middle of the room, lying on some dirty straw and covered by some old blankets, were Ginger and Ballantyne. At the side of the room, against a window, Bland lay on another bale of dirty straw. Next to him were spaces for two more beds.

I went first to where I could see Ginger's red hair poking from the blanket. He did not know that I was there until I pulled back the blanket from his head. His eyes opened wide at seeing me. His white face glistened with sweat and looked whiter surrounded by the red of his beard and uncombed rough red hair. His blue eyes softened when he said, 'Hello, Fred.' His voice was not the voice of the Ginger I had known with the laughing Yorkshire accent. It was that of a weak tired man.

Ballantyne must have heard us, and pulled back the blanket from his head. His face too was the colour of parchment, set against his black hair and beard. 'Hello, Fred,' he greeted me in a weak sickly voice with the barest trace of Scottish accent. 'How nice to see you again.'

'Hello,' I greeted both of them, 'and what the hell is holding you two down? Come on, let's have you up and about like you used to be,' I joked. But they did not laugh, not even a grin. They both rolled over onto their backs as I sat between the two of them.

'Come on, lads, tell me all about yourselves.' I tried to draw them out, but for a moment they lay still and silent, looking up at the roof.

Then Ginger began. 'Fred, we're sorry about the messages and the signs. We wanted to leave some and make signs for you to follow, but Johnny said that it would be a giveaway and anyway,' – he paused – 'he didn't think you would get through.'

'That figures,' I said.

'Friend got in with some Chinese bloke, who asked him to escort some refugees eastwards.'

'How many?' I cut in.

Ginger took another breath, 'About three hundred.'

'The stupid bastard,' I muttered half to myself. 'Go on,' I urged Ginger.

'The bandits were waiting for us, dug in, on some high ground. Their two first shots killed the Indians.'

'Stop,' I almost shouted. 'Don't tell me, they were the two front scouts!'

'How did you know that, Fred?' asked Ginger, raising his head.

'Never mind,' I said. 'Carry on.'

Ginger dropped his head back and went on. 'The whole bleeding lot panicked and got in our way. After the first two shots, we couldn't do a thing.' He paused again. 'Ballantyne and I tried to get on the flank and fire into the side of them, but we heard Friend shouting. We went back and found that he had been hit.' Another pause. 'He told us to bring him back to this place. We had lost everything, the mule and all.' He hesitated again. 'Bally was the only one who hadn't put his money in with the rest on the mule.'

'Where are your rifles now?' I asked, looking around the room.

'The Chinese army came and took them from us,' replied Ginger.

'Who had Jock's Tommy-gun when you were ambushed?' I asked.

'Nobody,' answered Ginger.

'How come?' I asked.

'Well, when Jock died,' Ginger went on, 'Friend dismantled it and threw it away. He said we wouldn't need it.'

Ballantyne then spoke up for the first time. 'I told him not to throw it away, but he wouldn't listen.'

'How stupid can a man get?' I asked myself out loud. 'Just one burst from it and the bandits would probably have run.'

The talking had done Ginger a little good for there was some colour coming back into his face, and he was now sitting up.

'Tell me what happened to Jock?' I asked, looking at one of the walls.

'When Johnny decided to turn south,' Ginger began, 'Jock played merry hell with Friend. He said that we were not playing fair with you in not leaving any signs and messages of where we were heading. Jock was going to turn back and try to locate you, but he got that fever.' Ginger stopped and swallowed hard. There were tears in his eyes as he went on. 'Do you know, Fred? It's very funny, but right up to the end Jock kept on calling for you.'

I sat in silence looking at my feet. A lump had come into my throat. Ginger continued talking. 'He said that you were the only one who could save him. That is why, Fred, I'm very glad that you have come.'

'Well,' I said, 'I don't know what help I can give you, except get you to come out of these filthy beds and get moving around. When did you have a decent meal last?'

Ballantyne raised himself up on one arm and said, 'We have been here for three weeks, and all we had to eat is just rice and what looks like cabbage.'

'How much money did you say you had, Bally?' I asked the Scot.

'Two thousand rupees in ten notes,' he replied.

I put out my hand. 'Give me ten, and I'll go and bring back some fresh fruit and other stuff for you to eat.'

'I haven't got it, Fred,' he said. 'Johnny took it all off me. He said he was to have charge of everything.'

'He did what?' I shouted. 'He had no right to take that money from you. The colonel gave you that money for yourself, to do what you like.'

Bland had now come and joined us, and I asked him, 'What do you think about this lot, Bill?'

'Well, he shouldn't have taken all of it. That is a fact,' he replied.

'Were you two fit when he took the money?' I asked the two of them.

'Yes, we were,' they both answered.

'And he wasn't, I suppose?' I asked.

'No! Far from it,' Ginger came back. 'He had been hit in the eye and hand. We had to lead him!' Ballantyne nodded in agreement.

I glanced at both Bland and Lacey. There was a smirk on Bland's face, while Lacey just shook his head and looked down.

'And where is Sergeant Friend?' I asked.

Bland answered, 'He's in the room across the veranda.' He pointed his finger. 'He never comes in here. He stays there all on his own.'

I got to my feet, walked out and went into the room opposite. The sergeant had his back to me. He was looking out of an open window. He never moved. He must have heard me enter, for my boots made enough noise, but he stood still. From behind him I could see that he had got his arm in a black sling.

I went to him on the right hand side. 'Hello, Sergeant,' I greeted him.

He half turned, and I could see that he had also got a black patch over one eye. It looked comical, but I did not laugh or even smile. 'Oh, so you got here at last then!' he snapped, as though I had been late on parade.

'Yes, Sergeant, I got here,' I snapped back, 'and it's no thanks to you!'

'What do you mean by that?' he asked, going red in the face.

'I mean the messages and signs that you promised to leave for us,' I came back at him.

'Er-oh-er, I ran out of paper,' he stammered.

'What about verbal messages then?' I snapped.

'Well, er, I couldn't trust the villagers, could I?' he stammered again.

'And I suppose you couldn't even trust Father McGovern, either, could you, Sergeant?' I asked him slowly, and watched his face as he tried to find an answer.

He never answered my question but turned to me fully and said, 'Look, you don't have to stay here, if you don't want to.'

I went closer to him, and almost putting my face into his, said, 'Sergeant, I'll go when I cannot help them, those two in there, any more.'

'They're alright,' he said casually. 'They don't need your help.'

'I'll decide that, Sergeant!' I threw back at him.

He turned back towards the window. For a moment there was a silence.

'You have some money belonging to Ballantyne, I believe?' I asked him.

He turned and almost screamed at me. 'I have got no money belonging to him. It belongs to me! He lost all his money on the mule.' His face was scarlet.

'Well, Sergeant, from what he tells me, you have two thousand rupees of his, and I want ten rupees now,' I said, being a little cheeky, 'so that I can go and get some fresh food for them to eat.'

'Oh no, you will not, I shall not give you any money to go and spend,' he glared at me with his one good eye. 'They are getting quite sufficient to eat.' He turned back and faced the window.

'Is that your final word?' I asked.

'Yes, it is!' he snapped.

'Alright, Sergeant,' I said, 'but if those two men die here, it will be through your stupidity and selfishness.'

I turned and walked to the door. I then stopped and turned back to him. 'Oh, and by the way, what happened to Jock's Tommy-gun?' I asked.

I had taken him by surprise. Again he began to stammer. 'Oh–er, the spring broke, so I threw it way. Yes, that's right, the spring broke, and I dumped it.'

I chuckled loudly and walked out.

On my return to the other room, Ginger and Ballantyne wanted to know what had transpired between me and Friend. I told them of his attitude towards giving up any of the money, and that I had my own views on why he wanted to hold on to the cash. I asked, 'Have you any money between you?' Both men answered that they had got none. I wanted to hang on to the few rupees I had just in case I did make a move and go off on my own, a thought that had crossed my mind often while walking alone. I asked where Smith, the other man of the party, was, but Ginger and Ballantyne assured me that he did not have any money either. I turned to Bland and Lacey and asked how much we could muster between us.

'I have five rupees,' Bland answered.

Lacey said, 'I've got nothing, you know that, Fred.'

I took out the blue paper roll from my pocket that contained the sixty rupees. With Bland's five that made a grand total of sixty-five rupees. Turning again to the two sick men, I asked, 'Who is the best person to go to in Tiu-Tien, who may help us?'

'There is a man who owns the bread and cake shop. He always gave us a few cakes and things until Friend stopped us going there,' Ginger informed me.

'Bloody hell!' I swore. 'Has he been fixing bleeding bounds as well? Come on! Take me to Tiu-Tien,' I said to Bland and Lacey.

We had to walk a mile and a half to reach Tiu-Tien, which was a similar sized town to Man-Ying. It was a new town built when it was decided to abandon the old one – where the lads were staying – because of so much fever and disease.

We found the bakery quite easily, and the cheerful-looking, middle-aged man inside answered my greetings with a smile. Two or three local women were in the shop making purchases. The man asked me to wait on one side.

As soon as the shop emptied he asked what he could do for me. From my pocket I took out one of the five rupee notes and spread it before him. I asked him if he would give me Chinese yuan in exchange for it. He looked at it for a few moments and then shook his head. In a pitiful and pleading voice I said, 'Wor-mun-yow jung-gwor-chien, liang-gor, ying-gwor-bing, sher-dah-dien, boo-how, ta-mun-yow-cher-fan, nee-gay-wor-shing-shur?' ('We want Chinese money to buy food for two English soldiers who are very sick. Will you give it to us?')

For a moment he stood and looked at the three of us. He looked down at the rupee note and back at me. Suddenly he nodded his head and waved his hand for me to follow him into the back of the shop.

I did not expect above two and a half yuan, but when I showed my gratitude at three yuan he put into my hand another half yuan. At this gesture, I almost kissed him. His face broke into a big smile at the way I embraced him, and he led me back into the shop. There he began sorting over a number of cakes from a tray, wrapped them in paper and handed them to me. I asked him how much, but he waved his hand, saying, 'Wor-boo-yow-chien.' ('I want no money.')

After thanking him we found a stall where they sold meat. Picking out a long thick piece, I asked the woman seller how much. 'One and a half yuan,' she answered. I shook my head and said that it was too dear. The woman then turned and pointed to another piece. 'One yuan,' she said. I then began to tell her about our two sick friends. At last she gave me the larger piece for one yuan. From there we went to the fruit stall. Here again I told the same story and got more for our money.

We returned to the sick men. First I made them eat a raw egg each. Then I gave them a couple of cakes. Smith, Bland and I cut up the meat and potatoes and put the whole lot into one big pot. We cooked the cabbage separately. When the stew was ready we got two bamboo bowls and poured some of the thick rich soup into them and took them to Ginger and Ballantyne. 'Here you are,' I said, 'soup for starters.' After they had finished that we got plates of rice and onto it we dished out the stew. For sweets we chopped banana and cakes. The amazing thing was that they ate everything. They said that it was the first time in weeks that they had really fancied what had been put in front of them.

After the meal Ginger asked if we could help him get on his feet. Bland and I duly obliged, only too glad to see he was making some effort.

It certainly proved my point that all they wanted was at least one good meal a day. After that we went down to town every day, but as is usual we began to be a nuisance and we could hardly get anything as time went on. We became known as the English beggars.

I went to the sergeant and once again pleaded with him to spend some of the money that he kept, but he flatly refused to even listen to what I had to say.

I told Bland and Lacey that I was intending to make my way back to Man Ying, try to pass the place where we had been ambushed, and push northwards on our original plan. They both readily agreed to come with me. So, after our evening meal I went to the sergeant and told him of our intentions. I also reminded him of the colonel's last words to us, that should any man jeopardise the rest, then he was to be given twenty-four-hour grace, and then left behind. I said that we had given them all the time stated, as he had done when he left Bland and me. He fully agreed to this, wished us 'all the luck' and hoped that we would meet again in India. I told him that we would be off at dawn the next day.

We said our goodbyes the next morning to Smith, Ginger and Ballantyne. We then went to the sergeant to say goodbye. It was barely light. He got up from his bed and to my surprise he shook me by the hand. 'Good luck,' he said smiling, 'and watch out for the saubur. He is a big man and the leader of the bandits around here. It was him who ambushed us.'

'Where does he hang out?' I asked.

'Oh, anywhere between here and Man Ying,' he said with a grin on his face.

I wondered why he was grinning when he said that.

Chapter Twelve

A Tempting Offer

The sun came up slowly, the thick mist which lay over the river gradually vanished and after two hours marching we came to the village where I had spent the night in the pagoda. There was a small market, and with some of the remaining coins from the notes I had changed I bought some bananas and rice cake to see us through the two days' march to Man Ying. Bland put the purchases in a bag he was carrying and we set off again.

It was just after noon. I was on a small bamboo bridge which crossed a stream, and glanced back to check that both Bland and Lacey were still following. Lacey was about twenty yards back and Bland about the same distance further away. Satisfied, I carried on. At the same time I looked for a spot where we could stop and have a rest. At last I found a nice grassy bank beside a small clear-running stream in the shade of some trees, sat down, and waited for the other two. Lacey arrived and sat beside me.

'Blimey Fred, isn't it hot?' he gasped out.

'Where's Bill?' I asked.

'Oh, he'll be here in a tick,' he answered, and lay back on the grass.

Ten minutes went by, then another five, and still no sign of Bland. 'Are you sure he's coming?' I asked Lacey with some concern.

'Yes, he was on the bridge the last time I saw him,' he answered, getting to his feet.

'Well, he should have been here by this time,' I said, getting up. 'We're going back to have a look for him. You look to the left and I'll keep my eyes on the right.'

We both made our way back to the bridge. 'You stay here and I'll go over to the other side,' I ordered. 'If I see him, I'll give you a shout. You do the same if you see him.'

But there was no sign of Bland anywhere. I went to some people working in the fields close by and asked them whether they had seen a bearded Englishman. They said no. We eventually went back to where we had stopped for a rest, in case he had got past us somehow, but again there was no sign of him.

I climbed a tree and sat high in the branches and had a good look around. Some distance away I saw a person walking across the fields of growing rice, towards what looked like another Mission. I shouted at the top of my voice, 'Bill!' The person stopped and looked in my direction. I shouted a second time, but the person ignored my shout and disappeared behind the wall of the building.

I got down from the tree and said to Lacey, 'Come on, he has gone to that big white building over there.' It was about half a mile away. We hurried through the trees towards the building, which had a high tower with what looked like a bell in it. Around it was a whitewashed wall. The path took us to a door in the wall. The door was open so we entered into a yard. At the base of the tower was another door. I knocked hard. After a few moments we could hear the slip–slop of sandals approaching. The door opened and a wrinkled old Chinese woman came out. She was obviously surprised at seeing us, for her eyes opened wide and she stepped back with a start.

'Have you seen an Englishman?' I asked in Mandarin.

She shook her head and said 'No!'

Being thirsty, I asked the old lady if she could give us a drink of water. She waved us into a room where she told us to be seated. We both sat on high wicker bamboo chairs and she disappeared through a beaded curtain, leaving us alone.

I glanced around at the décor. Tapestries hung on two walls, and along the wall opposite the door was a long and high bookcase. I rose from my seat and went and looked at the books. To my utter surprise the case contained books by Shakespeare, Milton, Byron, Shelley, Keats, Dickens and other well-known poets and writers, while on the lower shelf were large red bound books on English law. Further along and on the bureau were photographs of cricket teams like those of Eton or Harrow. I drew Lacey's attention to all this, but he was not interested.

The old lady returned with a tray containing two glasses of what looked like ginger beer and two large slices of pink melon. Behind her came a young Chinese man in thick horn-rimmed spectacles and wearing European clothes on the top half of his body, Oriental ones on the bottom part. He greeted us in Chinese and held out his hand for me to shake. I took his hand and returned the greeting. Lacey did the same. I then thanked him for allowing us to rest in his house. He replied that this was not his house but his uncle's. I went on to tell him that we had lost our friend. He told us that he had not seen any other Englishman.

It was getting towards five o'clock in the evening, so I ventured to ask the young man, 'May we stay the night here, so that we can make a search for our missing friend tomorrow?'

'I shall have to ask my uncle,' was his reply. He left us, and Lacey and I set to devouring the juicy melon and cold drink.

It was getting dark as we sat waiting for the return of the young man. The old woman went around the room lighting small oil lamps that cast weird shadows.

After some time the young man returned and handed to me a small piece of paper. On it was written in English, 'Please come with the bearer of this note.' It was not signed, but whoever it was must have had a good education by the style of the writing. So without any hesitation we got to our feet and followed the youth.

It was fully dark as we followed him in an east–northeasterly direction, which meant that we were going nearer to Man Ying. I was still very concerned about the disappearance of Bland, but I was equally puzzled to know who we were going to see.

We had been walking along the top of the paddy fields for about half an hour when I saw lights some distance away. The young man stopped, pointed at the lights and said, 'That is the place.'

We entered the village which seemed to be ablaze with lights. There seemed to be many people there awaiting our arrival.

I had a good look around to see if there were any Europeans in the village, but could see none. All were Orientals and dressed as such.

The young man led us to a pagoda, which was also brightly lit. Before entering we removed our boots and socks. Our guide motioned us towards some chairs set at a long table. Then he disappeared.

There was plenty of activity as young girls and women went about the task of placing dishes of all kinds of food on the long table. Some of the girls glanced at us sitting there, and giggled among themselves.

'Well, it looks as though we are going to have something to eat,' said Lacey, licking his lips at the sight of the numerous dishes of fruit and other food.

'Looks more like a bleeding banquet to me!' I replied.

Leaning over to whisper, Lacey said in a low voice, 'I wonder who this bloke can be?'

Before I could answer, our guide reappeared. He walked straight toward us and, leaning down, asked us to stand, which we did.

Everyone in the room stood and faced the door. In strode a well-built man dressed in a white open-necked shirt and white trousers. His hair was jet black, as were his eyes, which had a piercing look as if he knew what one was thinking. His face was round and flabby with a double chin and a sallow complexion like a half-caste's, making the eyes seem even blacker. He was taller than both Lacey and me.

As he neared us he put out his fat stubby-fingered hand in friendship. I took the extended hand and shook it as warmly as he did. In perfect English he asked our names. I told him mine and introduced Lacey.

'I'll bet you chaps are devilishly hungry, what?' he said.

'Yes, sir! We are,' I answered with a broad grin. 'Thank you for asking us to come and join you here. And what do we call you, sir?' I asked.

'Me?' He pointed to himself. 'Just call me Saubur.'

He smiled and watched my face. I tried not to look surprised by covering up with a wry grin and answering as calmly as I could. 'Very well, Saubur, but this surely is not an English name, is it?'

'No, it isn't. It's an Oriental name,' he smiled, still watching my face.

'When I got your note written in that very good hand,' I flattered him, 'I thought you could be either English or American.'

'Well, let's cut out the chat for now,' he said, waving a thick podgy arm towards the table and chairs. 'Let's dine.'

He moved to the head of the table while Lacey and I sat on his left hand side. A woman sat on the corner between me and the saubur, and another young woman sat on my left between Lacey and me, then another woman sat beside him. Opposite me sat our young man and guide with a very young woman on each side of him. Another young man had joined the party and sat opposite Lacey. All the women had that Oriental beauty and were all of our age or maybe a little younger. But my mind was not on the girls. I was deep in thought at what the sergeant had told me about the saubur. If what the sergeant had told me was true, then we both had got to be very careful or we might not get out of this place alive.

The feast began with the saubur banging his chopsticks on the table and shouting, 'How-Lah,' to which everyone also shouted and got stuck into the food. Two young boys with large jars went around the table pouring out the clear water-like rice wine into everyone's glass. This wine, even drunk in moderation, can knock you out in a very short time if you are not used to it, as we had found out on a number of occasions prior to the beginning of hostilities. Drinking a glass of water the next morning to ease the dryness in the throat makes you drunk again!

I looked at Lacey. He was swigging it down as fast as his glass was filled, but I refused it completely. One of us had to stay sober. I made the excuse to the saubur that I had just recovered from a bout of malaria and did not wish to bring it back on by drinking alcohol. He was a little put out by this at first, but when Lacey, who was lisping a little already, confirmed what I had said was true, he seemed to accept it.

During the meal the saubur spoke to me in English about the war and things in general, but when he spoke to our young guide he spoke in a language which was foreign to me, not Mandarin. This, I was sure, was so that I would not know what they were talking about. They periodically glanced at me as they chatted. I was sorry that they knew that I could understand Mandarin.

During the conversation with the saubur he asked me where we were heading, and where we had been. I explained to him what we intended to do, and told him how some weeks before we had been robbed of all our belongings and money. I put emphasis on the word money. It was during this line of enquiry that the saubur said he was sorry about what had happened to Sergeant Friend and the others. He then asked where I was at the time.

'Oh, I was at Man Ying, laid up with the fever,' I answered, which was not an untruth, and which he may have known anyway.

'They were ambushed by bandits, you know?' he said, showing no sign of sorrow.

'Yes, Sergeant Friend told me all about it,' I replied.

'They stayed here for a couple of nights,' he said. 'We had some great time,' he added, smiling to himself.

It made me wonder if this bloke was playing cat and mouse with me. At times he seemed genuine, at others not. I did not like it when he talked in the foreign language with that young nephew of his.

He surprised me with his next statement. 'Do you know, Fred,' – he looked at me with his eyes squinting like black slits – 'that Sergeant was a bloody fool.'

'Oh, why is that?' I asked, looking at him, and at the same time silently agreeing with him.

'Because,' he began slowly, 'I told him that it was dangerous to go that way.' He paused for a moment, put some food in his mouth, took a sip from his glass, then continued. 'But that stupid fool ignored me and my warning.' He took some more food from one of the dishes and ate it. Then, looking at me, he asked in between chews, 'Why is it that a man like him gets the stripes?'

'Don't ask me a question like that, Saubur,' I said. 'Ask those people who dish them out.'

After that, the saubur brought the women into the conversation, but this time he spoke in Mandarin. Lacey was still tipping the wine back and was beginning to get quite drunk. The thing that began to worry me was that he might get fresh with either of the women next to him. I would have rather he got blind drunk than start something like that, but one could not tell with Lacey.

Once, when I picked up my glass to drink what should have been water, I smelt the wine. I pretended to drink, and as I put the glass back onto the table

I 'accidentally' knocked it over. I begged my pardon and said that I was sorry to all around me. The saubur then said something to his nephew in that strange language.

I was enjoying the food. There was plenty to go around and certainly a variety. I was making the most of the opportunity, for I had no idea when we would get the next meal.

Then the saubur stopped eating, looked hard at me with his cold dark eyes and asked, 'Fred, how would you like to stay here with us?'

'What?' I asked in amazement, taken completely by surprise.

'Well,' he began, 'you seem to be an intelligent sort of fellow. You speak the language pretty well. My nephew here tells me that you are an NCO. I will pay you well and feed you well, as you have been fed tonight.'

'But, but,' I stammered, trying to get a word in.

But he continued, 'Are you married, Fred?'

'No, I'm not married,' I answered, at last getting a chance to speak.

'Well, then, you can have any woman here, except this one.' He patted the woman on his left. 'You can have two, if you so wish it.'

'No, thank you very much,' I replied. 'But tell me why you want my services?' I was watching him closely.

'Well, Fred,' he began, 'for many miles around here there are bands of marauding robbers and bandits.'

I nodded in agreement, but said nothing.

'I want to protect my property against them,' he continued. 'Should they try to attack me, I want someone like you to train some of my servants and people to do the right thing at the right time.' He paused and stared at me. 'What do you say?'

I did not answer immediately, and thought what action he would take if I refused, and whether or not he was genuine. Was he hinting to me that he was the number one bandit in the area and wanted to keep off intruders to his territory? I had to tread extremely carefully here, I thought, or else both Lacey and I could end up in a shallow grave. From what I could see, this man had very few scruples and might stop at nothing to get what he wanted. For what seemed an eternity I held back from answering him. I glanced sideways at Lacey. Looking at the big drunken sod, I thought, what use is he to me now? He was grinning all over his face and his beard was covered with fat and grains of rice. He was swaying back and forth, with a glass of wine in his right hand and his left arm was around the shoulder of the woman on his left. Well, I thought, if it is our last meal, at least he is enjoying himself.

'I can understand your predicament, Saubur,' I said, picking my words very carefully, for after all, our lives might depend on what I said next. 'Can you understand the position that I am in?'

'What do you mean?' he asked, bringing his black eyebrows down into a frown.

'I mean, Saubur, that I owe allegiance already to my king and country, to which I swore an oath, and it is my duty to try at all cost, even my life, to make every attempt to re-join the first British unit that I come into contact with. I am deeply sorry that I can in no way repay the wonderful hospitality that you have shown to my friend and myself. I am sorry, but I must refuse your proposal.'

He leaned his big bulky frame back in his chair, shook his head slowly and said, 'I cannot, for the life of me, understand you British.' He slapped the table with his two palms. 'You are being knocked for six all around the world with no sign of winning, and you sit here and talk about oaths and duty!' He dropped his head and shook it from side to side as if in disgust at my answer to him.

'Yes sir, we are taking a beating.' I leaned forward, getting a little more confident. 'But we haven't fought that last battle yet!' I grinned at him and waited for his next comment.

It seemed that what I said and how I had said it had eased the situation, at least for the time being, for he raised his large frame out of the chair and said, 'Well, I suppose you'll want somewhere to sleep.'

We all rose from the table, and I answered, 'Yes, please!' As an afterthought, I asked, 'Could you supply me with a guide at sunrise to go and look for our lost friend?'

'Don't you worry about that, it will be taken care of,' he told me, putting his arm across my shoulder.

He called to one of the boys who had waited at the table and spoke in that foreign tongue. It was obvious that he was giving the boy some orders. Without another word to us, the saubur left the building, and the boy motioned to us to follow.

Lacey was the worse for drink and had to have my help to walk. 'Why didn't you go easy on that rice wine? You bloody fool!' I grumbled and swore at him.

His answer was, 'Itsh the besth time I'ff had frr a long time.'

'Do you realise who we are with?' I asked, trying to make him see sense.

'Who cares?' he sniggered.

The boy led us to some cattle sheds and motioned us to wait. When he returned he was carrying a couple of blankets. He led the way up a bamboo ladder to a hay loft above some stalls, dropped the blankets and indicated that this was where we were to sleep.

Fred at the Bush Warfare School, 1941.   Fred and his mates.

Fred and his mates.

Bill Bland, Fred and Jock Johnson.

Local guides at the
Bush Warfare School.

Kitting up.

Getting the mules ready.

Preparing to move out.

River crossing.

On patrol.

Meeting up with elements of the
Nationalist Chinese Army.

Rangoon Railway Station.

Pegu to Waw railway line along which the POWs were force marched.

Rangoon Jail from
the air (USAF).

Typical village house in Waw.

Photo of Fred taken from film of
released POWs near Waw, April 1945
(US archive).

Rangoon Memorial which has the names of those men lost with 'no known grave'.

Peter, Dorothy, Faith and Fred in Hong Kong, 1991.

I struggled to get Lacey up the ladder with the help of the boy. Lacey fell flat on his face in the corner and I covered him over with one of the blankets. I thanked the boy who turned and went back down below. In no time Lacey had rolled over onto his back and was snoring like a pig.

I then set to work gathering enough straw together to make a 'dummy' alongside where my companion was sleeping, covered it with the blanket and placed my bush hat as the head. Somehow I still did not trust the saubur. After that, I selected the darkest corner and covered my legs and feet with straw. I sat and waited. What I waited for, I had no idea, but the two Orientals talking in that strange tongue at the table made me very suspicious. I sat perfectly still, for the least movement made a creaking noise. It seemed hours. Lacey was snoring his head off.

My eyelids began to get heavy as I sat there in the darkness. I had begun to nod when I heard a slight noise from one side of the loft and became alert. My eyes tried to pierce the blackness, and then I saw it. A large rat was sniffing about. Slowly it moved towards where my friend lay, unconscious of the intruder. I let out the breath that I had been holding so as not to attract attention, and watched the dark long-tailed creature as it stood on its back legs and explored the covered body of my friend. I relaxed a little. The sudden tautness to my nerves had caused me to break out in a cold sweat, so that I was soaking wet, but I couldn't help a grin as I watched the animal pull itself up and sit on Lacey's heaving belly. For a moment it sat there, seeming to enjoy the motion, then it slid down between Lacey and the 'dummy' and went out of sight.

I awoke with a start. I was lying on my side. The grey light of dawn had penetrated the loft. Quickly I crawled over to the blanket-covered humps, disarranged the one covering the 'dummy' and shook Lacey. 'Come on!' I shouted at him. He gave a grunt. 'Come on! We have to look for Bill,' I shouted, shaking him. I then crawled to the ladder and looked down. At the bottom with his feet through the first rung was the sleeping boy. I gave the ladder a shake and the boy jumped from the bed, looked up at me and grinned.

Collecting the blankets we descended the ladder and handed them to the boy. I motioned that we wished to wash, and he led us out to a well in the now deserted village. There he left us, returning a few minutes later with two towels. He had obviously had his orders to guide us in the search for Bland, for after a while he went ahead of us leading the way to a number of villages. We went in a circle. No one had seen an Englishman. No one even knew what one looked like, as they had never seen one. They were most surprised when we told them that he looked like us.

We returned to the village at about one in the afternoon to find a meal had been prepared for us. The saubur came to us as we ate and said, 'So, you have had no luck then, Fred?'

'No,' I answered, 'it seems that he has just vanished into thin air.'

'Was it too warm for you last night, Fred?' he asked looking at me hard.

'Warm? No, not really,' I answered, a little puzzled.

'Then why didn't you use your blanket?' he asked, looking me straight in the face.

'Oh, well, err..,' I stammered, being caught out and not knowing what to say. 'It was a bit warm up there,' I lied.

'Your friend slept alright,' he nodded to Lacey.

'Oh, he would've slept under any conditions with the wine he'd drunk!' I laughed, trying to change the subject. The man's face broke into a smile and he nodded his head. So, someone had been up to have a look at us while we slept!

I quickly got off onto another track by saying, 'I'm afraid that we must be off and make our way to Man Ying. Our friend may be there and waiting for us.'

To this the saubur agreed, saying, 'Alright, but I do wish that you would change your mind and accept my proposition.'

'I'm sorry,' I said, 'but I cannot.'

'Look, I'll tell you what I'll do,' he said, leaning over the table. 'I'll make you a better offer. You can have anything that you require, both you and Lacey. And furthermore, I will get some men to go out and scour the land and bring your friend, err, what's his name?'

'Bill,' I cut in.

'Bill. We'll bring Bill back here and then you can decide between yourselves what you want to do. How does that suit you?'

I could not answer, not straight back in all honesty. I had to think. We had another fifteen hundred miles to go, and the further we went the harder it had to get. We, two of us that is, if we did not find Bland in Man Ying, had to go over some of the toughest country in the world with little or nothing.

Then I looked at the man sitting before me. Was he a villain, this well-educated, well-spoken and well-mannered man, or was he having me on and going to use me for other purposes if I accepted? Then the words of the colonel came back to me, wise words of an old campaigner. 'Don't get mixed up with any rabble!' Friend had, and look how he had got on!

'No, Saubur,' I said, 'I'm sorry, I cannot accept. I must carry on and try to get to India and to join our forces.' I stood up and put out my hand to show him that I left him in friendship.

He took it and said, 'Fred, I think you're a fool, but not the same sort of fool that your sergeant is. Good luck!'

Lacey then shook his hand, and we waved farewell as we left the village with a young boy showing us the way.

The young boy walked with us for a good hour and put us back on to the now familiar road to Man Ying. We evaded two villages and slept out under the trees. We did not wish to get into any more trouble, as we had been informed that some of these villages were very religious and did not like foreigners.

We got in sight of Man Ying about three in the afternoon. It cost me one yuan for the two of us to get across the river. On arriving at the Mission, our first question to the French priest was, had he seen Bland. To our dismay he had not. The priest advised us to go to the YMCA and ask there, but he said for us to be very careful, as they had now become 'very aggressive' towards everyone.

Lacey and I discussed this on our own. We thought that perhaps we had misunderstood the priest. We put it down to the fact that we had to converse in Chinese with him and that we had misinterpreted his words.

The next morning Lacey and I made our way to the YMCA. To our surprise it was decked out with red banners with both black and white Chinese characters. As we entered, four men wearing fur hats and long overcoats with red armbands came forward and asked what we wanted. They spoke in Mandarin and were very abrupt.

I asked them whether they had got any information about an Englishman. As I spoke, the young man whom we had seen before came out of a rear room. He was very apologetic and said that he had not heard nor seen anything of our friend.

On the table was a large amount of all types of rifle ammunition, some .303 and some .280, also some .45 to go with Colt automatic pistols or Thomson submachine guns. Along one wall, behind the four men, there stood a number of rifles. Among the rifles were six British Army Lee-Enfields. Two of them had the light woodwork of those issued to the Indian Army. The two Indians with our party had had similar coloured rifles, plus the other four made me think that they had at one time belonged to Friend, Ginger, Smith and Ballantyne.

I casually stepped around to the young man and took hold of one of the rifles to look at the butt plate, which would give me the regiment, but as I gripped the steel band around the muzzle there was a sharp click-click behind me. I turned and looked. A man with a fur hat stood directly behind me pointing an automatic pistol at me. 'Boo-dzor, boo-dzor!' (Don't move) he snapped.

The young man shouted to me, 'Leave them. Please come away!'

I allowed discretion to overrule any thoughts of heroism, let go of the rifle and walked outside the hut. 'They are our bloody rifles!' I almost shouted.

The young man followed us out. 'I am very sorry, but I cannot help you anymore. So will you please go away?' He was pleading with me.

'Who are those people?' I asked.

'They are the new People's Republic of China Movement,' he answered.

'Oh, so that's what the priest was on about,' I snapped, and with Lacey following I led the way back to the Mission.

It was not fully dawn when we were awakened from our slumber by a loud noise coming from the courtyard. We both went out to see what was happening, and found the priest surrounded by a mob of excited people. We asked what was wrong and were told that the Japanese had come over the mountains in the night and crossed the river about thirty miles to the south.

Lacey said, 'That's done Sergeant Friend and the others, then.'

'Yes,' I answered, 'it seems that we moved off just in time, doesn't it?'

'I wonder what happened to Bland,' he said.

'I just haven't got a clue,' I replied, 'unless he got cold feet about coming with us and turned back to stay with Friend and the others.'

'Well, whichever way it is, he's in trouble somewhere,' he muttered.

'Yes,' I said, 'and we can't do a bloody thing about it, not now anyway.'

As Lacey and I walked back to finish our disturbed sleep, Lacey asked, 'What are we going to do now then, Fred?'

'Well,' I said, 'the first thing to do, I think, is go down into town and ask if this New People's Republic want us to help them in any way, as they seem to be the ruling forces in this area. At least we can say that we did offer.'

'I'll do what you do, Fred,' said Lacey.

Later that morning we again went down into town. This time there was chaos. People were running everywhere, carrying large packs and bundles, some with young children and old people. We had seen the same thing time and time again in Burma over the last few months. We made our way through the crowded narrow streets to the YMCA, which was now besieged with people. Forcing our way through we were once again confronted by the same people in fur hats. A young man came forward and asked what we wanted.

I asked him to tell the leader, whoever it was, that we had come to offer our help, as we had heard the bad news. We tried to impress the young man that we were specialists in certain types of army work, and that given the right equipment we could help them, but we must have some kind of arms for our own protection.

The young man turned to the fur-hatted men and told them what I had said. After some talk among themselves, and some laughter, they turned back. Without the young man translating, I knew that they did not require our help, so I said to Lacey, 'Come on, we are not wanted here.'

As we walked back to the Mission, Lacey said, 'Hey, Fred! I wonder if that Saubur fellow meant that lot back there when he said other bandits.'

'So! You were taking notice after all, weren't you?' I sneered at him.

'Well,' he said, 'I only caught snips of what that bloke was saying, the morning before we left him.'

Back at the Mission I went straight to the French priest and said that we would be leaving him early the next morning and that we hoped this time we would not have to return. We thanked him for all that he had done for us. Once again he warned us of the dangers that faced us. I was not so much afraid this time of being robbed, but of someone waiting their chance to get revenge on me for what I had done, for we must pass that same place again on our way to Tengchong. Lacey was a little afraid of going the same way. 'I don't like it, Fred,' he said, 'they could be waiting for us anywhere.' I had to agree with him, but asked him what alternative had we got. He fell silent and just followed behind.

Chapter Thirteen

On to Tengchong

We went with great caution up the hill, not stopping for any breaks, and when we got in sight of the village where we had spent the night we cut away from the track and skirted around, trying not to make any noise. We then slept the hours of darkness hidden in the jungle and away from the track, just in case anyone had heard us.

We then had to get past the bridge where we had been robbed, and began to climb the hill to the bridge just as dawn was breaking, going very slowly and keeping a sharp lookout. I waved Lacey into the cover of the trees while I went on ahead from tree to tree until I could see the bridge. I looked all around to see if there was any other way that we could cross, but the jungle was thick and impassable. No wonder the robbers picked this spot, I thought.

I crouched behind a tree and listened intently, but all was as quiet as the grave, so I waved to Lacey to join me and whispered to him that the best thing to do was to go across one behind the other as fast as we could and get into the thick brush on the other side. He nodded his agreement.

We more or less dashed from our cover and once on the bridge our boots made a noise like a big bass drum as we trod on the rough planks. I glanced down at the spot where I had stabbed the robber, and there was a distinct brown stain with some smaller stains going away from it. I then made for the trees as soon as I could, with Lacey fast on my heels. Going in and out between the trees we scrambled up the steep incline, not daring to look back.

We then went as fast as we could to get out of sight of the bridge, only too eager to put as much distance between us and that never-to-be-forgotten place.

We had eaten all the food the French priest had given us, and on the second night out in the jungle, high up in the mountains, we huddled together beneath a large tree, covering ourselves with the many leaves strewn around to keep out the damp cold night air.

With the coming of the dawn we were on our way again. The air, although clearer and cleaner, was getting thinner, and we found that we were having more difficulty in breathing. We also found that the air was chillier, and at times we were shivering, but this helped to make us keep on the move.

Towards noon we had a respite, for the path began to wend its way down the side of the mountain and across a wide valley. But after a while we began to climb again up the side of another mountain.

I had stopped to look to see where the path was leading us when I saw a movement high in the trees to my right. I was ahead of Lacey by about fifty yards or more, and stood perfectly still, looked away, and let my eyes slowly turn back to where I had seen the movement. I turned and began as if to exercise my arms, while waiting for my friend to catch up to where I stood. Now and again I casually turned to where I had seen the movement. I distinctly saw it again, so I dropped flat to the embankment on the high side of the road, which was on the right and the same side as the watcher. Now I could see him, but he could not see me. Lacey came up and dropped beside me.

'Don't look now,' I said casually, 'but we are being observed.'

'What? Where? Who?' he asked in a panic.

'Lie flat on your face,' I told him, 'and I will tell you where to look. At the same time, see if you can see any others. But whatever you do, keep yourself well behind the bank.'

As Lacey rolled over onto his face I kept my eyes on the man. It was obvious that he had lost sight of us for a moment, for he changed his position and came lower down the slope, moving between the trees. All this time I was giving Lacey details of where to look. I could now see plainly that the man carried a rifle of sorts.

Lacey whispered, 'I've got him, Fred. He's got a rifle. What do you think?'

'Yes, I had noticed,' I answered quietly.

'What do you intend to do, Fred?' Lacey asked, getting a little excited.

'I don't intend to do anything at the moment,' I replied. 'I'm going to let him make the first move. You haven't seen any others, have you?'

'No, and if there had been, they would have shown themselves by now, don't you think?' answered Lacey.

'He must be on his own,' I whispered, 'and he must have been watching us for quite some time. We will lie here, taking turns to watch for about half an hour. If he doesn't come to us, we'll go to him.'

'You're taking a chance, aren't you, Fred?' said Lacey, looking at me.

'Well, someone has to make a move sometime,' I replied. 'We cannot sit here forever, can we? I'll bet your stomach is beginning to rumble, isn't it? I know mine is.'

I rolled over onto my back, to give Lacey first watch, and had a catnap, but it did not seem very long since I had closed my eyes when Lacey gave me a nudge. 'Fred, look! He's coming down.' Picking his way between the trees and peering, the man came down the side of the mountain. He had begun shouting, and coming nearer he began waving his arms. Both Lacey and I looked around us to make sure that he was calling to us and to no one else. We could not see anyone, so we both stood up. Again he called, and waved for us to go to him.

'Perhaps he was waiting for us, and when we stopped he got impatient,' I said.

'Could be!' Lacey agreed.

As we neared the man he waved us to follow, which we did.

He wore the customary blue wide-bottom trousers and black cotton tunic, and was barefooted. A black woollen hat was pulled down on his head, while across his chest hung a bandolier with ammunition stuck in it, but it looked to me that the ammunition was too large for the rifle, an old-fashioned breech-loader with a long barrel partly covered with a wooden stock.

We followed him until we came to a small and what seemed like a little-used track. This led us into some very thick woodland and scrub. Every now and then, he turned to see that we were still following. As if by the stroke of a magic wand we came out of the dullness of the trees and into a wide open space surrounded on three sides by tall cliffs that seemed to reach to the sky. The cliffs were even more surprising by their whiteness, as if they had been carved out into a huge sculpture. Here and there dashes of green grew between the ragged clefts. At the base of one of the cliffs was a large door, which was opened by an unseen person as we approached. We passed into a large hallway hewn out of the rock. Off the hall there were a number of passages. Oil lamps hung around the walls, and daylight shone through a number of slits in the walls on the same side as the door. Around the walls hung swords and shields from a bygone age. At the far end of the hall was a long wooden table, and squatted around this were men dressed in the same kind of clothes and each armed with a rifle of some sort.

Our 'guide' led us down towards the long table. As we passed the squatting men they made some comments and laughed out loud, which caused me some consternation. I whispered to Lacey, 'What do you make of all this, Len?'

'I don't know,' he answered shakily, 'but it looks as though we are in some kind of bandits' den.'

'Yes,' I replied, 'it does seem that way, doesn't it?'

We stood before the table. Now and then I turned and looked around me. Our 'guide' had disappeared into one of the side passages. The squatting men were now staring at us hard, as though they resented us being there. I thought that at any moment they would get up and do something drastic.

Then from one of the passages came a well-built man. He wore a white turban on his head and had a dyed-red beard, his eyes were black and half closed into slits, and he was clothed in a white robe which made his enormous body seem even larger. He issued an order and our 'guide,' who had reappeared, dashed away and returned with rough wooden seats.

'Sit down!' he ordered us in broken English. Lacey and I sat facing the large man. I looked and looked again at those familiar dark piercing eyes. Then I noticed the fat podgy hands as he clasped them in front of him on the table, and was certain.

As if having difficulty in finding words to speak, he asked, 'You, from where come you to?'

His voice was low and gruff. I had recognised him, but did not show it. I dared not, for here we were both at the mercy of the saubur, and he could do what he liked with us. So, I did not smile at his attempt to disguise his voice and his good English. I leaned forward and quietly said, 'Man Ying.' I said nothing else, but kept looking at him.

'To where now go?' he asked.

'Tengchong,' I answered. Lacey had not said a word, but just fidgeted on the seat next to me.

'Tengchong!?' he said, as if surprised. 'Many, many lee (Chinese miles).' He shook his head.

'Yes, it is many, many miles for us to walk,' I agreed with him.

'And after Tengchong, where you go?' he asked, still trying not very successfully to disguise his voice.

'We go to India,' I answered.

'India!' he shouted. He roared with laughter. 'India!' he repeated. He tapped his turbaned head. 'You English are sick in the head!' Then, breaking into Mandarin, he said, 'I will give you some food.'

I thought that it was my turn to do some acting, for we had not said a word about understanding Chinese. I glanced at Lacey, then back at the saubur, and said in English, 'I'm very sorry, but we do not understand.' I watched his face closely.

'Oh, so you cannot speak Chinese,' he said with a grin. I knew then that I had guessed right, and that he knew it as well. He said that he would give us shelter for the night.

After a very good meal, the saubur asked us when we were going to continue our journey. 'Now,' I answered.

'But I have already told you that you can stay the night,' he pointed out, his English improving rapidly.

Lacey looked at me disapprovingly, but I shook my head and told the big man, 'You have been very kind to us, but we have a very long and hard journey before us. We must make use of every hour of daylight that we can.'

I was a little surprised that he offered no resistance, but furnished us with a guide who he said would show us back on to the trail that would take us to Tengchong. 'It is an eleven-day march,' he informed us. Then, dropping the attempt at disguise altogether, he said in earnest, 'Do not come this way again or you will be shot on sight.'

The guide led us by different routes and paths to the other side of the mountain and bade us farewell as we made our way down towards the valley below.

The saubur had given us some food to take with us, and we made this last us for three whole days. We did not see a human being in the whole of that time. Food was very scarce in the mountains, and we had to resort to the long-bladed grass that we had been shown at the Bush Warfare School to be edible. The only difficulty with this was that it tended to cut the tongue and the inside of the mouth. Down in the valleys we lived off the wild fruit growing there. The large pear-like fruit of the papaya was particularly filling.

We must have been well over half way to Tengchong when, at the top of a rise, the sky became overcast and thick low cloud appeared. I shouted to Lacey, who was some distance behind me, to get a move on, as we needed to find shelter from the coming storm. I set a quicker pace, striding down the steep incline, but then it was as if the whole heavens had opened up and we were engulfed in torrential rain. In a matter of seconds I was soaked to the skin.

The path crossed a small stream. On the opposite bank, about three feet above the stream was a sandy ledge, and on this was a cave about four feet high, wide at the base but going to almost nothing at the top. Quickly I jumped the stream, pulled myself onto the ledge and peered inside. The cave went back into the bank for about five or six feet, and inside was dry. This, I thought, would do us for shelter for the night. On the floor were some dry leaves and grass, which I gathered to start a fire. I had peeled off my wet clothes by the time Lacey arrived. I went back out into the lashing rain naked, hunting for the driest pieces of wood that would get the fire going. After getting enough firewood I began collecting some large boulders to close up the entrance, as we were going to be there for the night.

Except for the pangs of hunger, I was quite enjoying myself, splashing about in the cold water of the river. Lacey had come out and seated himself near a small waterfall. I had stopped collecting boulders and was now attempting to 'tickle a fish.' I lay flat on my stomach. A fish came, and I 'tickled' its belly, but when I went to grab it it slipped through my fingers and swam away. So I picked up a large boulder, raised it above my head and, swearing at the fish, threw it down in the water, and then turned away, angry and very hungry.

'Look, Fred!' shouted Lacey. 'You've stunned one.'

I turned back quickly. There, flapping about on the surface of the water was a fish about a foot long and three inches wide. I dived into the water, grabbed it, made my way back to the bank with my prize, and began tearing it to pieces with my teeth. The scales and bones dug into my lips and gums, causing them to bleed, but I was so ravenous that I took no notice. Lacey broke the silence by saying, 'Give me a bit?' to which I replied, 'Get your own ****ing fish!'

The rain was still falling as darkness came upon us. We built up the entrance with boulders from the inside and left a small gap at the top for the smoke to get out. Our cotton trousers had dried, but my shirt and jacket were still very wet. We had made a drying 'horse' from branches and over these we draped our wet clothes. The fire was burning well. Some of the wood we had gathered was a little damp, which caused the fire to smoke quite a bit, but as it dried out and the flames caught it lit up the small cave. We lay one on each side of the fire, I with my head near to the entrance and Lacey the other way around. There was very little room to move, but we were dry and warm.

We talked about past events, though Lacey naturally kept off the subject of why we were there in the first place. We wondered even more about what had happened to Bland and how far Captain Brown's party was in front of us. We also wondered how the colonel and the others had fared, and if they had managed to get over the Irrawaddy to safety.

When I leaned forward to place a fresh piece of brushwood on the fire I heard a low throaty growl above my head. I sat up and half turned to look up to the gap at the top of the boulders. The topmost stone began to wobble, and for a moment I was transfixed as I watched it being pushed by some unseen animal then overbalance and fall inside near the fire. From outside came ear-piercing howls as if other animals were shouting encouragement to the one who had dared to push the stone from its place, then a large wolf-like head and forepaws appeared at the now enlarged hole for a brief moment as if to take stock of the occupants of the cave.

I gripped a burning stick and, getting into a kneeling position on the side of the entrance, waited. Once again the rocks shook as the animal put its weight on them. And once again the wolf-like head appeared at the gap, emitting a low growl and showing long fangs and two rows of white teeth.

Quickly I raised the burning stick and thrust it at the animal's open jaws. The night was rent with a terrific snarling, squealing and yelping as the animal moved rapidly away. I could hear it snorting and snivelling as it made its hasty retreat.

I replaced the stone and sat for some time in silence, until eventually we both fell asleep.

The coldness around me caused me to awake with somewhat of a start. The grey light of dawn had crept into the cave. Lacey was turning restlessly, and I could hear the rush of water outside. The floor of our cave was wet and in some places nearly an inch deep in water. I pushed out the top boulders and looked out. What had been a slow gurgling stream was now a rushing torrent, bubbling now and then over and across the ledge where the entrance to our cave was.

The rain had stopped, so we gathered our clothes and picked our way along the ledge to drier ground. We got dressed and hoped that the sun would soon be up to dry our clothes as we walked.

Our path took us up into the pine forests. We reckoned that at this point we were about 150 miles from Tengchong, and hunger was biting into our insides. Lacey was complaining of pains in his belly as if he were the only one who was hungry, and this caused us to fall out, so I pushed on ahead. It was only when I rested and he caught up again that I knew he was still with me. The raw fish which I had eaten by the river was all I had had for three days, but Lacey had eaten nothing. I felt a little ashamed that I had not shared the fish with him, but then in the next minute I was saying to myself, 'Well, it's his fault that we are having to go this way,' and I would forget my shame.

We must have been very high up, for the air, though cool, was difficult to breathe. I found that I needed more rests. My legs were beginning to get stiff, especially after sitting for a while. It was during one of these rests that I took the opportunity to look back and down into the lush green valley far below us. A river ran between the high mountains like a silver strip of ribbon glinting as the sun moved across it. Beyond, spread out, were the green carpet-like plains, all of different colours. Oh, I thought, if only I had the time to really enjoy the beauty and serenity of this landscape!

The thought that kept me going was that on the other side of the mountain there had to be a village or even a rest house where for one night at least we could be under some kind of shelter.

Many times we both fell to our knees, too weak to walk any further, and then we would crawl on all fours. It was always in the back of my mind that we must keep going.

At the summit of the mountain we stood together and surveyed what lay before us. There was no sign of habitation. Our eyes searched the trees, looking for any tell-tale spiral of smoke that would tell us there was someone, somewhere, but we saw none. The narrow valley that lay before us was covered with trees so thick that one could barely distinguish individual trees. Beyond were more mountains, not as high as we had come over, but still high enough.

The sun was sinking over to our left as we made our way down the steep mountainside. Strangely, some of the weakness had left me, and so it seemed also with my companion. We were being helped along by the descending gradient. I stopped and caught hold of my friend's arm. 'Look, Len, smoke, isn't it?' I asked excitedly, but unsure my eyes were not playing games. A thin wisp of smoke seemed to hang in the air just above the trees some distance below, and then get blown away by the wind. Lacey agreed with me. We were almost running when we turned a bend in the path and came upon a small bamboo hut. We stood for a moment, and then with caution, I went one way and Lacey the other, so that we came to the open door from either side.

We both stood in the doorway of the hut. The smell of something cooking almost sent me mad. Sitting on the floor, facing the door, was an old man with long flowing beard and hair. His eyes almost popped out when he saw us, but he rose to his feet. He just stood and stared at us. He was dressed in a flimsy white shirt which had seen better days, and dark loose cotton trousers. His feet were bare. In his right hand he held a long-bladed pointed knife. His clothing had me guessing as to what language to use. I began with Chinese, but this drew a blank look. I then tried Urdu, but this too drew a blank stare. What next, I thought? I sat down near the fire and waved him to do the same. After all, I thought, if you are going to fight a man, you don't ask him to sit down with you. Lacey sat too. Then, taking the man's left hand in mine (he still held the knife in his right hand), I shook it to show friendship. At this he immediately smiled, showing a row of yellow teeth. He must have understood that we meant him no harm, for he picked up the bamboo pot, placed it on the fire and began stirring it with his knife.

The contents of the pot had begun to boil, giving off such a wonderful smell that my stomach began to make incredible sounds. The old man looked at both Lacey and me, got to his feet and went outside. Lacey looked at me, then at the pot, then back at me. We both sat there with our mouths watering. The man returned with three large leaves. He spread these out and spread the contents of the pot on each of them in equal shares. By this time it had got quite dark, and we scooped whatever it was from the leaves with our fingers. There was some meat and a number of leafy vegetables – of what kind, I had no idea. The meat tasted very much like rabbit, but it seemed much smaller. Whatever it was, it eased the hunger pains and we were very grateful. We sucked at the small bones until they were almost dry.

After the meal the man left the hut, returning sometime later with an armful of wood for the fire. Both Lacey and I left him making up the fire, got down in a corner of the hut and went to sleep.

When I roused myself Lacey was already awake and sitting by the glowing fire. It was already daylight, but the air was quite cold. I went and sat by the fire.

'Where's the old man?' I asked.

'I don't know,' he said. 'I woke up while he was making up the fire, then he went outside.'

I had to go outside to relieve myself. Between us and the next mountain was a sea of grey mist. It swirled around like a gigantic wave as it caught the wind. I turned to the side of the hut and at my feet saw the remains of a skin of some animal. The tail was long and thin. I picked the skin up by the tail. It was a greyish black and short-haired. The head was missing, but from the shape of the body I would make a guess at it being some kind of rat. I realised that was probably what had been in the pot the night before. When I went back inside, I did not say anything to my friend. I saw no point in telling him. What did it matter now, anyway? We had eaten it seven hours ago, and if the chance came again, I would eat it again.

Our host returned, and to our surprise he had around his neck a snake, a large python. It must have been eight feet in length and about three inches in diameter at the thickest part, though the head was missing. He laid it on the floor of the hut and at about the thickest part cut into the belly and began fetching out all the undigested food still in the gut. We saw fur from some kind of animal, and there were masticated bones and also feathers.

The old man then began to cut the snake up into cutlets about two to three inches thick, and stuck bamboo skewers through the meat. He then held them over the fire. We watched what he did and did the same. The fine skin shrivelled and burnt, peeling back to expose the fat underneath. We kept the cutlets turning so that the fat ran on to the hot side and cooked them more quickly.

Whether it was because of hunger or not, the snake meat tasted like something one only dreams of. It was delicious. The nearest thing I could think it tasted of was chicken.

While we sat around the fire cooking more cutlets, I tried by sign language to make the old man understand where we were heading. I said 'Tengchong' and pointed in the direction of northeast, and he nodded his head to show that he understood. I then pointed to the sun and to the east and made an arc with my arms to show him the rise and fall of the sun. He copied what I had done and put up three fingers at first, and then four. So I reckoned that he meant between three and four days to Tengchong.

The sun was well up when we bade our hermit friend goodbye. We had stuffed our pockets with most of the rest of the snake, which he had wrapped up in leaves for us.

On the lower slopes and plains we managed to find wild maize. This went down well with the snake meat. So we did not fair too badly for the next two days.

We saw and encountered all types of animals, but we saw no more people and I thought that this must be the worst part of our journey. Sometimes I thought that we had taken the wrong track, but the rising sun in the morning and the stars at night always showed me that we were going in a general northeasterly direction.

We had crossed two more mountains and had slept on the side of the third. By noon of the next day, I estimated, we should be able to see Tengchong, thus reaching it in the middle of the afternoon.

We were climbing the mountain that we thought would give us a view of Tengchong. It was just before noon, and Lacey had dropped behind. By the side of the road I saw a mound of earth, about six feet in length and fenced in by some roughly cut sticks, which were drawn together at the top, forming an arch. There was a rough cross made from two tree branches. I went closer to look at the words cut into the wood. Unconsciously I read them aloud: 'Tpr. R. Sharp died Ju … 1942.' The weather had erased half of the month. I sat down beside the grave and tried to think what month it was now. I had completely lost all knowledge of time. Then my mind went back to the man who lay beneath the mound. Sharp, the joker, always ready with a quip, always trying to bring a laugh to something that was dull and black. He would always come out with a witty remark, and all would seem better.

As I sat daydreaming of the past and enjoying those moments when we had all laughed and joked with each other, drank and made merry, Lacey came slowly up the hill. I glanced down towards him, and all the prejudice forgotten over the past few months came rushing back. I hated the man, hated the sight of him and did not want to even speak to this despicable louse. My hands clenched and unclenched in temper and anger for what he had been responsible for.

Lacey asked me, 'Who is it, Fred?'

'Sharp!' I grated out between my gritted teeth. 'Another one for you to carry on your back!' I stood up to face him as I said it.

For a moment Lacey stood silent, looking down at the grave, then, lifting his head to look at me, he said, 'You can't forget it, can you, Fred?'

'No! I bloody well can't!' I rasped at him, turning away and walking on up the slope.

Tengchong was on the slope of a long mountain range stretching far to the north. We knew that this range of mountains ran parallel with the border of Burma, which was about twenty-five miles to the west.

I had hardly spoken to Lacey since we had passed Bob Sharp's grave, and I entered Tengchong well ahead of him. A teahouse was the first thing that I saw, on the edge of the town. There I sat and ordered a cup of tea. Lacey arrived and also asked for tea. By this time a small crowd of people had gathered around us. I knew we looked dirty and unkempt, with beards and long hair poking from beneath our hats. I thought that they are looking at us because we were English. Perhaps they had never seen Englishmen like that.

As we sat drinking our tea and ignoring the watching crowd, two Chinese soldiers armed with rifles came and stood one each side of us. I tried to draw them into conversation, but they would not have any of it. We finished our tea and rose to go.

'Boo-shu-gworler!' ('Don't move!') one of the soldiers rapped out.

'Way-shemma, wor-mun boo chugworler?' ('Why can't we move?') I asked.

'You no go, no speak,' he answered, motioning us to sit down.

I ordered two more teas. Lacey and I sat and talked, sipping our tea and completely ignoring the two guards. After about a quarter of an hour there was a shout from further up the street. The soldiers motioned us to go with them. We pushed our way through the crowd and walked up the cobbled street with the two soldiers on either side of us.

They led us to a large wooden bungalow. There, standing on the veranda, was a smartly-dressed Chinese officer, complete with a sword and shining Sam Browne belt. As we neared the bungalow, he turned and went inside. Our guards motioned us into a spacious room, where the officer was seated at a highly polished table. There was also a well-built Sikh officer leaning at a window and looking out. He had two pips on his shoulder straps.

To him I said, 'Do you speak English, Sir?'

'Yes, I do,' he answered in a well-cultured voice.

'Then Sir, can you please tell me why we have been placed under guard?' I asked, turning towards him.

'That, I'm afraid, was a misunderstanding,' he answered very politely.

'But surely, Sir, they must have known we were English?' I came back quickly.

'They are not taking any chances,' he replied. 'You are probably unaware of the fact that the Japanese have penetrated across the whole of the frontier.'

'We knew that they had crossed the Taiping River about fifty miles to the south of Man Ying, but that was about two weeks ago,' I said.

'So, you didn't know that Man Ying had fallen, then?' he asked.

'No, sir, but I expected it,' I replied.

'And that is where you have come from?' he asked.

'Yes, Sir, and I didn't expect a reception committee like this,' I answered. The big Sikh smiled slightly.

'And where are you heading for next?' he asked.

The smile left his face and a queer look came into his eyes when I answered, 'Sima, Sir, then on to Sadon.'

'After that, where to?' he asked.

'We shall carry on north, to Sumprabum, and west into Assam,' I continued, not giving him a chance to interrupt. 'We shall then follow the Brahmaputra River until we run into a British garrison.'

I was getting a little fed up with this questioning, as we had not eaten a decent meal in eleven days. I gave the information as if I was rehearsing it. I knew where I was heading for, and I wondered to myself if they knew where they were going.

The big Sikh stopped me by saying, 'You realise the risk that you are taking, of course, by going back into Burma.'

'Yes, Sir, but we have managed this far,' I replied, 'and I see no reason to alter our plans now.'

For a while there was silence. He looked at the Chinese officer, who had not spoken a word. I had no idea if he understood English. 'You also realise that the country is very rough and mountainous,' continued the Sikh, in a friendlier voice now, as if trying to warn us of the danger we were going into. 'There are very few villages,' he went on, 'and very little food, plus the fact there are roaming bands of dacoit bandits who would kill you just for the fun of it. They hate everyone, even themselves.'

'Yes sir, we have taken all that into consideration and we both fully understand the position.' I was adamant now and feeling very hungry.

The Sikh was either speechless or thinking of something else to say to put us off going any further, so I cut in on the silence by saying, 'Sir, you must realise that we have the shortest part of our journey to accomplish. Besides, we are aiming to catch up with Captain Brown's party who are ahead of us.'

'If you are referring to the captain that I think you are, he and his party went through here about seven weeks ago,' he said.

'Blimey!!' I almost shouted in amazement. 'That is a long while ago, isn't it, Len?' I turned to Lacey who had up till then been silent. He mumbled in agreement. Most likely he was thinking of the food he could be eating.

The Sikh officer then turned to the Chinese officer and told him what I had said in Mandarin. The Chinese officer then gave orders that we were not to leave the village until he said we could go. We were not prisoners and could move around the village as we wished, but we were not to go outside until a guide was found to take us some of the way northwards. The guide, we were told, would put us on to the right road that would bring us to a place called Bataum, which was just inside the Burma frontier.

For three days and nights we were supplied with food and tobacco. We hung around the small mountain village, going for small walks so as to keep fit for the journey ahead of us. If we ventured too far from the village or its bounds, a shout from the trees would tell us that we were being watched. After the first day the people began to get used to us and would stop and chat and give us sweets or fruit. The waiting around, however, got on my nerves as I thought of the time already wasted. Lacey found a place where he could get free drinks, and once or twice came back a little drunk, but I never said anything to him about it, as I thought it was up to him. Me, I was ready to move off at any time, night or day.

Chapter Fourteen

Fortress Sima

On the fourth day of our stay at Tengchong we were asked to go to the Chinese officer's bungalow once more. The Sikh was there again. I saluted as I entered, and my salute was returned by both him and the Chinese officer, who was seated behind his highly polished table. The Sikh informed me that a guide had been found and that we could leave at dawn the next day. The Chinese officer then got up from his chair, came around the table, held out his hand and wished us a safe journey to India. I took his hand and thanked him for everything.

Then it was the Sikh's turn, but he said, 'I think what you are going to attempt is pure madness, just the two of you and unarmed.'

All that I could think of for an answer was, 'Do you, sir?'

'Yes!' he answered.

'But then, sir,' I went on, 'that's why the British have never been defeated, I suppose.'

His eyes flashed and a grim smile parted his lips as both Lacey and I saluted and marched away back to where we were staying.

At dawn we were ready and waiting outside the bungalow. Quite a number of people had gathered in the early light to see us off, as we had made quite a few friends. Out of the bungalow came the man who was to be our guide, a short stockily built Chinese, dressed in a white open-necked shirt and khaki shorts, and with nothing on his feet. In his hand he carried a short hunting-bow, while across his back was a quiver full of arrows. In the belt at his waist was his long dha, or sword, for hacking down branches and other things. He was clean shaven, and a broad grin came to his face as he approached us. After our greetings, we moved off. We turned back now and then to wave to those who had come to bid us farewell until they were out of sight.

The guide stopped only when he wanted to, and moved very fast although seeming only to go at a casual pace. Many times he waited for us to catch up with him and did not seem at all put out by any delay. He had perhaps been given strict instructions by the Chinese officer to have patience with us and wait.

He showed us his prowess with the bow late in the afternoon when we had eaten the rice packs. He obviously thought that it was time that we had something else to eat before darkness fell, and brought down two large wood-pigeons with his arrows. Skewering them through the neck with a stick, he carried them on his shoulder until he saw a third wood-pigeon and brought that down too.

When we stopped he soon had a fire going, skewered the three birds individually and gave one to each of us. We held them over the flames of the fire and allowed the feathers to burn, leaving the bare flesh to cook in its own fat, and turning them over and over until they were done. At the same time we cooked some maize that we had collected on the way.

We rose at dawn and got going again. After two hours or more the guide led us along a rough mountain ridge, thickly covered with trees, to a fork in the track. Here he stopped and, pointing his finger and waving his arm, said 'Burma.' Then, pointing down the left-hand track, which was going in a northwesterly direction, he said, 'Bataum!' After thanking him we watched as he made his way back along the track. When he was out of sight I turned and led the way.

Bataum, we reckoned, was about thirty-five miles away, which we thought would take us at least two days of marching. It all depended on the type of country that we had to get over, and again, with no guide to get food out of the air for us, things could become very difficult.

Crossing the rough mountain ridge soon had us tired. How high we were we had no idea. All that we could go by was the foliage of the different trees. We thought we were up at about ten thousand feet. The night seemed to come down more quickly, and we tore off tree branches to make some sort of shelter from the night air that got cooler as the hours of darkness went by. Neither of us slept much. I dozed on and off until dawn came, bringing with it the warmth of the sun.

We had been walking for about two hours, just following the track which meandered up and down, and I was well ahead of Lacey when I saw a bamboo hut further along the track. I thought at first that it was a village but when I reached it I found that it had been built as a rest hut for lonely travellers. I sat down by the stream that ran close by the hut. When Lacey arrived I growled at him and told him that we could have used the hut the night before if we had carried on a little longer.

'You aren't blaming me for that, are you?' he asked angrily.

'Yes, I am!' I shouted back. 'You're always lagging behind. We could have been here before dark if you had kept up.'

'I think I'll shut up,' he said. 'You seem to have got off on the wrong foot this morning.' He lay back on the bank and fell silent.

'Yes, you do that!' I ranted at him. 'We'll get on much better.'

'Well, I like that!' he said, tutting. 'We've walked hundreds of miles together and I doubt if we have spoken civilly to each other more than a dozen times.'

'Well, Lacey,' I shouted and glared at him, 'if you don't like it, you can always go on your own!'

'You wouldn't like it on your own,' he said with a smirk, 'no more than I would.'

I stood up. 'Lacey,' I shouted, 'you're kidding yourself!' My temper was rising. 'If it hadn't been for you, I wouldn't be here anyhow. You!' I went on pointing at him. 'You depend on me, not me on you, and I'll prove it.' With that I walked quickly away, leaving him still sitting by the stream.

All day I travelled alone, only now and then looking back to see if he was coming along behind. He kept his distance from me until dusk began to fall, and then he began to close the gap between us.

I selected a spot to bed down for the night. Lacey came along and got down on the opposite side of the track. The next morning I set off as quietly as I could, leaving him asleep. I was very tired and hungry as I climbed the steep rise which brought me into Bataum.

It was midday, and the sun was blazing down. This had brought on a great thirst. At the first hut I arrived at I managed to crawl into its shade, completely exhausted. The door opened and an old man came out and looked down at me. 'Pani mea lager,' I gasped out. The old man waved me inside the hut, and I struggled to my feet and went into the cool and dark interior.

The old man handed me a bamboo pot of cold water. I drank greedily. As I drank, I saw that there was a second man inside the hut lying on a bed in the furthest dark corner. This man rose from the bed, looked at me and said something to the old man which I could not catch.

After I had drunk as much water as I wanted, I lay back on the floor and closed my eyes. After a short time I felt hands going over my clothes as if I was being searched. Keeping my eyes still closed, I lifted my arms above my head to give the searcher more scope. I then said, 'Teek hai, teek hai, dekna dow picer nay hai!' ('Alright, alright, look inside I have no money!') The hands stopped groping. I opened my eyes to see the old man kneeling beside me.

The old man did not know what to do with himself. Unknown to the two men, my roll of notes was tucked into the lining of the sleeve of my jacket, so that when I had raised my arms it had passed detection.

The look upon the old man's face must have triggered off some sniggering from me. In an instant I was simply rolling on the floor with uncontrollable laughter. The old man moved quickly away as if I was possessed of a devil and sat cringing in a corner. The other man, now easy to see as my eyes had become accustomed to the dark, had sat back down on the bed, staring at me as I rolled from side to side in laughter.

Tears began to flood my eyes as new outbursts of mirth engulfed me. Every time I looked in their direction a new wave of laughter came.

My mirth began to subside, and I sat looking at the two men in the darkness of the hut. I wiped the tears from my eyes and face, just chuckling now and then. In Urdu I asked them if they had any food to give me. They said they had none, but that if I went further into the village I would see a large bamboo hut. There I might get food, for that was the headman's house.

I walked out, now a little refreshed, made my way to the hut indicated, mounted the bamboo veranda and walked to the open doorway. My boots had made enough noise to be heard inside, and a youngish man who looked Indian came out. He had a white turban around his head, a small growth of hair on his chin and a thin line for a moustache. He wore a sleeveless army pullover over a white dirty shirt, a pair of dirty khaki shorts, and open-toed sandals. Around his waist was an army webbing belt, and stuck in this at an angle was a long-bladed knife with a beautiful carved ivory handle.

I spoke in Urdu and asked if he could give me some food. Without any hesitation he invited me inside, where he motioned me to sit near the fire in the centre of the room, but I picked a spot away from it and in the cool.

The young man took a short hunting-bow and a handful of arrows and left the hut. I sat gazing at the glowing fire and various ornaments that hung around the room and wondered if he had at one time belonged to an Indian regiment, had got this far north and then had decided to stay. At the back of my mind there was the feeling that I had seen him before somewhere, but I pushed it away as pure fancy.

I was getting fidgety and impatient. The hunger pains were not any help either. Then there came the sound of a cough from what looked like a pile of old rags in the opposite corner of the room from where I was sitting. I sat still, the sound of a cough came again and the pile of rags seemed to move slightly. Curiosity got the better of me, for I got to my feet and went to the piled rags, which I found were sacks and skins, knelt down beside them and gently lifted the covers. A girl's pale face, almost white, looked up at me. Dark rings showed around the bottom of her black, almost coal-like eyes. Her black hair fell untidily about her as she raised her head from the rough pillow. For a moment she stared at me in wide-eyed fear. Then a puckered frown came across her forehead, and the stare in her eyes slowly changed from fear to a wan smile, which showed her white well-kept teeth.

'Toom Taunggyi our hau ou?' she asked in a weak voice.

Now it was my turn to frown. 'Yes,' I answered, a little puzzled, 'I am from Taunggyi.'

She then lifted a thin yellowy brown arm from beneath the covers, and with her hand covered the lower, bearded part of my face. This puzzled me even more, until she said, 'Toom Taunggyi hospitali admi hai?' Then she threw back the covers and showed me her chest. A smell of rotten flesh came up from the clothes. I glanced at the spot she tapped with her fingers and saw the cloth covering a wound. It was then that I realised that this was the same young woman who had been taken away by her husband from the hospital in Taunggyi, hundreds of miles away from here, the night a Gurkha got shot.

I looked closer at the smelly wound. It still had the same dressing which had been put on at the hospital. I carefully removed it, hardly daring to breath, in case I hurt her.

I was on my knees with my head bent forward as I did this. Suddenly, strong hands gripped at my shoulders and pulled me backwards so that I was lying flat on my back, with my head between the feet of my attacker. I looked straight up into the face of the young man. He stepped to the side and, in a flash, put an arrow in his bow, aiming it right at my heart.

The face of the young man had hatred all over it, and at that moment I lost all will to live. The woman was screaming and shouting, but that didn't register. I had had as much as I could take. I gripped my jacket with both hands and pulled it apart so that my chest was bared. With one hand I tapped near my heart. 'Go on! Shoot! Go on!' I shouted. Then I made out what the woman was screaming about, that I was from Taunggyi Hospital and was trying to help her. All this passed through my almost-numbed brain. I was still looking at the young man's face. Slowly the hatred left it and he relaxed the bow string and lowered the arrow point, turning away like a schoolboy being caught doing something wrong.

For a few moments I lay still. Sweat was pouring from me. I was completely exhausted and I could not move. It was obvious that on returning to the hut and seeing me bending over the woman, the young man had thought I was about to take advantage of her.

Slowly I gathered myself, got to my feet and stood facing him. But he would not look me in the eye. I spoke in Urdu, telling him that I required a clean cloth and hot water with plenty of salt. 'I shall also need this,' I said, snatching the knife from his belt. He jumped back and stared at me in fear and raised the still-loaded bow. I smiled and shook my head. I then went and cut some short sticks of bamboo from outside.

When I came back in he was putting a large steel bowl on the fire. He had also got some white cloth and a bamboo pot containing salt. I sprinkled salt in the water and tore the cloth into strips. The water did not take long to come to the boil. The young man stood back as I cut away the old dressing. The woman had two wounds, one in each breast. One was almost central, but just below the nipple, while the other was to the side. She had been hit by two fragments. The wounds were now full of pus and inflamed. The one in the centre was the largest, so I tackled this first. Using the bamboo skewer wrapped with the cloth and soaked in the salt water, I probed out the yellow pus. I looked at her pale face, screwed up in agony, and gave her a sympathetic smile, but carried on probing until I made the wound bleed. I then did the same with the other wound, placed dry pads across both wounds and used strips to hold them in place. As I began to rise, she gripped both my hands together and kissed them. It was her way of saying thanks.

While I had been attending to the woman, unnoticed by me an old man had come into the hut and sat beside the fire. After some time, food was prepared.

As we ate, the old man asked me, 'Where are you heading?'

'India,' I replied.

'India?' they all asked in amazement.

'To go there you must first go to Sima,' said the old man.

'The Japanese are there,' butted in the young man, his eyes widening. 'They will take you and put you in prison, and maybe they will kill you.'

'Is there no other way?' I asked.

'Go back!' they both answered together, and pointed down the mountain.

'How long have the Japanese been in Sima?' I asked, thinking about Captain Brown and his party.

They were not sure. One said nine days and the other said ten.

In that case, I thought, Captain Brown had got through before the Japanese had arrived.

I was eating a bowl of rice with vegetables and meat when Lacey ambled up to the door. Forgetting our tiff, I shouted to him to come in and get tucked into the food. As we ate, I told him what the two men had said about the Japanese being at Sima. I had not noticed before, but his face and eyes seemed to be puffed up. Looking at him closer, I asked him if he felt alright.

'Well, I do feel a little funny,' he replied. 'My legs seem to get stiff after I have rested.' He changed the subject and asked me, 'What are you thinking of doing, Fred, if the Japs are at Sima?'

'I haven't quite made up my mind yet,' I answered, 'but I am not turning back now after we have come this far. We'll get a good night's sleep here and see what tomorrow will bring.'

Although we were in reasonable and comfortable surroundings and I was as tired as I had ever been, sleep would not come. I tossed and turned, going over the problem. Meanwhile Lacey lay on his back, snoring his head off.

The decision was whether to return to Tengchong or try to get past the Japanese somehow or other. I thought that they could not keep watch over the whole of the jungle. I also wondered why they had suddenly come up this far.

This question was nagging at me. It was now five months since Burma had fallen. Perhaps they were expecting a drive or an attack from the northeast and had manned an outpost to give them warning. If so, we might be able to slip past them, as we were coming from the south. They would not be looking for anyone coming from that direction.

I do not know if I slept, but when daylight came I had made up my mind that we were going to go on, Japanese or no Japanese. I still lay where I was when the two men rose, got the fire going and cooked tea and rice. The young woman also raised herself up on one elbow and asked for tea. I lay with my eyes open, looking up at the roof, trying to plan how we could get past the barrier that faced us.

After we had eaten, I asked the two men to sit outside with me. Sitting on the edge of the veranda, I asked them to give me as much information about Sima as they could. I asked them to sketch in the sand what I would see. They told me that there was an old fort which was previously used by the British, overlooking a deep ravine that was the frontier with China. Only one track led up to it, going right past. The fort, a few huts and the main part of the village were all on the right-hand side of the track.

The two men believed that there were about thirty Japanese garrisoned in the village. They did not know whether they were using the fort as billets or not. There was a wire fence to the north of the village that the Japanese had put up and patrolled. The garrison changed every so often and came from a town down in the valley called Washung, on the banks of the Irrawaddy, about thirty miles away. I asked them question after question. They told me that the fort was the first thing we would see as it had a high square tower that you could see above the trees as you got near. Then came the crunch question. I asked if there was anyone in the village who could take us past the wire or who might help us get past. 'The only man who may help you,' the old man said, 'is the headman who was deposed by the Japanese. If you could contact him, he might give you some sort of help.'

It was forty-six miles to Sima, they told us, and it was right at the top of a mountain. They warned us to be very careful how we approached it, for if the Japanese had put a man in the tower he would see us from a great distance away. They also warned us to take care as there was a fork in the track before we got near Sima, and the wrong path led straight down into the valley to the Japanese HQ.

I bade farewell first to the young woman and then to the two men, thanking them both for their hospitality and help. We set off just after noon. I told Lacey that there was no need to hurry, but that at the same time we must be on the alert, as we were back again in enemy territory. I reckoned that, taking it nice and steady, it would take us about three days.

By dusk I estimated we had covered a good ten miles. If we did twenty the next day we would be within striking distance of our objective by the afternoon of the third day.

I warned Lacey that should anything happen he was to get away as fast as he could and I would do the same. I told him to keep about three yards behind me at all times. We tried our best to walk as quietly as we could and at the same time listen for any sound other than those we were now used to. I set a steady pace, having two stops and eating the wild peaches that grew thereabout and also the plentiful wild plantains. For the second stop we went into the jungle and away from the track, following a small stream. Here we took our boots off and washed our feet in the cool water and dried them on the broad leaves of the plantain trees.

We were in no hurry, as I did not want to get within sight of the tower before dark in case there was a watching guard. Dusk is a bad time to see clearly anywhere, let alone in the jungle.

As darkness began to fall on the second evening out from Bataum I looked for a suitable spot where we could rest for the night well away from the track and into the cover of the trees. I reckoned that we had now covered a good thirty to thirty-five miles, leaving us about twelve more to go. If we had been told correctly, we should be near the fork about mid-morning or around noon. There we must be very careful as we would then be within only a few miles of Sima.

Before setting off the next morning we drank and washed in a stream. The puffiness around Lacey's eyes was even more noticeable than before. His whole face was swollen and he could barely open his eyes. I asked him if he felt alright, and he said yes, except for stiffness around the calves of his legs. I asked him to let me take a look. When I pressed the swollen skin with my thumbs, the depressions remained, leaving great dimples in the skin.

'Did you get bitten by something?' I asked him.

'No, not that I know of,' he replied.

His legs were swollen like tree trunks. He had to remove his boots to walk, but as we walked the swelling seemed to go down remarkably. The skin around his legs was getting stiff every time we rested, and I could feel the water-like fluid underneath it.

My idea was to get past the fork just before noon, then rest up in the heat of the day and get within sight of the fort towards dusk. My calculation came unstuck somewhat when after about two-hours marching, and not too fast at that, we came to the fork in the track. With plenty of time on our hands, I found a nice shaded spot away from the track, among some tall teak trees. Fallen leaves on the ground made a deep brown carpet. It was against one of the teak trees that we both settled down. The track was about twenty yards away, but not visible from where we were. After a short while sitting there, I must have dozed off. It seemed no time when a hand was clapped over my mouth. I opened my eyes to see Lacey with his fingers to his mouth telling me not to make a noise. He then pointed towards the track. I could see Japanese troops marching past, heading away from Sima, with mules loaded with equipment. We both sat there, hardly moving a muscle, until they were completely out of sight.

For a good half hour we sat in silence in case other Japanese troops were following on behind. Even after a good while we still only spoke in whispers. I asked Lacey how many Japanese he thought we had seen. He made a guess of between twenty-five and thirty. This needed some thinking about. I rested my head back against the tree and thought it out. If they had all left and no one remained in Sima, our troubles were over and we could get through. But if a relief had gone up earlier in the day, then they would be fresh and on their toes. On the other hand, if they had marched the thirty odd miles up here, they would want to get their heads down tonight.

I made up my mind that I would risk it. Only one thing was worrying me. That was Lacey. His legs had got much worse during the day.

I reckoned that we had about six miles to go to get to Sima. So in a whisper I told him to get a little closer but keep clear of the track and stay in among the trees on the right-hand side, the same side as the fort. That way we should see the tower through the trees. We picked our way slowly through the dense jungle, using every bit of cover, stopping now and then to listen. Everything was quiet. Even the birds seemed to be on our side for this last and most dangerous leg of our journey.

It was late in the afternoon when, through the trees, I saw the tall grey tower of the fort with its battlements and gun ports, just like in a Foreign Legion film.

Red tiles or slates covered the roof. On the other side of the track, through the trees, I could make out a number of small huts perched high on the hill. I sat for quite some time watching the tower for signs of movement, the sort a man on guard makes when he has nothing else to do. When I tried to rise to my feet I felt awful stiffness in my legs. I lifted my trousers and looked at my legs. They were swollen almost beyond recognition. Oh, no! I said to myself, not now! Not after we have come this far.

Lacey came near me and said, 'Oh, so you've got it as well now, have you?'

'Come on! Let's get moving before our whole bleeding bodies seize up and we can't move at all,' I said, more in despair than anger.

Walking stiff-legged we managed to climb a small incline, keeping in the cover of the trees. To our right we could hear the rush of water cascading down to a great depth. This told us that we were near the ravine. As I walked, to my relief, for some reason the stiffness went from my legs and I found that I could walk normally. I glanced at Lacey, but he was still having difficulty walking.

Darkness came as we made our way through the trees towards Sima. Keeping well to the side of the track we got to the top of the hill and crept around the ravine-side of two huts which showed a glimmer of light. A little further on we came to the dark wall of the fort. I edged my way quietly along the small gap between the shrubbery and wall, going away from the village to the eastern side, and Lacey followed. We could now hear the water as it tumbled into the ravine more clearly. I stopped now and then to listen for any footfalls that may be on the other side of the wall, but heard none. So far there was no sign that the fort was occupied. When we got to the northeast corner I stretched up my arms and gripped the top of the wall. Standing on tiptoes, I pulled myself slowly up until I could see the dark shape of the barrack rooms inside. There was not a sound.

I whispered to Lacey to stay where he was at the northeast corner so that I could easily find him again in the darkness then, creeping cautiously, I moved along to the corner facing the village. I could hear girlish laughter and giggles coming from the huts across the track. Keeping close to the ground I peered around the corner. As I did so, a door in one of the huts opened, sending a beam of light onto the ground. I froze. A Japanese soldier in his puttees and breeches and open-necked shirt came out into the darkness. His cigarette glowed against the side of the hut as he drew on it while he relieved himself.

I kept perfectly still, hardly moving an eyelid. Turning around, he drew once more on his cigarette and did up his flies. It seemed as if he was looking straight at me, but he drew on his cigarette once more, flicked it away and went back inside. I relaxed and put my head on my arms with a sigh of relief.

Towards the northern part of the village, standing alone was the headman's bamboo hut with glimmers of light seeping out. It was raised about two feet above the ground on stilts, and by the light I could make out the track as it wound up the hill. The hut was on the left of the track and about twenty-five yards from the brush that ran parallel with the track.

I made my way back to Lacey and told him to stay where he was. I then went in a northerly direction, keeping the sound of the water on my right until I thought I was opposite the hut, then crawled through the undergrowth to the edge of the brush and went a further ten yards from the track. I could now see the hut more clearly, but I had misjudged and was about ten yards short of being directly in line with the hut. So, back I went into the thick brush, crawling almost all the way on my belly. Once again I crawled towards the track, and this time I was almost opposite the hut. For a moment I lay flat and rested, looking both left and right to make sure that no one was about. The noise coming from the other huts told me that the Japanese were using them as billets. This, I thought, might be in my favour. I lay in the brush, not knowing what to expect, when I made my dash across the track to the hut. Although the evening was getting cooler, the sweat was oozing out of my body. I had also begun to shake a little, possibly from the tension of what I was about to do. Come on, I said to myself, pull yourself together! It was then that I got to my knees, dug my toes into the earth and, rising up onto my hands, dashed across the open ground, striding over the track and diving full length under the hut. I had moved fast, and it left me breathless and panting. I remained there, quite still, for some time, until I had regained both my breath and my composure.

I wriggled about a little to try to see through the bamboo floor. Chinks of light penetrated through the strips. I turned over onto my back, so that I could look straight up. Then I heard a creak as someone moved above me. There was no sound of talking, so I presumed that whoever was above me was alone. It seemed hours, but it was only minutes, before I risked tapping on the floor above me. At first my tapping was weak and there was no response. I tapped again, this time harder, and there was some movement above. I tapped again, and heard a scuffle and more movement. Finally I forced a gap between the strips of bamboo, and then forced my hand through. Someone gripped my fingers. Quickly I withdrew them, then a voice came down to me in Urdu, asking who I was.

'English,' I whispered.

'Don't stay here. Go to the trees. I'll come to you,' came the reply.

Without another word I dashed back to the edge of the brush as fast as I could. I did not have long to wait. An old man, the headman, came creeping through the shrubs and we immediately made our way to where I had left Lacey near the wall of the fort.

Quickly and not wasting any time I asked the man if he could get us past the road block, or if he knew a way around it. He explained that the Japanese had erected a wire fence in a half circle. He had no idea how far west, but it was guarded up the track about a quarter of a mile by four men with a machine gun. They were changed every day in the morning. All of them stayed for one month at a time. This accounted for the party going down, I thought. I asked him if there was any chance of going along the ravine, but he said no, as it was about a one hundred feet sheer drop to the river.

He then said that his brother was coming later and wished to join his family who lived in the northwest. 'He would probably take you,' he said. He then told us to wait where we were and he would tell his brother about us. In the meantime he would bring us both food and something to drink. He said that he could not be gone long from his hut as someone might want to know where he had been, as he was being watched day and night.

About an hour had passed when we heard someone coming towards us through the trees. We both concealed ourselves just in case it was someone other than the headman. But it was he, laden with a sack of food and a large bamboo pot of steaming tea. The next time he came was about one o'clock in the morning. This time he brought another man who he said was his brother and who would show us a way past the wire.

Our guide, from what I could see of him in the dark, was a very rough-looking man. His hair stood out in a frizzy style, he was bearded, and one could hardly see his face. He wore a dark brown skin-like jacket with no sleeves, showing a pair of muscular arms, and for trousers wore what looked like cut-off pants tied at the waist with a leather thong. The old headman left us, shaking our hands and wishing us well. Our guide then motioned us to follow him. He led us back down the hill, the way we had come earlier.

Keeping well into the trees and down past the huts on the fort side, we were about a mile or so away from the village. We crossed the track going due west for about half a mile, then turned north. Our guide stopped us with raised hand now and then. He went forward alone and upon return motioned us to keep down. After about ten yards of crawling on hands and knees we came to an entanglement of barbed wire. From the east, and carried on the slight breeze, came the murmur of voices. Our guide began pulling clumps of earth away from beneath the wire. Eventually there was a large enough gap for a man to crawl under. He lay on one side and motioned me to hold up the wire while Lacey crawled through. I went next, then came our guide. Lacey had moved away a little, but I stayed and watched the man replace as much earth as possible so that the gap would not be seen. I then knew that this man had done this before.

For about half an hour we followed this man through the thick jungle. None of us spoke. It was amazing how he picked his way in the darkness. I am quite positive that without his help we could never have made it.

We were climbing what seemed a steep hill of rough jungle. Then at the top we came to a piece of flat land. After a few yards we came to a track. Here our guide halted, pointed up the track northwards and spoke the only word he had spoken the whole time, 'Sadon.' Both Lacey and I turned and looked up the track, and when we turned back to thank him he had vanished without a word. I would dearly have liked to at least say thanks.

Chapter Fifteen

Betrayal in Sadon

As the dawn began to break we were a little happy that once again we had got past the Japanese lines. I said to Lacey that, as we had less to worry about now, we could take our time and would rest until the afternoon, for we were tired after the night's events and extra walking. I knew that Lacey was feeling the strain from his swollen legs and feet. I thought that the extra rest would help him.

We found a nice shady spot with a clear running stream. We got down and soon both of us were asleep. When I awoke, the sun was well over its zenith and it must have been about two in the afternoon.

I crawled over to Lacey, but I stopped for his face was unrecognisable. It was about three times its normal size, totally blown up. His eyelids were swollen as well. Only his ears had remained the normal size. In comparison to his head, they looked like mouse ears. I leaned over and gently tapped his arm. His eyelids barely moved.

'Is that you, Fred?' he asked.

'Yes,' I answered, 'Can you see me?'

'Yes, I can a bit.'

'Can you get up?' I asked, then added, 'I find that the swelling goes down after I have been walking for a little.'

'Alright then,' he said, 'You help me up, and I will have a try.'

I helped him to his feet, and with him resting his arm on my shoulder we began a slow walk. After a while he walked on his own. I noticed that I, too, had some stiffness in my legs. I wondered what it was that had affected us in this manner.

After two days of walking, with very little food, we got into a very weak state. The situation was not being helped by the continuous climbing.

Milestones appeared at the side of the road telling us how far we were from Sadon. We rested at the fiftieth milestone. There we slept on the third night from Sima. In the morning, as the sun came up, I tried to rouse my companion, but he could not move. I tried every means I could to get him to his feet. I even called him and his parents all the dirtiest and filthiest names I could think of to try to get him to his feet, but he would not budge.

Unable to get him to use his own effort, I dragged him by the shirt to the nearest tree. There with his back propped against it, inch by inch I raised him until I had got him onto his feet. Then bending forward, I allowed him to fall over my back. Being weak myself, I struggled putting one foot in front of the other. I watched the milestones as they came into view. Forty-nine went slowly by, and forty-eight came. I rested with my load against a tree at the side of the track at forty-seven. I sat on the milestone itself with my friend across my shoulder. At forty-six I collapsed in a heap, unable to go any further.

In this road, in that lonely part of the world, with no one but the birds and the animals as a witness, I knelt and prayed to God to give me strength to carry my friend, this man who I had blamed for all our suffering, who I had said would carry all the guilt on his back, and here I was praying for the strength to get him to safety.

After a rest and using the same method as before, I again got him onto my back, but this time like a sack of coal. With rests I got the milestones down to forty-three. Here Lacey began to feel a little better, and after a rest he helped me by getting onto my back himself. Darkness was upon us as I reached forty-one. Exhausted, I lay by the side of the milestone. When dawn came, Lacey appeared much better and managed to rise with me. I suggested that we do a trot. I explained that with the sweating of carrying him I had lost all the swelling. We linked arms and jogged along in this manner. The track was running quite flat at this point. I thought if we could keep this up, we would soon be near Sadon, but suddenly Lacey stopped and said, 'I can't go any further like this.'

'Alright,' I said, 'we'll walk.'

At the thirty-ninth milestone he again refused to go on. 'Come on! Get on my back,' I said.

With rests we passed the thirty-seventh milestone. About halfway to the thirty-sixth he shouted, 'Put me down!'

'No!' I shouted back, 'I've got you in a comfortable position.'

'Put me down!' he shouted again, shaking my shoulders.

'No!' I shouted and trudged on.

'Alright, you bastard,' he shouted, 'You've asked for it.'

His hands gripped me around my throat, squeezing the breath from me. I stopped walking as his hands got tighter. Then, giving me a mad chuckle in my ear, he said, 'You've blamed me for everything, haven't you, Fred? Well, let's see you get out of this.'

The blood was roaring in my ears, flashes of light were coming and going before my eyes. I could not breathe. I let go of his legs with my hands and quickly flung them above my head. Reaching up, I gripped the long hair at the back of his head and at the same time heaved forward, bending my body down so that the whole weight of him came over my head. He came down with a crunch onto his back. He lay flat, his hands and arms spread wide. For a moment I staggered, trying to get the breath back in my lungs. I shook my head to clear the flashing lights that were still before my eyes. I dropped to one knee in order to get some respite and to regain some of my strength.

Opening my eyes, I saw Lacey turn over onto his face, and then, shaking his head, he rose to one knee.

The thought in my mind as I watched him was that he had had me for a fool, he had been acting. I got to my feet and with murder in me I said, 'So! Lacey, you wanted to kill me?'

'No, Fred! No, I didn't mean it,' he said, shaking his head.

'You were going to kill me' I said, advancing towards him.

'No, Fred, No, I wasn't,' he said, putting one hand up in front of his face.

'You have been building up to this, haven't you, Lacey?' I snapped.

'No, Fred, I haven't,' he whispered, shaking his head.

'You've had me for a mug!' I snapped, 'And I fell for it.'

'I didn't mean it, honestly,' he said, looking up at me.

'Get on your feet,' I rapped out, 'we'll settle this once and for all, here and now. Either you'll kill me, or I'll kill you! Get up!'

Slowly he rose to his feet, watching me all the time. To me he seemed larger than he had before. His big ham-like fists were ready. His body was bent slightly forward. A scowl showed on his face.

'You won't get away with this, y'know,' he muttered between his teeth.

'You have got the same chance as me,' I answered. 'Besides, who's to know? There's only the jungle to witness it.'

I advanced a step at a time with my left hand and foot forward. I thought, I must keep away from those long gangling arms.

I was almost within arm's reach when he lunged forward with his right arm. I ducked under it, stepped inside and drove my left fist into his stomach. He dropped both his hands. With every ounce of weight that I could put behind it, I swung my right fist to his unprotected jaw. His head twisted, his eyes rolled, his knees buckled and he fell forward. I stepped back and sideways to allow him to fall in a heap at my feet.

Had this been one of the many amateur boxing matches I had been in I would have jumped for joy at flooring an opponent of this size and weight, but instead

I just stood and looked down at the still form. I walked to where my hat had fallen, picked it up and put it on my head. I then picked up his hat, and as I walked past him dropped it on the back of his head. Without looking back I walked on up the track northwards.

After about fifty yards I stopped. Suddenly, a feeling of sympathy for the man I had left lying on the track came to me. I stood perfectly still for some time. I was unable to make up my mind whether to keep going and forget Lacey or go back and help him. Somehow a voice said, 'He is your friend. He is a human being after all.'

I turned and walked back. He had rolled over on his back. His arms were outstretched. My pace quickened. Just before I got to him, I was running. Dropping to my knees, I bent over the still form, gripped his shoulders, lifted him and shook him and called his name.

He was breathing, but his eyes were closed. I lifted his head and cradled him in my arms. After a while he opened his eyes and said, 'I knew you wouldn't leave me, Fred.' A smile spread across his face. A lump came up into my throat, choking me. Tears welled up in my eyes as I looked down on the pale grimy bearded face.

'I nearly did, Len, you know,' I muttered.

'Y'know, Fred,' he spoke in a weak voice, 'You're a good bloke, but you've got a vile temper.'

'Yes, I know, Len. And it will land me in some trouble yet,' I replied.

We sat there on the track in the gathering dusk. All around us was a wilderness. Lacey lay in my arms asleep like a child. His face was at peace as he slept. As the darkness gathered about us I vowed that I would stop blaming him for what had happened and for our plight.

I awoke lying flat on my back on the track. Dawn was coming over the eastern side of the hills. I roused Lacey and asked him if he would try to walk. With my help he got unsteadily to his feet, and like a drunken man he staggered along. Slowly we trudged on, passing the thirty-fifth milestone. At the thirty-second he stopped and said that he could go no further. 'Please Len. Please try!' I said and helped him up on the track. 'Len! Len! Please help me to help you,' I pleaded.

He sank to his knees, almost pulling me down with him. 'I can't go on. I can't go any further, Fred,' he almost cried. I sank down beside him, weary, hungry and dejected.

After a rest I gathered my strength, dragged him to a tree and got him standing. Then in a fireman's lift I got him on my back and staggered along the track. This time I tried to keep my eyes off the milestones, but every time I looked up from the track my eyes searched for the next stone.

I staggered to the brow of a hill under my heavy burden. The sun seemed to be picking me out, for its rays were beating down upon me. The sweat was pouring out of my body. The one good thing, I thought, was that it would keep that dammed swelling away.

Besides hunger – for we had had hardly anything to eat since leaving Sima four days before – water seemed to be scarcer in these parts of the jungle. The moisture had been sweated out of me.

A little way down the slope I saw the next milestone. There, I thought, I will rest and go in search of water. I was surprised when I saw that it was the twenty-fifth. I lay Lacey down at the bottom of the hill and went in search of water. To the right of the track, about twenty yards away, was a clear running stream. Along its banks, vegetation which looked very much like water cress grew abundantly. I drank from the stream and grabbed a handful of the bright green stuff and chewed at it. At first it tasted slightly bitter, but after the first taste one got used to it. I grabbed some more and stuffed it into my mouth.

I went back to Lacey who had once more fallen into a kind of coma, and I was able to wake him. Gripping him by the shirt and walking backwards, I managed to drag him to the water's edge. There I doused his face. He showed signs of consciousness, so I went and grabbed some handfuls of the 'cress' and tried to make him eat it. But he spat it out and said that I was trying to poison him. We rested there by the water's edge for a good hour. As I tried to lift him to get on our way again it seemed that all my strength had gone from me. I could hardly lift him into a sitting position, let alone to his feet.

After some more rest I regained my strength and dragged Lacey back onto the track. There I looked for and found two stout branches, and twined the softer twigs together so that it left me with two shafts. I pulled Lacey onto the branches so that he sat with his back to the shafts. I then got between the shafts and dragged him along that way. In this manner I managed to get him over the brow of the next hill and within sight of the twenty-fourth milestone.

My rough carrier had by this time become no more than a bare bunch of twigs, and Lacey was saying that it was hurting his backside. I pleaded with him to stick it out until we got to the next milestone, as the road was at that moment flat and smooth.

We reached the milestone and rested. Lacey lay in the bush while I went looking for food. The pangs of extreme hunger were hurting my innards. I could find nothing. I searched even for the roots of the trees for just one edible morsel that might ease the hunger pains.

I peeled off the bark of one of the trees and chewed on that, but it was so bitter that, as hungry as I was, I could not bring myself to swallow it. I made my way back to where Lacey lay and sat there. After a while I woke him and said, 'Come on, let's have another go.'

Once again I got him on my back, but the lack of food was testing my strength. I was beginning to weaken. My pace was getting shorter and I was hardly moving.

At the twenty-third milestone I fell to my knees, unable to go any further with Lacey on my back. For some considerable time we both lay on the track in the afternoon sun. While I lay there I decided that the best thing to do was for me to go on alone and get help, otherwise neither of us would get to Sadon.

By the position of the sun it must have been about three in the afternoon. I dragged Lacey into the trees behind the milestone so that he would be easily found by anyone looking for him.

I set off for Sadon feeling a little happier and, funnily enough, not so hungry. The track wound its way uphill through the virgin jungle. It seemed no time that the sun was disappearing behind the hills to the west and dusk was upon me. I must not stop, I thought, or I might not have the energy to go on. The only stop I made was just a small pause to grab a fallen branch from a tree to drag behind me. This was to create enough noise to frighten away any wild animals that I thought would not hesitate to attack a lone man at night.

When the track went downwards I lengthened my stride, but I had to be slow and steady when I went upwards, for as I climbed I was left with only one side of the track to walk for fear of losing my footing and plunging over the side. Darkness was closing in on the jungle as though someone had pulled a huge blanket overhead. As I climbed higher the air became harder to breathe and I was beginning to stagger.

I could hear the snarls and growls of different wild animals that must have wondered who the fool was to trespass upon their territory in the dark.

Birds suddenly shrieked as I walked into their tree, disturbing their peace. This caused my hair to stand on end more than once.

To take my mind from the presence of the animals I began to sing at the top of my voice. This did not last long for I soon got out of breath as I climbed ever upwards.

The track was now invisible and I was stumbling from side to side in the inky blackness. I knew that on my left-hand side there was a drop of hundreds of feet, and should I make one false step that would be the end of me. So I attempted to keep as far to the right as possible. But I was tripping over unseen roots, bumping into trees and scratching my face on branches, which almost blinded me.

I strained my eyes to see the track through the inky blackness that seemed to cover every inch of the jungle before me.

For a moment I stopped. I do not profess to be a religious person, for I suppose I am more a devil's disciple than anything. But I dropped to my knees, closed my eyes and prayed that I be given help to guide me to safety so that I could send help to my friend.

When I opened my eyes, to my utter amazement, there on each side of the track were lights. For a moment I could not believe my eyes. I thought that I was having hallucinations until I went to the lights and looked closer. They were luminous plants. I bent and plucked some and held them in the palm of my hand, and sure enough they glowed in my open hand.

I stood looking up the black ribbon of track with the lights on each side. I still could not believe that this had just happened. Perhaps, I thought, they were there all the time and I failed to notice them. But no, that would not do. I had peered into the darkness for any sign of the track, and they had not been there then. So why did they appear at that precise moment, when I asked God for some help?

I walked on quite easily. All that I had to do was keep between the rows of green light.

Eventually a dull grey light began to show itself over the large hump of mountain to my right. With the coming of a new day one seems to get new energy from somewhere. I strode on downhill towards a rough wooden bridge that spanned a small stream. I discarded the branch that I had dragged behind me through the night.

Quickening my pace I strode across the wooden bridge, my boots making a clattering noise, breaking the still morning air. With three paces I was across to the other side of the river. There in front of me, standing on the edge of the stream, was a huge animal, of the mountain-lion type. I stopped still and stared at it, and it stared back at me for a moment. Then in one movement it had turned and vanished off into the undergrowth.

I looked at the trees to where it had gone, but could see no movement. When I walked to the river edge where it had been I could see plainly in the mud the paw marks of a large cat.

Further upstream was a suitable place for me to drink. I splashed the cool water over my head and face and rubbed the water into my long beard and whiskers. Refreshed, I set off in the full daylight.

The first milestone that I passed said eight miles to Sadon, which meant that I had covered fifteen miles since leaving Lacey. I thought that this was not so bad, considering the type of ground I had come over, and in the dark at that.

I was coming to the sixth milestone when I saw a flock of vultures circling in the sky high above the trees. I turned and looked in the opposite direction and thought of Lacey, but the sky was clear in the direction where I had come from. As I went on I wondered who the poor soul was. His bones would have been picked clean by those scavengers. That is, if it was a human being.

The path rose very steeply as I came to the fifth milestone. Once again the strain on my tired legs and body were beginning to take its toll. I went to the side of the track, took off my hat and sat down. For some unknown reason I turned and looked behind me. There, a little way back in the trees, was an array of sticks drawn together at the top, forming a canopy over a mound of earth. At the far end was a rough wooden cross.

Getting to my feet I went and read the rough-cut name. It was Lockington, the man who always entertained us with his piano playing. Slowly I retraced my steps and sat down again. I could picture him sitting at the piano, laughing, with his blue eyes, pencilled moustache and light brown curly hair, with one curl always falling over his forehead, while we sang to the music he played. I looked down into the valley where Lacey was lying. This time all the hatred had gone from me, no ill feeling towards him, nothing. Some lines I had read somewhere came to me. 'The dead are dead, let us who still live see to it that their ranks are not swelled.'

I rose to my feet and without a backward glance went up the hill. Whether it was the heat of the day or the tiredness that had really caught up with me, I began to stagger about as if I was in a drunken stupor up the steep incline, and the hunger pains in my stomach seemed to be tearing my insides out.

I passed the fourth milestone. Through the trees above my head I could see the bungalows perched high on the side of the mountain. To me they looked barely a quarter of a mile away, but with the track winding around the mountain it was actually four miles. This gave me the idea of taking a short cut and going straight up, but it was my undoing. I used up more energy trying to climb up through the thick jungle of tangled brushwood and trees. I was also slipping back at times further than I had climbed. Eventually I gave up and made my way back to the track again. Suddenly the jungle and the track began to dance and the ground shot up before my eyes and I fell down. I raised myself on my hands and knees and began to crawl along on all fours. How long I went in this manner I have no idea. Once again I fell flat on my face in complete exhaustion, unable to move a muscle. For some time I lay, taking in deep breaths in order to get some strength back.

Then, rising up on my arms, I looked and saw that I was at the second milestone. Gathering all the strength that I could muster I dragged myself to a tree and pulled my body upright. I then went along pushing from tree to tree and stopping now and then to gather my fading strength. It was through half-closed eyes that I saw the number one milestone.

I was again down on my knees, trying to crawl. As I looked across at the white stone with black letters, the sign had become a mocking face. The word 'Sadon' became the eyes, 'one' the nose and 'mile' the mouth. It seemed to be grinning as I passed it.

I gritted my teeth, shut my eyes and with all the available strength I had in my body I staggered up the steep hill. With my body bent forward I managed to put one foot in front of the other. When I turned a sharp bend I saw buildings of the village higher up in front of me. Mustering all the energy I had, I climbed the hill. Across the track was a five bar gate. Onto this I collapsed. As I did, two dogs came barking and yelping, and I fell into darkness.

I awoke lying on a rope bed in the middle of the village. People of different nationalities stood around me. They talked in groups. As I looked around from my lying position I could see Chinese, Indian, Burmese and also Anglo-Indian.

Nearest to me was an Indian woman. She held a glass of milk in one hand, and in the other a saucer with an egg on it. I sat up, took the milk and the egg. I drank the milk greedily and gobbled the egg in one go. I took the second glass of milk more slowly, washing down the egg in my mouth. I turned around in my sitting position to take in my surroundings. Behind me, about thirty yards away, a large bonfire was burning. I looked at the sky. The sun was up. I thought it strange, a bonfire on a day like this? Perhaps they were burning some rubbish, and I discarded it from my mind.

An Anglo-Burmese woman came to the front of the circle of onlookers and asked in perfect English, 'Are you alone?'

'Yes, but I had to leave my friend, who is sick, twenty-three miles back. He needs help.'

'Alright, don't worry about your friend. We will have him brought up,' she assured me.

She turned and spoke to a number of men, who went off in all directions. Turning back to me, she asked, 'When did you leave your friend?'

'Yesterday afternoon,' I replied.

'Then you must have walked all through the night,' she said questioningly.

'Yes, I have,' I answered.

There was a murmur among the onlookers as what I said was passed around. The Anglo-Burmese woman was speaking again. 'If you will come with me, I will get you some proper food, a bath and some clean clothes.' She then beckoned me to follow. Unsteadily I rose from the bed and followed her. On the way, she told me her name was Miss McRae. She led me to one of the bungalows a little further up the hill. There were others waiting at the door, a fat elderly Burmese lady, a girl of about seventeen and a young Burmese lad of about twelve years of age. Miss McRae introduced them as the Kin-Maung family. The young girl's name was Nita.

After a meal, a good hot bath and some clean clothes I felt once more as fit as a fiddle and on top of the world.

Miss McRae and Nita showed me to a smaller bungalow which they said was mine until my friend arrived. They said that it would be about three days before he would be brought to the village.

I ate and slept well with the knowledge that I was safe. All I had to do was wait for Lacey to arrive. With the same treatment I was getting, Lacey would be fit in a couple of days and we could go on to our next objective, Sumprabum, a mere twenty-one miles away, where we had been told there was a British garrison of Indian troops.

In the afternoon of my second day in Sadon, Nita Kin-Maung accompanied me on a walk. We strolled up the hill in the direction that would take me to Sumprabum. We sat on a high crag looking to the north. Sitting there we took in the landscape. Just below, the sun shone upon the lush green valley. Then there were the smaller mountains and foothills, specked in all colours. Further on in the far distance were the vast Himalayas rising like a huge grey wall stretching from east to west in all their majestic glory, changing colour as the clouds went across.

Sitting there up on that crag I thought that I had the world at my feet. I turned to Nita and said, 'Nita, I'm raring to go and get back to India.'

The young girl sitting beside me said in a soft sweet voice, 'Fred, why don't you go? Go now!'

A little surprised, I looked at her. 'I can't, until Lacey comes,' I answered, and was a little surprised by the look of sadness on her face. Then, without another word, she rose to her feet and ran back to the village.

I was so taken aback that I sat there for some time. I could not understand what had upset her. I pushed the young girl from my mind and gazed northwards and down onto the track that would take us to Sumprabum.

Early the next morning Lacey arrived, being carried on a bamboo litter by four men. After giving him a good meal and a bath they brought him to the hut we had been allocated. I made him comfortable on the veranda then went back inside to read some magazines I had been given.

About fifteen or twenty minutes later there was some shouting and commotion outside, and I heard Lacey calling me. I jumped to my feet and rushed to the veranda and saw a crowd of men. They were trying to drag Lacey away. I saw red, and my blood was boiling. Without thinking of any danger I set on to them with my fists and feet. I know that I planted one on the nose. The blood spurted across his face as he fell back. One took to his heels, and another let go of Lacey. I went for the remaining one, but he too let go of Lacey and moved back.

Lacey, still being weak, fell to the ground. I stood near him with my fists at the ready. I thought there were only four, but as they stood in half circle in front of me I saw there were six. They had drawn their dhas. A big man who stood at the back, dressed in the national costume of Burma, stepped forward. His eyes looked in opposite directions. I immediately named him 'boss-eyed.' I thought he must be their leader. From his waistcoat pocket he took out a folded card. He came within a yard of me and held the card out for me to see. I glanced at it and saw that it contained some Japanese characters and the insignia of the Japanese, the red sun. Below, in English, I read, 'Represents the Imperial …' That was as far as I read. I took one step forward and knocked the card to the ground. It fell at his feet. 'Pick it up, you boss-eyed bastard, and I'll put my boot right into your face!' I had it in my mind that if I got him, the others might run. I stood waiting for him to make his move. His face had turned into a hateful snarl. The knuckles on his hand clasping his dha went white. He raised it menacingly.

At that moment Lacey, who was on the floor to my left side, shouted, 'Watch out, Fred!'

But it was too late. Something crashed down upon the back of my head. I saw 'boss-eyed' grinning. I tried to get my hands up to go for his throat, but they would not respond. The trees began to spin and the ground came up and hit me in the face.

I could hardly open my eyes. The pain in my head was terrific. When I did open my eyes I did not know whether it was getting dark or getting light. I was in a sitting position with my back to the wall of a hut. I could not move my hands. They were tied behind my back. After a time of sitting still and trying to clear my head I searched with my hands to try to find the knots of the cords that bound me, but I soon realised that the cords had been taken through the bamboo wall of the hut and tied from outside.

I looked across the room. In the half light I could see Lacey.

'Len! Are you alright?' I shouted.

'Yes,' he answered.

'Are you tied up?' I asked him.

'Yes, but they didn't hurt me like they did you.'

'Who hit me and with what?'

'It was that bloke you hit on the nose. He hit you with the handle of his dha. That big bloke told me that they would have killed you, but they would have got only one hundred rupees for you dead. Alive they get two hundred. You were very lucky, Fred. They all wanted to kill you, but the big bloke stopped them.'

'What about the villagers? Didn't they try to do anything?'

'No one came near. It was as if they were all afraid.'

Although my head was still hurting, it slowly dawned on me that the bonfire that was burning the morning I arrived must have been a signal to those down in the valley that we were there.

'Well, Len, it looks like the end of the line for us, doesn't it? And here I was thinking that we had made it.'

Lacey was silent.

I went on talking mostly to myself. All that effort, was it worth it? We had got this far, and then to be caught like this, and by traitors? At this point I fell silent. I wondered what Lacey was thinking.

My head had eased slightly, and I began going over what had happened the last few days. I went back to what Nita had said when we sat on the crag. Was she warning me then? Her words came back to me. 'Why don't you go now?' I thought about it over and over. But why didn't she tell me outright? Was she afraid of someone?

My mouth became suddenly dry. I began to doze. I must have fallen asleep, then awoke and dozed again. Each time I woke I could hear Lacey as he tried to alter his position with a sigh.

I had got a terrible thirst when I again awoke. There was some light coming into the hut. As the dawn approached, Lacey was slumped forward but fast asleep. Movements outside told me that the villagers were awakening and going about their daily chores.

About two hours after sunrise I heard a woman's voice outside the hut in conversation with a man. The door was flung open by one of our captors. An Indian came in and set down a tray with food and a jug of steaming hot tea with two cups. As the Indian went out, in came Nita Kin-Maung. The door was shut behind her.

She stood and looked down at me and at Lacey. She was a beautiful girl, with jet black hair, dark almond eyes and a small mouth. Our eyes met as she turned her gaze back to me.

Slowly I shook my head and said, 'If this had not happened to me, I would never have believed it.' Her gaze dropped to the floor, and she covered her face with her hands. In a very nasty voice, I asked. 'What's it like to be a traitor?'

Her shoulders began to shake as she sobbed into her hands. She dropped to her knees and continued to sob. Her head almost touched the floor. 'I didn't want it to happen,' she sobbed. 'I am sorry, Fred, I am sorry.' On her knees she came to me and threw her arms around my neck. Her tears wet my face.

'Why didn't you warn me?' I asked. She released her hold on me and sat back on her heels, wiping the tears away from her eyes with the back of her hands.

'I wanted to, but Miss McRae said that my father would be punished by the Japanese if they found out.'

'Where is your father?' I asked.

'He has gone to the Japanese headquarters at Myitkyina,' she replied.

'So, he's a collaborator, and I suppose it was his idea to light the signal fire as soon as I arrived here?' I said.

She did not answer but dropped her gaze.

'What about the other British soldiers? Did this happen to them as well?' I asked her.

'No!' she almost shouted. 'They went on after a few days, but someone must have informed those men,' she pointed to the door, 'that the British troops had passed here. They told us to light the fire the next time.'

What she told me also tied in with the roadblock at Sima. Information must have been passed back that stragglers were getting through, and this was their way of stopping them.

'Well, the tea is getting cold, and I cannot eat with my hands tied behind my back.'

She rose and went to the door and knocked. After a few moments the door was opened slightly. She had a few words with someone outside, and the door was closed. I felt the cords slacken on my hands and I was able to move from the wall. She went to Lacey and helped him with his bonds while I sipped a cup of tea. We ate and drank. She stood against the wall of the hut looking at us but not saying anything.

After I had finished eating I rose to my feet and stood in front of her and said, 'You know, Nita, that you are a very beautiful girl. I am most sorry that we have met under these circumstances.'

I really meant every word I was saying. I also felt some pity for her for the situation she was in. She turned her face to the wall and began to sob again. Going near her I placed my hands on her shoulders, more to comfort her than anything else. She turned around suddenly and held me in a close and tight embrace, kissed me full on the lips and more passionately than I had ever been kissed before. 'I'm sorry,' she sobbed, 'I am sorry. Oh, I am so sorry.'

'Never mind. It wasn't your fault. Anyway, it is too late now,' I tried to comfort her.

'Fred, don't try to run away,' she pleaded, 'or they will kill you.'

'Well, if they don't, the Japs will.' I said softly.

The door opened. The Indian came in sheepishly, hardly looking up, bent down and took the tray away. Nita went to the door, turned and said, 'I'll never forget you, Fred.'

'And I shall never forget you, Nita.'

As she opened the door I asked her to ask Miss McRae if she had ever heard of a woman called Cavell. The girl turned around and frowned. 'Cavell?' she repeated the name.

'Yes, that's the name.'

'Alright, I will ask her,' and she was gone.

Lacey, who had been seated and silent all the time, said, 'Do you know, Fred? I think she has a crush on you.'

'It's a bit late to show it now, isn't it?' I answered.

Chapter Sixteen

Ruthless Barbaric Animals

Four of the men came into the hut with their dhas drawn. Two of them made me go into a corner and the other two took Lacey out. When these two returned they tied my hands in front of me and led me outside. Lacey was sitting in a bamboo litter, which four villagers hoisted onto their shoulder. The cord of my hands was attached to the litter by a long rope which allowed me space to walk behind.

As we set off down the hill I turned and saw a number of people watching us go. Among them was Mrs Kin-Maung, Nita, her young brother and Miss McRae. With the slackened rope I was able to turn to them, sweep my hat and bow as if I was ending a Shakespeare play. Then the rope tightened, and I was forced to walk on.

We had been walking for about two hours when 'boss-eyed' called a halt. He went to the side of the track and looked down. I went forward as far as the rope would allow and looked down also. There was the skeleton of a man, lying flat on his back. The vultures had picked the body clean. My mind went back to the day I had seen the birds circling in the sky. This then must have been the unfortunate victim. 'Boss-eyed' saw me looking and grinned. A pith hat was near the head. I tried to get my foot to it. I wanted to see if there was a name inside, but the rope was not long enough, so I pulled a little. 'Boss-eyed' swore, lifted his foot and booted the skull away from the rest of the bones, sending it into the undergrowth. He then roared with laughter. I said with a scowl, 'Your head will roll like that when the British return.' The laugh vanished from his face and he came towards me with his dha. He then changed his mind and waved the party to go on.

It was in the afternoon that we arrived on the plains. The carriers and escort together with 'boss-eyed' all carried food and water. Lacey and I had neither. I asked for water but 'boss-eyed' shook his head and grinned. It was obvious that as long as he handed us over alive he did not give a damn.

As the afternoon wore on and dusk began to fall we entered a small village. I reckoned that we had covered about twenty miles. We stayed at the village for the night. Lacey and I were put into a large hut. Our hands and feet were bound. We could hardly move the way we were trussed up. Lacey was given a little water and food, I suppose to keep him alive for the rest of the journey.

As for me, the men just jeered when I asked for refreshments. I suppose it was because I had fought them and made them look fools in Sadon.

At dawn, still trussed up, we were put onto a bullock cart. 'Boss-eyed' sat up front with the driver while two of the others sat one on each side of Lacey and me. The rest of the gang were sent away. The track that we took was quite flat and went in a southwesterly direction through some very thick jungle. The bullocks were sent at a trot and kept up the same pace all morning.

In the afternoon 'Boss-eyed' ordered the drivers to stop for him and his two men to stretch their legs. We were dragged from the cart and laid at the side of the track, and 'boss-eyed' ordered the driver to turn the cart around and go back to their village. When the cart was out of sight, 'boss-eyed' and his two men stood over us with drawn dhas. A cold sweat broke out of me as they all moved closer to us. They looked down as we lay helpless on the grass at the side of the track.

The whole of my body began to quake as I waited in fear and bewilderment for what they intended to do to us.

The expression on my face and the licking of my parched lips must have given away my feelings. 'Boss-eyed', being the nearest, spread his arms wide and stopped the other two. I thought that he was going to do the job himself. With all my remaining strength I tried to get loose from the cords that bound me. I wriggled and rolled, trying to loosen the bonds, but exhausted I lay still, looking up at his grinning face. The other two men laughed and chatted between themselves at my effort to get free.

'Boss-eyed' stepped forward and raised his dha above his head. I closed my eyes and waited for the blow that would take me from this world, hoping that it would be quick. Instead I felt a saw-like cut at the cords that bound my hands. I kept my eyes shut. The cord around my feet was cut as well. I opened my eyes and saw 'boss-eyed' bending over Lacey and cutting his bonds.

I sat up completely bewildered by this sudden turn of events. 'Boss-eyed', standing back, shouted 'Up! Up!' and waved his dha menacingly. I got to my feet and helped Lacey up. 'Boss-eyed' then pointed along the track and ordered us to march. I soon realised what was happening. The Japanese were not too far away, and 'Boss-eyed' wanted it to look as if there had only been three of them to bring in the two of us.

Lacey was leaning heavily on me so that I was almost carrying him, and with three men walking behind with their dhas drawn I had very little chance of making a run for it.

After struggling along for about a mile we came in sight of a small river. The track led onto a bridge, and on the bridge was the enemy. The Japanese sentry saw us, turned and waved and shouted to others beyond the bridge.

As we got near the bridge, others joined the sentry. All were grinning and pointing at us. Some were slapping their sides and laughing as though they were watching something very comical being acted out for them. As we stepped onto the bridge I looked neither left nor right. As we passed the Japanese some spat at us, others kicked at our legs and some slapped our faces, but with Lacey hanging on tight we kept going across the bridge. More Japanese were lined up on both sides of the road after the bridge.

We were halted opposite a large red brick building, like a kind of barracks. Here we were made to stand. After a while a small Japanese officer complete with sword and black riding-boots came out. As he came near, I drew myself up and, as smart as I could be, gave him a salute. He stopped still and returned my salute, holding the handle of his sword with his left hand. Then he seemed to be inspecting us. The Japanese officer half stopped in front of Lacey, with his right hand pointed at his swollen legs. I stepped forward and bent slightly to look where he had pointed. The next instant I was reeling from a blow from his left hand which sent me sideways against Lacey, knocking him to the ground. At this, all those watching gave a resounding cheer and clapped.

The officer then issued a quick order, and one of the onlookers fetched rope and some thin twine. Behind us was a tin hut. We were bundled into it. They tied Lacey to a pole in the middle of the hut while they made me hold out my hands and tied my thumbs together with the twine. One of them stood on a stool and made me reach up. They then secured me to a beam in the roof with my feet barely touching the ground. At first I groaned in agony, at which they pulled on the twine more, so I tried to bite back the agonising pain by gritting my teeth to stop any sound coming from my mouth. I bit on my tongue. I did anything that would stop me causing them any more enjoyment.

They were satisfied that the binding was tight, but it was not enough for them that I hung there in agony. The little yellow bastards had to line up to either slap my face, spit on me or kick me. I could stand the slaps, spits and kicks, but as each one touched me it sent me either spinning around or swaying from side to side supported only by my thumbs, which sent stabs of pain shooting through my whole body.

Between the winces I opened my eyes and saw two European girls standing in the doorway. They seemed to be twins, for they were very much alike and wore identical pink flowered thin dresses. I assumed they were British who had failed to get out of Burma. The girls must have been brought to witness what happened to any British soldiers taken by the Japanese. On seeing me hanging by my thumbs they shrieked in horror and covered their eyes, but were forced to stand and watch as I hung there.

All went quiet after a time. Everyone left except for four Japanese with rifles. I assumed that this was the guard.

Whether I had stretched or the string had eased under the strain, I found that after a while I could almost get the soles of my boots onto the ground. For how long I was left hanging I cannot say, but the whole of my time was occupied in trying to take the strain from my thumbs. Now and again I looked at the four Japanese as they sat at a table at the end of the hut, hoping that they might have a little pity on me and cut me down. Darkness was beginning to fall, and one of the Japanese lit an oil lamp.

I was reaching up on my toes to ease the pain in my thumbs when I overbalanced and spun around and gave out an uncontrollable cry of pain. I regained my footing quickly and kept quite still in an attempt to regain my breath. I closed my eyes and tried to shut out the pain that I felt. When I opened my eyes one of the guards was standing before me. He issued an order to one of the others who got a stool and cut me down. I immediately fell to the floor. I lay at the feet of the man who had given the order to cut the string from my thumbs. I looked up and said, 'Thank you,' to which he replied in broken English, 'Uppu, Uppu!' motioning me to my feet without any sign of pity. I then had to stand with my back to the post that Lacey was tied to. The post went right through the corrugated roof. I was tied facing the table where the guards sat. Soon the guards' food was brought to them. The smell alone was enough to drive me mad for it was now two whole days since I had eaten or had any drink of any sort. The guards ate their rice mixed with vegetables from their mess tins. This they swilled down with hot tea.

One of the guards, who wore horn-rimmed spectacles, came and stood in front of me. He too spoke in broken English. 'You like eat?' he asked.

I hesitated at first, then nodded and added a weak 'Yes.'

'You like, also, drink tea?' he asked.

Once again I nodded and said a careful 'Yes.'

'All Japanese soldier finis, I give you,' he said, smiling.

'Thank you very much,' I said, returning the smile.

The Japanese walked back to the table and said something to the others, and getting all the leftover rice into one mess tin he mixed tea with it and stirred it altogether. He then came to me and dashed the whole soggy mess into my face, saying, 'Inglis want! Inglis got!'

The Japanese who had given the order for me to be cut down must have been in charge, for he jumped up from the table and let go with a tirade at the man for what he had done.

Once more all went quiet in the hut. I was trying to get my tongue to some of the rice that had stuck to my face and beard, but the salt in the rice only caused my thirst to be more severe and greater.

Then in the distance I heard a rumble. The guards heard it too. Was it bombs? I listened again, straining my ears. Another rumble. Was it gunfire? Or was it just rolls of thunder? There was another rumble, a little closer. I wanted so much for it to be gunfire. I was praying that it was gunfire, but my hopes were dashed in the next instant as I heard the first pitter-patter of heavy raindrops falling on the steel roof above my head. Slowly the pitter-patter increased in volume until the rain came down in torrents. I watched at the open doorway as the streams of water cascaded from the roof and ran like a curtain into the drain outside. The rain was also running down the post behind me. Raindrops were falling upon the bush hat that I still had on my head. All this seemed to aggravate the thirst and longing for just a spoonful of the precious liquid which at that moment I would gladly have given my life for.

I twisted my head in every way possible in an attempt to catch just one droplet. I imagined that I could get my head down to my bound hands that by now were saturated. I looked down at my feet and there was a pool forming. I began to get hallucinations that I was knee-deep in a swimming-pool, and I tried to bend my head down so that I could duck my head under the blue-coloured water. It seemed that my tongue was too big for my mouth and that the roughness of my dry parched mouth had now developed spikes which protruded from my dry tongue, making a rasping noise. I closed my eyes but I could see pictures of places I had been where I had swum and bathed at my leisure. I found myself grating out in a voice which I did not recognise as my own. 'Water! Water! Water!'

I heard a scraping noise from a distance. I opened my eyes and saw the guard commander coming towards me with a small tin. He held it in front of me, level with my mouth. I thought it was a trick and I shot my head forward to grip the tin in my mouth. Instead, I knocked the tin and its contents from his hand. The Japanese cursed me. I tried to say sorry, but could not. The Japanese turned and dragged the tin along the drain to fill it again. This time I waited. He gently poured the contents for me to drink. Once more he went and filled the tin, and I drank the water from the drain as if it was the best wine in the world, which to me it was. I thanked the man who had at least shown some form of humanity.

Lacey suddenly murmured. Looking around I could see that he was on his knees with his head lolling forward. The guard commander pointed to Lacey and shouted to the other guards. They came and looked at my friend, and one of them asked me, 'Your friend sickah?'

'Yes, he is very sick.' I answered.

I turned my head towards Lacey and saw them cut the rope that held him and lay him in a dark corner of the hut. As they returned to the table one of them stopped in front of me and said, 'Nippon soldier kind to sick English soldier, Nippon not kind to you.'

The rain fell all through the night. I was soaking wet from the drips as they fell through the roof. I dozed off now and then only to awake sharply as my legs gave way beneath me.

Dawn was coming up when a bugle close-by heralded reveille. As the sound of the bugle died away the guard commander came and cut the rope. The first thing that I did was to pick up the rusty tin and put it under the drips near the post and go to Lacey. He had come to, and asked for water.

The Japanese watched my every move. I went to put the tin under the drips again. They shouted and pointed to the faster ones falling from the roof into the drain. I hesitated as I thought that they wanted me to do something that they could hit me for, so I returned to the slow drips, but they insisted that I take the tin to the faster drips by the doorway. There by the faster drips I took the opportunity to wash off the rice and other stuff from my face and beard.

Later, two Japanese officers came into the hut and ordered us to take off all our clothes. I was amazed and so were the Japanese at the sight of Lacey. His stomach was swollen like a pregnant woman and his testicles were the size of a football. His legs were as thick as tree stumps so that you could not make out the kneecaps or calves of his legs. His ankles were completely unsightly and out of all proportion.

One of the Japanese officers was dressed in a white coat and had a stethoscope hanging around his neck. He asked me in perfect English, 'Why do you not have beriberi?'

'Beriberi? What is that?' I asked, puzzled.

The Japanese officer pointed to Lacey's swelling and said, 'That is beriberi. But why don't you have it?' He asked again.

I was as puzzled as he was and so could not answer him. The Japanese held a quick conference and then told us to get dressed. The Japanese in the white coat, acting as an interpreter, said, 'We are going to ask you a few questions and we want you to answer truthfully. We shall know if you are lying and we shall not hesitate to have you shot.'

The two officers sat at a table. I stood before them.

'First, where have you come from?'

'Sadon.'

'Is that where you were living?' was his second question.

'No,' I answered.

He repeated everything in Japanese.

'Where were you living before you went to Sadon?'

'In the jungle,' I answered truthfully.

'You lie! You lie!' he shouted, and banged the table with his fist. 'Where did you come from?' he came back at me quickly, trying to catch me out.

'We came from Taunggyi,' I answered. I thought that would give him something to think about, and that whatever I said would make no difference after all this time.

'From Taunggyi,' he repeated with a frown and very puzzled look. 'And how did you get to Sadon from Taunggyi?' he asked slowly.

'We walked,' I answered, laughing inwardly.

'You walked!' he shouted, and nearly fell off the stool. After regaining his posture he interpreted to the other officers who looked completely shocked. He turned back to me and asked, 'Do you want to die?'

'No, I don't want to die,' I answered.

'Then stop trying to be clever, and tell the truth,' he said, and scowled at me.

'But sir, I am telling the truth,' I said politely.

He looked at my face as I answered him. His hands clenched and unclenched, making his knuckles white. 'How long have you been hiding in the jungle?' he stared at my face and asked.

'What day of what month is it, sir?' I asked, again politely.

'You don't know?' he shouted in amazement.

'No sir, I don't know what day it is today, and I cannot in all honesty answer truthfully how long we have been in the jungle.'

There was a long and slightly heated discussion between the two Japanese officers. The one in the white coat faced me again. 'It is the twenty-fifth of October,' he told me.

I was taken aback, for I had no idea that the months had gone by so quickly. 'Then we have been walking for over six months,' I told him.

'Where?' he came back quickly, trying to catch me out.

'Between Taunggyi and Sadon,' I answered casually.

'Which way did you walk from Taunggyi?' he asked.

'We came mostly by jungle paths,' I replied, trying to dodge the question.

'But you could not have come through. We have our soldiers everywhere.' His voice was full of contempt and pompousness.

I did not want to court trouble and tell them that we had passed their troops on more than one occasion, so I kept silent.

The Japanese in white was speaking again. 'We think that you have been dropped by parachute in the last few days to spy.' He paused. 'So we have decided to send you to Myitkyina. There you will be executed.' His face broadened into a grin. 'That will be two more Englishmen less in the world,' he added, and the grin turned into a wide toothy laugh.

I looked back at both men. I do not know if I showed what I was thinking on my face. Had they known my thoughts I would have been killed right then and there without a second's hesitation.

I found out later from one of the Japanese guards that we were at Washung.

Later in the morning two Japanese armed with rifles came to take us to the river. There we were ushered on board a river steamer and made to sit down on some sacks. I had to half carry Lacey. It took us about half an hour to get across the river and to Myitkyina. As the ferry chugged its way across I thought of our friends who had decided to go across the same river, all those months ago. I hoped that their crossing was better than mine.

When we reached the bank we were marched from the ferry down a long road to a red brick-built house at the corner of two main streets. The house was slightly larger than the others in that area.

We were ordered into a large room with a highly polished table. There were four uniformed Japanese who wore swords and a white armband with red characters. This, I knew from our Chinese instructors, was the mark of the dreaded Kempeitai. We had been told that to fall into the hands of these people was the worst thing that could happen. So, I resigned myself to the worst. I did not give up hope, but certainly feared the worst. I could not help myself as the whole of my body began to shiver. I turned and looked at Lacey, but he was merely trying to stand and it seemed he had no thought for anything else. His face was a complete blank. At that moment I kind of envied him, for he had not realised the danger that we were in.

Our escorts passed all the information on to the four, and as soon as that was done our escorts were most rudely despatched out of the room. Even though I did not understand the language, it seemed that these four were most arrogant even to their own men. So I thought, what mercy are we to expect?

The four Kempeitai officers then turned their attention to us. Thoughts were racing through my head. I told the truth, and they called me a liar. If I lie like the blazes, they can do the same as if I tell the truth and they don't believe me.

What about Lacey? Will they question him first, or will they start with me? Lacey might just say the wrong thing unintentionally and drop me in it, but then so what? They will probably kill us anyway. I'll lie a bit and I'll tell the truth where it would not matter.

The four Japanese came towards us. Staring hard, they talked among themselves. The tallest of them stepped in front of me. He took his hand off his hip and pointed his finger at my belly. I kept my eyes on his face. He said, 'Inglis ka?' in a questioning voice.

'Yes,' I nodded, still watching him.

He then said something in Japanese that I did not understand. I frowned and shook my head to show that I had not understood. I was watching him carefully. I saw the blow coming and got ready to receive it. I stood rigid as his right hand smacked against my left cheek, forcing my head to the right and causing a ringing in my left ear. Quickly his left hand came up and sent my head in the other direction, then again his right and his left, his right and his left. Faster and faster came the blows. I took them, still standing. Harder and faster the blows came. He was using the heel of his hand now. I closed my eyes and clenched my teeth which had now begun to rattle. My temper was boiling over. My fingernails were digging into the palms of my hands as I squeezed my fingers into hard fists. I forced my hands to my sides and said to myself under my breath, I must not lose my temper, I must not lose my temper. I must hold on, I must hold on. I kept repeating this to myself, but I was staggering under the furious blows.

Then there was a crash on my left and the blows stopped. I opened my eyes, which had filled with tears forced up from the restraint of holding back my temper. The other three Japanese were standing over Lacey, who had fallen to the ground. The one who had been hitting me pointed to my friend and asked, 'Sick ka?'

I nodded and answered, 'Yes.'

One of the others looked at me and asked, 'Byoki ka?'

'Yes,' I answered. I had learned my first word of Japanese.

One of the Kempeitai went away and returned with two armed men and a length of rope. I was ordered to get Lacey to his feet. Once again our hands were tied and a noose put around both our necks. I was then pushed outside with Lacey dragging on the rope behind, while one of the armed men tugged the rope in front. We were paraded through the streets. Rain had begun to fall. The guards stopped to put on their waterproofs. We were taken to a wooden barracks. The smell of food was torture.

One of the guards went into a bungalow while the other sheltered under the veranda. Our rope was tied to one of the uprights of the veranda. I stepped onto the veranda to get out of the rain and pulled the rope attached to Lacey's neck. I shouted to him, 'Come in out of the rain.' The Japanese guard jumped forward, his rifle at the 'on guard'. I ignored it and pushed my stomach against the barrel and, with a curse, walked forward. To my utter amazement the Japanese stepped back. His face changed from a snarl to one of fear. He looked both ways to see that no one had seen the incident, and walked back against the wall of the bungalow. Well, I thought, so this is the great conquering Japanese army who are afraid of nothing.

The other guard came out and we were taken further along the road to another bungalow. There our ropes were taken off and we were told to sit on the floor. There was an officer with a sword, which he took off and laid on the desk. He told me to sit on the chair opposite, which was much lower, so that he was looking down at me. Lacey lay on the floor with his eyes closed.

The officer spoke in perfect English. He said, 'You must answer all the questions I ask you truthfully.' As he spoke he took the sword from its scabbard and laid it on the table. 'I shall know whether you are lying or not.' He watched my face through half-closed lids as he spoke.

He began with me. 'What are your name, rank and number?'

I gave them without hesitation.

'Now, what are your friend's name, rank and number?' he asked.

I had to turn to Lacey and give him a shove with my foot so that he would answer.

'Now, what is your unit?' he glared at me.

'I'm afraid I cannot answer that, sir.' I said.

'What!' he shouted, 'and why can't you answer me that?'

I thought I was pushing my luck. But what could I tell him? I could not say a Commando unit that had attacked the Japanese on the Thai frontier. I had to think fast. 'Well, sir,' I began, 'according to the Geneva convention–'

He banged his fist on the desktop and shouted at the top of his voice. 'We do not recognise the Geneva League of Nations! So, you will answer my question or die!' He picked up the sword from the desk and began to twirl it around his head using both of his hands.

At first I thought that he had gone completely mad. I had to gamble on the fact that my friend would not be questioned. I had to make up something quick, for the Japanese was asking again, 'What is your unit?'

I answered quickly. 'We did belong to an administration unit,' I said, praying at the same time.

'Administration unit? What is that?' he asked, frowning in disbelief.

I thought, bloody hell, he is never going to believe that in a month of Sundays.

'Well,' I stammered slightly, to gain time, 'it's a unit that supplies all other units with helpers.' As I said it, I thought, oh blimey, that's too daft, why didn't I think of something else?

'That is very funny. I have heard of many units in your army, but this is the first time I have heard of that.' He was looking at me very oddly. 'What do you mean helpers?'

'Well, like hospital orderlies and cooks and tent riggers and cleaners,' I went on in a voice that I did not think would have convinced anyone. I just sat there looking at him with the best poker-face that I could put on, but hoping that he would not ask the same question.

'Tell me, then, why I have never heard of it?' he asked, leaning forward and laying the sword down again.

'Oh,' I came back readily, 'it only began the early part of this year.'

'Oh, I see. That's something else that I have learned about your army,' he said smiling. Then he asked casually, 'And what hospital have you served?'

'Taunggyi, sir,' I replied quickly.

'The military one, I suppose?' he queried.

'No, sir, the civil one,' I answered.

'Oh, and why is that?' he asked in wonderment, his eyes widening.

'Because your planes came over and bombed the town, and there were many civilians killed and injured. So we were ordered to go and help at the civil hospital.' I said this with a great deal of pleasure and satisfaction. There, I thought, get hold of that.

But a moment later I almost regretted being so cheeky, for he picked up the sword again, got to his feet and stood over me threateningly. 'You lie! You lie!' he raved at the top of his voice, almost screaming. I sat there trembling, thinking that I had gone a little too far this time. He raised the sword above his head and swung it in an arc from the right side of his head and stopped it at the side of my neck. I could feel the cold steel as he drew the blade towards him. I felt a slight pain as the sharp blade cut into my flesh. I was staring at the man. Slowly, and to my utter amazement, a smile spread across his face. He put the sword down, dropping his gaze, and said quietly, 'We do not bomb civilians.' I remained silent. I thought it to be the best thing to do at that moment.

His next question was easier to answer, and my answer gave him some satisfaction and pleasure. The question was why had we walked and not used transport. I told him that we had been shot up by his planes and we had to abandon our trucks. He asked how we had been captured in Sadon. My answer gave him extra pleasure, and he said, 'We have our helpers, too.' He was beginning to be friendlier, but I became more careful with my answers. I thought that any time now he was going to come with some catch questions as he might think that I was off my guard. He even put his sword back into its scabbard.

Then, suddenly, his face changed back to one of hatred, and he asked, 'Do you know Captain Brown?'

His question was so quick that I was surprised. I repeated his question to give myself a little time. 'Captain Brown?' I asked, putting on a frown. 'Captain Brown?' I said again as if in deep thought. 'Oh, yes, I did know a Captain Brown,' I answered him. 'But he should be safe in India by now,' I added with a smile. 'That is, if it is the same one that I know.'

'Why? How many Captain Brown are there?'

'Well, off hand I know two, and both of them were in Burma,' I replied, thinking, that's got you confused now, mate. At the same time I was thinking, how did he know about Captain Brown? Perhaps it might be the other Captain Brown, as I had spoken the truth. There were indeed two Captain Browns. The other Captain Brown belonged to an Indian Signals unit in Maymyo, and we had helped him get his car out of a ditch after a dance. To repay us he had taken us back to his place and given us drinks. Now, which one was this Japanese officer asking about?

'So, you know two Captain Brown?' he asked, surprised. 'Why are you laughing at me?' he glared at me and once more drew his sword.

Oh, blimey, I thought, here we go again, and I thought how nicely we were getting on.

'Yes, I do know two Captain Brown. It is a very common name.' I tried to cool him down and added, 'I have two sisters whose married names are both Brown, as they are married to two different men named Brown.' My two sisters were indeed married to two brothers named Brown.

'So, this Captain Brown, your sister's husband, maybe?' he was looking very hard at me. His question made me smile widely, which did not please him. He banged the table and shouted, 'Why are you laughing at me?'

I tried to explain that both my sisters' husbands were too old to be in the forces.

He stopped me and asked if I knew a Captain Brown.

'Yes, I did know a Captain Brown, but he was not in our unit.'

'Oh, that is very funny,' he said, raising his eyebrows and pointing his fingers at me. 'Captain Brown also went to Sadon, the same place as you! Did you and your friend plan to meet Captain Brown at Sadon?'

'No, we did not plan to meet anyone at Sadon.'

I could not understand why he had picked on Captain Brown. I tried to get him away from the subject, and said, 'We had not planned to go there, but my friend fell sick and I needed help, as you can see.' I turned and pointed down at the still form of Lacey.

What he said next shook me. 'And I suppose that it was pure coincidence that we caught you two and Captain Brown at Sadon.' He watched the uncontrollable change of my face and smiled a cynical smile. I would have smashed my fist into his face if I could.

He is lying, I thought, he's got to be bloody well lying. He is trying to trick me into saying something. 'Where is he, then?' I asked, trying to keep alert to his next question.

The Japanese officer stood up and began to slash the air with the sword, making a swishing sound.

'Is he here?' I asked.

He stopped the slashing and said, 'He was here, but we cut off his head like this.' He stood feet apart, gripped the handle of the sword, held it high above his head and brought it down to the floor with a great swish. His face showed an awful grin of satisfaction as he obviously could see the imaginary head roll from the imaginary body of the imaginary victim. After the demonstration, he once more placed the sword on the table in front of him and sat down.

Forcing a grin to my face and stroking my neck, I asked, 'And when do we die?'

At first he looked hard at me through those half-closed slanted eyes, then he slowly said, 'It will be very soon. We will not keep you waiting.'

Licking my now very dry lips, I thought, oh well, what have I got to lose, I might as well be cheeky. So I said, 'In our country, it is the custom that we give a condemned person a good meal before execution.'

'Yes, I am aware of that custom,' he said sadly, and shook his head, 'but we think that it is such a waste of food. So, I am sorry.'

The interrogation was over. We were again tied by the neck and marched back to the Kempeitai barracks. There we were made to strip naked. At the sight of Lacey's swollen parts the Japanese began to laugh and poke them with their bayonets. They showed some disappointment when he did not cry out with pain. We were led into a long hall. In the hall were a number of barred cells. The wooden bars reached from ceiling to floor. One had to get down on hands and knees to enter it through a small door, leaving one's backside wide open to a kick to push one in. The cell had one window. This too was barred and about eight feet from the floor. It was almost the length of the wall opposite the bars. The cell itself was about eight feet by six. The floor was concrete. The ceiling was about ten feet high. Inside, squatting against the left-hand side wall and near the entrance, were two Orientals. They were stripped except for what looked like ragged loincloths. They looked quite clean and not too badly off as regards to being fed.

Lacey and I took the right-hand side wall facing them. Lacey got straight down and lay on his back. I sat with my back against the wall, watching the two men opposite. They turned their heads sideways and spoke in whispers so I could not pick up what they were saying. I wanted to make sure that they were not Japanese put in as plants. I put my head in my hands and rested my arms on my knees, trying my hardest to hear what they were saying. Their shaven heads told me nothing, because both Chinese and Japanese had shaved heads and so did some Burmese. They did not talk much but just squatted on their heels. At times they both glanced over at me, but quickly averted their eyes when I looked up.

It was late in the afternoon when a guard came, unlocked the small door and called out to them 'China', and they crawled out into the hall.

About an hour later the two Orientals crawled back into the cell. They sat still until the guard had gone, then from beneath their meagre clothes they brought out a number of raw vegetables: potatoes, carrots and onions. Waving me into one of the corners of the cell that was hidden partly from the passage, they shared out their spoils. They tossed some to me. Halving my few scraps, I tapped Lacey who was asleep; he said that he did not want any. I made short shrift of the vegetables, eating them very fast, dirt and all.

It was after this that I tried to make conversation with them. They were Chinese soldiers. One, a short stocky fellow was quite jolly and always smiling. His name was Lieu Chang. The other always looked as though he had the worry of the world on him. He hardly smiled. His name was San Chien. He was taller and slimmer than Lieu.

Lieu seemed more ready to talk, so it was to him I became friendlier. He told me that he had been taken near the Chinese border some two months before, while Chien had been taken many months before him and had been here when he was brought in.

Lieu surprised me when he told me that in the next cell down the passage was an English officer. He told me also that when the guard took him and Chien out, it was to clean the vegetables for the Japanese meals, and that was how they managed to get them. He also said that they had to take food to the English officer. That was how they knew about him.

'Will I get any food?' I asked eagerly.

'It is according to who is on duty.' Lieu replied with a sad face. 'We also have to be careful when we go out and bring in stuff, as some of the Japanese are very cruel,' he informed me. 'They would think nothing of chopping your hand off if we are caught. We try to put a little away and to the side,' he said, pointing to the corner where two rusty small tins were.

'But they are empty,' I pointed out.

'Yes, we have eaten it all today,' he answered.

I looked at him. 'You gave me what you normally put on one side?'

He nodded his head and gave a wide grin and shrugged his shoulders, as much to say, 'There's another day tomorrow.'

I gathered that there were times when no food or water came at all. It was left to the Japanese guard who was on duty if he thought we should get something.

San Chien spoke in a low voice, 'Boo shaw wha!'

We could hear boots coming down the hall. San Chien had been standing at the bars listening. A Japanese stopped outside. 'Ingris meshi, China no!' he growled, then unlocked the small door and pushed in a small kettle and a bowlful of mixed-up rice and vegetables. It was obvious that it had been the leftovers and swill from the tables.

The two Chinese were again taken out and Lacey and I were left alone. The kettle contained water. I drank from it and moved over to Lacey to give him a drink too. I had to force him, and force him even harder to eat some food, but all he wanted to do was sleep. I tried my utmost to save some of the food, but it was like asking me not to drink the water of a pond I was swimming in when thirsty. When the Chinese came to take away the kettle and the bowl, I really felt ashamed that I had saved none.

As darkness began to fall on the cell and the air became cooler I tried to find the best position to lie on the flat concrete floor. The best place I found was to use part of Lacey as my pillow, but I found that as I turned over now and then through the night the cold of the bare concrete floor brought me awake, plus the fact that my hips were getting sore and hurting as I lay upon my side.

It seemed a very long night. I was glad when the dawn began to light up the cell. I noticed that the two Chinese had slept most of the night sitting in one position with their backs to the wall with their knees drawn up, resting their hands across their knees and laying their head on their arms. They stayed that way until the heat of the sun had warmed the floor of the cell. They then lay on the floor.

The two Chinese told me the British officer had been brought in some two months before Lacey and me. I asked them what his name was, but they said they had no idea.

A Japanese guard came and took the two Chinese out to prepare the morning meal. They returned with some hidden vegetables but did not eat them. Instead they put them in the tins and out of sight. They told me not to touch them, as a Japanese called Mundo was on duty. 'He is a very bad man. He would not give any food to us,' they told me. Sure enough we went that day without any food or water.

During the day I wanted to go to the toilet, as did Lacey. I asked the two Chinese what we had to do. They both shook their heads and said they did not know. They always managed to wait until they were taken out. I shouted for someone to come. Eventually a Japanese came with a bamboo stick. I was standing near the bars. I made the motion that I wished to make water, but the Japanese shouted and pushed the stick through the bars, making me back away. Lacey got to his feet, staggered over to the bars, gripped them and began to shout at the Japanese. I tried to pull him away, out of reach of the stick, but the Japanese whacked the stick down on Lacey's head and lashed his hands with it as they gripped the bars. With me pulling Lacey from behind we both fell over backwards to the floor with a crash. At this the Japanese roared with laughter. I could not control either my bladder or my bowels any longer, so I got down and squatted in the furthest corner, beneath the window. Lacey followed me, but was unable to squat and overbalanced into the mess that I had made. The Japanese stood and watched and pinched his nose with two fingers and walked away. I made apologies to the two Chinese and said that I was very sorry. Other Japanese came and they also pinched their noses, but did nothing to help and laughed at our predicament.

Later, in the afternoon, the two Chinese were taken out and put into another cell. Lacey and I were alone in the now stinking cell.

We were kept in that state for a number of weeks. Some days we got food, some days we did not. Not once were we allowed out of that stinking cell. We were not allowed to wash or go to the toilet.

Lacey's health was getting worse rapidly. He hardly spoke or held any sane conversation. His mind was also going. He woke me up one night in the dark cell and asked me to help him find his cigarettes and matches. I must have been in some kind of haze myself at that time, for I began to search for them until I suddenly realised that we had not had any fags or matches since our capture. I then cursed him for disturbing my sleep.

During the day I tried to keep myself fit by doing exercises and walking around the cell. One day a Japanese officer stood and watched me. He called me and spoke very good English. I pointed out the horrible conditions that we were in. I told him that it was not usual for prisoners of war to be treated as we were being treated. I told him that I was willing to work outside if I was allowed to. Here, I thought, I may have a friend. I would do almost anything to get out and get some fresh air.

The Japanese officer went away and came back with two of the Kempeitai guards. All three stood facing me. The officer spoke to the guards and then said to me, 'I have told them that you would like to come out for work. Is that correct?'

'Yes sir,' I answered and nodded eagerly. 'Yes, I would.'

The Japanese officer then turned to one of the guards and said, 'Mundo,' then spoke in Japanese. I knew then who Mundo was. The officer had given Mundo an order to find me some sort of job outside. The three moved away down the hall and out of sight. A few minutes later Mundo returned and undid the hatch for me to crawl out and into the passageway. I held myself in readiness for anything that might happen. I was cautious from what the two Chinese had told me, and I was on my guard.

Mundo was an evil-looking, stockily-built man with a flat nose and red face. One could see hatred in his eyes. He had a frog-like grating voice. He spoke very little English and expected everyone to understand Japanese. After locking the hatch he motioned me to follow him out into the bright sunlight and in view of the main road. I must have looked a real funny sight to the people who stared, with my long hair and bearded face in contrast to my pale white nakedness that had been starved not only of food but of sunlight and fresh air. I walked like a cat on a hot tin roof as I trod on the hot stones, my timid and tender feet not used to the heat. I ignored the looks of the staring people as they walked along or rode past me. I followed Mundo around to the rear of the house to what looked like a small outhouse. Mundo undid the latch and threw open the door. A look inside almost turned my stomach over and made me sick. The floor was completely covered with human excrement. In the middle of this there stood an enamel bucket, full to the brim with millions of yellow maggots crawling in it and overflowing into the mess on the floor, which was about two inches deep and spread out to each wall and the edge of the step.

Mundo turned to me and said in his best English, 'Goodoh, creen,' and pushed me towards the stinking horrible mess.

I turned to Mundo and asked, 'Shovel? Shovel?' I made the motion of shovelling, and asked again, 'Shovel?'

'No shoveluh! Goodoh, handoh.' He spread out his hands to show me that I had to do it with my bare hands.

I was aghast that I should be expected to clean that mess up with my bare hands. 'No!' I said shaking my head and walked away from the doorway.

Mundo's face became red and he screamed 'Goodoh, creen,' and tugged at a small holster on his belt. He pulled a small pistol from the holster and put it to my head and pulled back the hammer as he did so.

'Goodoh, creen! Speedo, speedo!' he shouted in that frog-like voice. I knew that it would have given him great satisfaction to have reason to pull the trigger. So with as arrogant a smirk as I could put on my face at forcing him to draw the pistol on me, I turned and gingerly put one foot into the mess on the floor, trying not to take too much of a breath as I leaned down to grip the handle of the bucket. Trying not to spill any of the contents of filth, I turned and asked where to take it. Still pointing the pistol at me, Mundo directed me to go further around the back of the building where a pit had been dug for the refuse. Into this I tipped the bucket, with Mundo looking on. I once more asked for a shovel, but was refused. The hateful little Japanese made me get down and scoop up the filthy mess with my hands and into the bucket until it was full.

This took three journeys. On my way to and from the pit, I had to pass a water tap. On the last journey, I took the bucket and began to wash it under the tap. At the same time I made an attempt to get the mess from both my hands and feet. Mundo had, for a few moments, relaxed his vigil upon me, and I was succeeding in getting rid of the mess off my body. When he realized what I was doing, he made me come away from the water tap and took me back to the cell once more.

Chapter Seventeen

Torture in Myitkyina

Sometime after my introduction to Mundo a brick was knocked out of
the wall under the window and level with the floor. Buckets of water and
brushes were pushed into the cell and I was told to clean up our mess.
This was after a Japanese medical officer had visited us. After we had cleaned up
the cell and got rid of the smell, Lacey and I and the two Chinese were all roped
together with our hands tied behind our backs and a noose was put around our
necks. Four armed guards marched us through the main streets of the town to
the bank of the Irrawaddy. Still with the noose around our necks and a rope
around one ankle we were allowed to clean the filth from our bodies and bathe.

I was more embarrassed by the sight of Lacey than I was for myself, for his
testicles and penis were swollen to an incredible size. His legs were more than
three times the normal size and his stomach was also swollen. I had to assist him
as we went along the road. Even our Japanese escorts seemed to be somewhat
ashamed as they marched along with us past the staring crowds of onlookers.
There were very few people along the route who thought it amusing. Many
showed their disgust by turning their backs, so as not to look upon the scene.
In my opinion the Japanese lost more friends and gained more enemies in that
town that day.

On our return from the river the two Chinese were put back into our cell,
which had been disinfected. Now we were also allowed to have a bucket in there
to do what we had to do. This was emptied every morning and brought back
clean by the two Chinese in turn.

One afternoon an air-raid siren went off to let us know that our planes were
on their way. Guns began to fire as the drone of aircraft came nearer and nearer,
and the scream of the planes could be heard as they made their dive for strafing
and bombing. It seemed to us that they were coming straight into our cell.
The building shook as a stick of bombs landed close by, dust rose into the air,
screams of wounded could be heard just outside, and then another wave came
over. I thought that the next would be right on us, and in the centre of our
cringing circle. We could hardly see each other through the clouds of dust that
had filled the cell. Then it was over. All went quiet as the sound of the planes
faded away and the guns ceased firing. All that we could hear were a number

of people outside moaning and groaning. Then above this I heard the shout, 'Ingris, Ingris!' I somehow sensed something was wrong and I got hold of Lacey under the armpits and dragged him into the corner where the two Chinese had put their tins. There was about eighteen inches of wall before the start of the bars. With my legs astride Lacey and pressing myself close to the wall, very little of us could be seen from outside. There was another shout coming from the hall, and I could hear the sound of boots running towards the cell. The footsteps stopped in front of the bars. A rifle barrel was pushed through and a voice shouted, 'Ingris, Ingris, mutta coy, mutta coy!' I never moved but pressed myself further back. The Japanese tried again to get his rifle around to where we were, but the bars stopped him. He then called the two Chinese who stood at the wall almost opposite, shaking from head to foot. Lieu raised a shaking finger and pointed in our direction. Once again the Japanese shouted and tried to get me to show myself. But seeing that I was not going to move he turned his rifle as far round in our direction as he could and fired. The noise in that enclosed space was deafening. The bullet struck the wall about a foot from my right shoulder, sending bits of brick in all directions. It then ricocheted from that wall and went diagonally across the opposite wall and flattened itself before dropping to the floor, making a kind of splat sound.

As the shot rang out there were shouts down the hall, and a number of Japanese came running from all directions and took the man away. I still did not move from my position until I was quite sure that all was well.

Some days passed after that incident, and the two Chinese were again removed from our cell. This caused me some concern for every time the Japanese did this, something always followed.

The two Chinese were taken from the cell at an early hour in the morning. At about midday I heard a terrific scream coming from a large room up the hall. Looking through the bars, my vision was screened by the two swing doors. I moved closer to the bars to get a better look. As I did, I saw a Chinese civilian being dragged out by Mundo and Tamura, the big Japanese who had slapped me the first day. These two were the bully boys and would stop at nothing, not even death. I moved quickly away from the bars as they dragged the struggling and bleeding man down the hall. Suddenly there were shouts. I moved back to the bars to see the injured Chinese dashing back up the hall and past where I stood and out into the sunshine, with Mundo and Tamura in hot pursuit, both men with their swords drawn.

A few moments later they returned with the luckless man. He had a deep gash, pouring with blood, in the right shoulder. As he went past I could see that he also had a long cut down his back. This too was pouring with blood and leaving large spots on the floor. What happened to the man after that, I do not know.

The day after that incident I was asked if I could do any carpentry. I said that I could do the basics provided I was given the tools. I was let out of the cell and taken down the hall to the bathhouse. There I was given a claw hammer, a box of nails which were about an inch and a half in length, a saw and some lengths of two by two-inch wood. I was told to put four legs onto the duckboard that was lying by the side of the large square bath.

The duckboard was about six feet in length and about two feet wide. The bath was raised about three feet from the floor and had steps up the one side for entering the bath. One end was against the wall. At the other end was a tap. Behind the steps and at the furthest wall was where the fire was put beneath the bath to heat the water. I looked at the bath and couldn't see any purpose for raising the duckboard to the height that I had been told. But I did not question them on the point and got on with the job, thinking that I might get a good meal out of it. Even when I had finished what I thought was a good sturdy job I was still puzzled, as all they had to do was walk down the steps onto the duckboard. The Japanese were satisfied, and I was taken back to my cell. I had two helpings of food that day. I thought perhaps they were bribing me for something.

At about eleven in the morning there were shouts of both agony and of denial. These then turned to screams. I had a peep through the bars and saw the same two bullies, Mundo and Tamura, dragging another struggling man down the hall, followed by another Japanese who was carrying a whip, or what looked like a whip. I moved away and waited. There were cries coming from the bathhouse, pleading for mercy, but the cries went unheeded. I walked around the cell, trying to blot out the cries of the man, but I could not blot out the agony that came up the passageway, for it brought me to a halt. The screams of that man were screams the like I had never heard before. They slowly died, as though being swallowed back into the throat of the person who had uttered them. For a moment all was quiet. Then I heard a guffaw of laughter and some loud Japanese being spoken, then quiet again. I went back to the corner quickly and sat down beside Lacey as I heard footsteps coming up the passage.

I was staring at the opposite wall when Mundo shouted, 'Goodho! Mutta coy, mutta coy!' I rose slowly to my feet, went over to the bars and faced the man that I hated like I had never hated anyone before. Mundo undid the latch and opened the door. I crawled out and stood up in front of him. He knelt and locked the door. At that precise moment I felt that I could easily have killed him with my bare hands. He stood up and motioned me to walk before him down the passage to the bathhouse. As I stepped inside the bathhouse the heat of the floor burnt my feet and the puddles of water almost scalded them. Then I looked towards the bath. The sight that met my eyes made me almost cry out in horror. I had seen death in many ways, mutilations of all kinds, but what was before my eyes was indescribable. The face was not that of a human being, although I knew it had been. The steam that was still hanging about didn't help the situation, for it came down on me and gave me a feeling of nausea. I had stopped in my tracks. The burning in my feet was nothing now. The slits for the eyes were still there and slightly open, but not looking. There were bright red patches over the face and chest. The skin was beginning to form into large white blisters.

I was given no more time to wonder, for both Mundo and Tamura got hold of my arms and said, 'Untie, untie,' and pushed me towards the man tied upon the duckboard. He was tied face upward, with his head directly under the tap. I began to weep as I knelt and tried to undo the cords that bound him. I could not make out whether the man was still alive or dead. I began by trying to undo the rope that bound the man's shoulders to the duckboard. My hands were shaking and as I glanced now and then at the still form I could not help the tears of sympathy for the poor man. At the same time I turned my head to look at the three Japanese who were standing nearby. I cursed them, their mothers, their fathers and their children, and hoped that the time would come, as I was sure it would, when they would get their true and just deserts.

I was not fast enough in undoing the ropes, so Mundo drew his sword and slashed the cord that bound the body. Tamura got his riding-booted foot to the frame and sent it over on its side. I jumped back as both frame and body fell over and made a dull thud as they hit the floor. Some of the blisters broke in the process, causing water to seep from them. With the cords now free of the body, the three Japanese began gesticulating at me and threatening me. They waved their arms, telling me to drag the man outside. At first I bent and got my arms beneath the arms of the body, but in my weak state I could not budge it. The dead weight was too much for me alone.

Tamura shouted to the third Japanese, who went up the passage, while I tried to move the body along the floor.

The third Japanese returned with Lieu, who went white at the sight. He looked at me in the manner that I had got to know which said 'hopeless'. Between us, with one on each leg, we pulled the body outside the building. There we left it, as we were told to do, and returned to our respective cells.

The following day there were more screams and sounds of torture. I saw a young man of about seventeen being taken to the bathroom and given the treatment, whatever that was. In the afternoon, eight Chinese of all ages crawled into our cell. Among them was the young man who had received the treatment.

He could hardly crawl and was holding his private parts and moaning and rolling over in agony. I asked him what the Japanese had done, but he shoved me away. I asked some of the others and they tried to say that the Japanese had cut him or put something on him. I thought they meant some kind of castration, which I had heard was common practice by the Japanese on the Chinese. The young man was in terrible pain. Later I found out that the Japanese had poured acid on his penis and testicles.

As we were now short of space I was forced to get closer to Lacey, who had by this time become very weak and hardly spoke. It was while I was trying to make conversation with him that the young Chinese man crawled to the bars, pulled himself upright, turned and, with agony in his face, dashed across the cell to the wall where the window was. He sprang with his arms up and grabbed the bars of the window, pulled himself up with his knees under his chin, and did a backward dive onto the floor. His head struck the concrete with a loud thud, and his back slammed on the floor. He lay still and his eyeballs rolled in their sockets. He had taken us all by surprise. A Japanese came by just as he was falling. When he saw what the boy had done, he began clapping and said, 'Very good! China acrobat, very good!' Then he went away laughing. By this time the youth was bleeding from the mouth. We had to pull him to one side of the cell because of the cramped space. One Chinese and I pulled the youth to the side near the hatch. As we did this his head left a trail of blood along the concrete.

Not long after that episode, with the youth still lying lifeless in the cell, a Japanese guard brought a large clean bowl, full of cooked white rice, together with a bowl of mixed vegetables in curried gravy. A kettle of sweetened tea was also pushed inside, and the Japanese stood and said, 'Goodoh, meshi, OK. China meshi nai, no give China meshi OK kah?' I nodded my head and pulled the two bowls and kettle into the cell. I then went back with them to Lacey. He refused to eat any food, but did drink from the kettle. I tried to force him to eat some of the food, but he would not.

As I sat there, eating to my heart's content, I glanced at the old man squatting on his heels opposite me. I looked around at all of them, and they were watching me hungrily as I scooped up the food with my fingers and stuffed it into my mouth. My eyes came back to the man who looked the eldest of them. I could see that he was eating every morsel with me as I lifted each handful to my mouth. I had been hungry and I knew what it was like to be hungry. I had suffered the pangs that the old man must be suffering now. I stopped eating from the bowl, went to the corner where the two Chinese had left their small tins in case of emergency, and filled one. Making sure that no one was watching I got down on one knee and slid the tin across to the old man. It went so far and stopped when it hit an uneven piece of floor a few inches away from him. He saw what had happened and swung first his right arm then his left towards the tin, but making no attempt to pick it up. What the bloody hell is up with him? I thought. Why doesn't he pick the bleeding thing up?

Although his hands went near the tin, his fingers never moved. Then I realised that he had no use of his fingers or arms, because of the way they had been trussed up beneath his armpits and hung for I did not know how long.

Throwing all caution to the wind I went across to the old man, picked up the tin and began pushing handfuls of food into his mouth as fast as he could swallow it, disregarding any Japanese who might be passing. The old man had eaten nearly all of the contents of the tin when there was a shout from the passage. 'Goodoh, no good, no give meshi, China!!' It was none other than that hateful Mundo.

Mundo gave a shout, and an officer and two other Japanese came up to the bars. 'Why have you disobeyed our orders?' the officer demanded in very good English.

'Because I was sorry for him,' I replied, facing them.

'Why are you sorry for them? They are not your friends, are they?' he shouted with glaring eyes.

'No sir, but they are human, and I know what hunger is like,' I replied.

'Oh, you do, do you?' The hatch was unlocked and I was ordered to crawl out. As I did I fully expected a boot to the head, but it did not come. I stood up with my back to the wall that divided the two cells.

'So, you like the Chinese savages?' the officer asked, staring at me and moving closer. All four stood around me in a half circle. I never answered, but began to steel myself for what was to come.

'And you do not follow orders given by your Japanese masters,' the officer continued, 'who have been kind to you and given you very good food.' He was glaring at me, and the temper was showing in his face as he went on, 'Is that how you repay the kindness?' His eyes were half closed as he spoke.

Before I could answer he was throwing blows at my face. The others immediately joined in. Some blows were going to my head, and others were knocking the wind from me in the belly. The blows to my head were making me bang my head against the wall behind me. My head was going from side to side one moment, then against the wall. I tried to get my arms up to protect my head, but as fast as I lifted them, they were knocked down. I felt a terrible pain as one of them trod on my foot. It was this pain that seemed to hurt me most, as I felt the wall slowly slipping up my back as I lost consciousness.

It hurt for me to even open my eyes. It was pitch black. I slid my tongue over my swollen lips and tasted the dried blood around my mouth. I felt stiff all over. I was also feeling much colder than I had ever felt before. My head was resting on something. As I tried to move, my shoulders felt like ice. I lifted up my one arm. It hurt, but I managed to get it above my head. What I felt then was deadly cold and damp. I pulled my arm down and touched the concrete floor. Slowly my eyes began to get used to the darkness, and I could make out the shapes of the others across the room and I began to hear their breathing. With some effort I raised myself up into a sitting position and, half turning, felt for what I had been lying upon. It was the corpse of the Chinese youth.

Gathering my wits, I could just make out the bars and I made my way on my hands and knees across to where Lacey was lying. There I snuggled against his warm body until daylight came.

As the light came to the room I tried to focus, and there bending over me was the old Chinese man to whom I had given the food. 'Ying-gwor, ying-gwor, nee shr howla wren, nee shr hun howla wren,' his squeaky voice was saying. 'English, English, you are a good man, a very good man.' He went on to thank me. I told him through my swollen lips to go back and sit down before the Japanese came.

I knew that I had got a couple of black eyes, for I could feel the puffiness around them. My foot was giving me some pain, and my whole body ached. Lacey woke from his usual stupor and said in a weak voice that he was glad to see me near him, as he thought that it was the last he would see of me after I was taken out.

I did not wish to talk too much, for my face gave me so much pain. The old man kept looking across at me with a kind of guilty look upon his face as though he was blaming himself for what had happened.

Lieu and Chien were brought from their cell to drag out the body of the young Chinese. As they did they both gave me looks of pity for they were in the next cell and had seen almost everything that happened. The Japanese came at intervals and taunted me with, 'Goodoh, no good, meshi nai,' meaning that food had been stopped being given to me as I was no good.

A few days after my beating a Japanese officer came into the cell and gave each one of the Chinese a pill to swallow. He said to me, pointing at their injuries, 'Malaria cah?'

'Yes, so is this,' I answered, and pointed at my injuries.

The Japanese only grinned and offered me some of the pills, which I refused.

A short time after that a Japanese NCO came into the cell. His name was Sato. He was not too bad, as the Japanese went. He told the remaining Chinese that they would be going back to their homes. This left Lacey and I on our own once again.

To my utter surprise Sato brought a large bowl of food into the cell, together with the kettle. Lacey wanted only water. Sato stood for a time inside the cell with his back to the bars. He pulled out a packet of cigarettes and threw it by my feet with one match. Then in quiet Japanese he began to talk. I did not understand what he was saying, but he seemed sullen and sad as he spoke. He stopped talking and left.

Lieu was sent in to take away the bowl and kettle. Sato came back and told me to get Lacey outside as we were going on a journey. Straightaway I thought of what the interrogating officer had said about a 'last meal' being a waste of food. I wondered if he had changed his mind about that. Outside in the passageway our hands were tied behind our backs and a blindfold put over our eyes. We were both led out into the sunshine, which I could feel upon my naked body. Hands gripped me and hoisted me upwards. I just put out my feet and felt floorboards beneath them. Then I was grabbed from in front by another pair of hands which pulled me forward a few paces and made me kneel. I put my head forward and touched something. I also felt someone near me on my right-hand side.

'Is that you, Len?' I asked.

There was a weak reply of, 'Yes, Fred, it's me.'

I heard the tailboard of the lorry being slammed up and latched. After a few moments the engine started up and we were on the move. I thought to myself, well, this is it, I suppose they have kept us hanging around for long enough, now this is it.

'What are they going to do with us, Fred?' Lacey asked in that low weak voice of his. 'Why have they blindfolded us?'

I could not answer the question, but I had my own idea of where and what was going to happen to us. 'I haven't any idea,' I said, 'and it's no use worrying now anyway.'

We both fell silent, falling against each other as the lorry went around bends in the road. After a time I got the impression that we were being driven around the same places. I could begin to recognise the sounds as we went past. But if we were going around in circles there could only be one end.

The vehicle stopped. This is it, I thought. I could hear quite a number of Japanese talking, and some of them were shouting and laughing. I wondered who would be first, or if we would go together. I was not given any more time to think. I was grabbed by the arms, lifted to my feet and turned around to face the other way. I was then shoved forward to the back of the lorry. Arms grabbed me again and made me sit. I found my legs were dangling over the back of the lorry, then a push from behind and I was on my face in the dust. I was lifted to my feet and forced forward. I felt a step with my foot. I raised it and felt another step with my other foot, then I was pushed forward again for a few paces and the blindfold was taken off.

I thought that I would be standing on some kind of platform that was part of a gallows, but instead I was standing just inside a room with two beds with mattresses on them. As I took all this in, Lacey was brought in and my hands were untied. I was completely taken by surprise and just walked forward without the Japanese pushing me from behind.

The door of the room was shut and locked behind us. There were bars on the one window but, amazingly, a blanket on each bed. Lacey had already occupied one of them and lay flat on his back. I turned to the window to look out at our surroundings. I heard the lock being turned and swung around as the door was opened. To my astonishment an Indian woman entered. She was wearing a royal blue sari. I rushed towards the bed and grabbed up the blanket to cover myself.

'It is alright,' she said smiling, 'I am a nurse. I have got to look after you.'

'Where are we?' I asked, looking around the room.

'You are in the civil hospital in Myitkyina,' she answered in perfect English, smiling still and showing a perfect set of white teeth. She looked me over and asked, 'Have you been fighting?'

'Yes, I suppose I have in a way, but I could not fight back.'

'Your friend is in a very bad state,' she said, turning to Lacey, 'and he is covered in lice. Did you know?'

'No, I hadn't noticed,' I answered truthfully. I looked closer at Lacey and then I could see his black hairy body was completely covered in crab lice.

'I'll go straight away and bring something back for those lice and something for your bruises.' She knocked on the locked door. It was opened from outside, obviously by a guard or hospital orderly. When she returned she was carrying a bowl of hot water, a bottle of meths, a tin of ointment and a roll of cotton wool. She said to me, 'I had better see if you have any lice on you.' I had not. The only reason that I could think of was that I was not so hairy and not as dark-haired as Lacey. 'How long has he been like this?' she asked.

I hesitated to answer, for I did not know how long we had been captive. 'I don't really know. What date is it now? What day is it?'

'It's the twelfth of December, 1942,' she informed me.

'Then he's been like this for about two months,' I told her.

The nurse began to swab Lacey over with the cotton wool soaked in the meths. 'Here,' she said to me, handing over the tin of ointment, 'rub some on your arms where the bruises are, and I will do your face later.'

Sometime later a Japanese came and ordered me outside. There I knelt down while he shaved every hair from my body, even my eyebrows. Later, the nurse brought in food. Again I tried to coax Lacey to eat, but he refused. The nurse also tried to tempt him, but he would not eat.

The next day, when she came to bathe Lacey, she brought me a pair of white trousers. Later, when she brought in some food, she also brought me a white shirt. I told her that I could not thank her enough for what she had done for us.

Early the next morning the door was opened and a man of small stature, dressed in a smart Western-type suit and carrying a small attaché case, entered. He had the face of an Oriental and at first I thought he might be Japanese. 'Hello, how are you?' he greeted me with a broad smile on his face. He put out his hand for me to shake and I took it. 'I am Mr Kin-Maung,' he then declared. For a moment I was dumbstruck. 'I have come to see how you are being treated,' he said.

After I regained some of my composure, I asked, 'How is Nita?'

'She is very well,' he replied. 'It was she who asked me to come to see you. You see, she has had you watched, and pleaded with me to get the Japanese to release you from the Kempeitai and send you to a POW camp.' He said this with a smile on his face.

'That was very kind of her, sir,' I replied. So, her crush on me was doing some good after all, I thought. But for all that, I could not push from my mind the thought that we had been betrayed. We could have been safely in British hands by now otherwise.

Mr Kin-Maung looked down at Lacey's bloated yet thin form lying on the bed, still with some lice in patches on his body. When he enquired of his health it was with bitterness in my voice that I said, 'Oh, he will die, but he would not have done so if I could have got him to Sumprabum,' I answered.

For a few moments there was an uneasy silence. Picking up his hat and case from the bed, he said, 'Well, I must be off.'

'Please give Nita my regards and tell her thanks,' I said.

As he walked towards the door he turned back and said, 'I will, and keep your pecker up. Old soldiers never die, you know?' He gave a smile as he reached the door.

I do not know what made me say it, but it was the first thing to come to my head in answer. 'No, but traitors do!' I said it with some hatred. His face went blood red. He snatched open the door and stamped out, slamming it behind him.

We had been in the hospital for four days. The nurse had brought hot water every day so that I could wash and keep myself clean. She bathed my friend twice a day with the meths. But his general health was getting worse. He was now beginning to ramble and was in a sort of coma.

Before the nurse came in the afternoon of the fourth day, Lacey opened his eyes and called me. I leaned over to hear his weak voice. 'Fred,' he said, 'I've seen all the lads, every one of them.' He raised one arm and pointed a finger towards the ceiling. At the same time tears fell in rivulets down the side of his face. For a moment I just sat and looked down. Tears welled up into my own eyes. I had to move away. I went over to the window and just gazed out. I was not looking at anything in particular, but just gazed more or less into space. Tears were streaming down my face, as my thoughts went back over the months that we had struggled to get back, the walking, the sleeping out in the jungle where even the natives would not dare to spend a night out, and being unarmed into the bargain.

I turned from the window as the nurse entered the cell. She went straight to the still form of Lacey who was making a funny sort of noise in his throat as if he was having some difficulty in breathing. The nurse came to me near the window and said, 'I'm afraid your friend will not last the night.'

But he did. He died just as the Japanese were blowing reveille.

TELEPHONE NO.:
SLOANE 9696

TELEGRAPHIC ADDRESS:
"WOMIREL, KNIGHTS, LONDON"

In replying please quote reference:

7 BELGRAVE SQUARE
LONDON, S.W.1

3 – 4 – 43.

Re. 5108868. L/Cpl. F.C. Goode. D.C.L.I.

Dear Mrs Goode,

Thank you for your letter giving us particulars concerning your son

We will certainly do our utmost to obtain news of him and if we are able to get any definite information we will let you know at once.

We sympathise deeply with you in your anxiety and hope that good news may come through before long.

Yours sincerely,

P.P. Margaret Ampthill.

Chairman.

M.F.

TELEPHONE NO.:
SLOANE 9696

In replying please quote reference: ED/MF

7 BELGRAVE SQUARE,
LONDON, S.W.1

Lance Corporal Fred Goode, 5108868,   15th August 1943.
Duke of Cornwall's Light Infantry.

Dear Mrs. Goode,

We have received your letter in which you make a further enquiry for your son. We are so sorry that no news has reached us since he was missing in Burma.

All possible enquiries will be made on your behalf, and should we receive any further news, which we are able to send you about him, we will write to you immediately.

Owing to the difficulties of the country in which he has been serving it is not easy to get in touch with our men in the Far East. You will therefore appreciate how long it takes for any information to reach us.

Please accept our deepest sympathy in your anxiety.

Yours sincerely,

PP. Margaret Ampthill.

Chairman.

Mrs. G. Goode,
16 Templeton Road,
Kingstanding,
B'ham 22.

The first two letters from the Red Cross.

Chapter Eighteen

Rangoon Central Jail

few days after Lacey had died and been taken away somewhere and buried, I was marched through the streets back to the Kempeitai barracks. This time I was dressed in a pair of white trousers and a white shirt, and had rolled up one of the blankets and tucked it under my arm. No one noticed.

In the barracks I was shown to a room in a basement. There Lieu and Chien each had a bed with sheets and blankets, and a bedside locker. There were no guards, and Lieu and Chien were dressed in new uniforms, complete with hats.

Sato greeted me and asked, 'Would you like to live down here like the Chinese?'

'Of course I would,' I answered.

'Then, all you have to do is sign this.' He pushed a typewritten paper towards me. I picked it up and read it. It went as follows: 'I... promise not to escape. I will help the Japanese to overthrow the British and United States Forces and I shall enlist in the British, Indian and Burma Independent Army.'

I dropped the paper to the table, looked hard at the Japanese officer for a second or two and asked, 'Can I go back to my cell now, please? It stinks in here.'

Sato smiled slightly and said, 'I didn't think you would sign it, but I had to try.' He then turned and shouted to the guard, who accompanied me back up the steps to my cell. It had changed quite a lot. The walls had been whitewashed and the floor had been scrubbed almost white. I was allowed my blanket to lie on.

Later I was taken down to that dreadful bath house. There I was allowed to wash and given a piece of cloth to dry myself.

Fred's Japanese POW dog tag. Japanese kanji (British Prisoner) and his Army No.5108868.

After that I was taken upstairs and told that for the next few days I would be helping to prepare food. That would be my job until I was to be transported to Rangoon, from there to be put on a ship to Japan.

During the time that I worked upstairs I was able to get hold of a good deal of food and drink. Sometimes I got caught and received a thumping. I never really minded as the punishment was worth the risk. At least I was getting food.

One day while working upstairs helping to prepare a meal a voice made me turn around sharply. It said, 'Hello, Corporal Goode. How are you?' It was Captain Brown.

I went to answer, but the Japanese who was with him said, 'No speaku, no speaku.' So I just nodded to him and gave a little smile and a wink. I noticed that he had his arm in a sling of black material. I wondered what had happened to him.

After about a week Sato came and told me to be ready to travel. I was taken out of the cell with a bundle of what little belongings I had managed to collect in that time. I stood outside in the passage. The cell next door was opened and Captain Brown came out. He too had a small bundle which he put under his good arm. We did not attempt to speak, but just stood there. Then along came Mundo and another Japanese guard. Both were in their best uniforms. Mundo was armed with a sword, and the other man carried a rifle.

With Captain Brown in front of me, Mundo on his right, and the other guard behind me we were marched to the railway station, where we boarded a train. We were in a reserved compartment. Mundo insisted on me being handcuffed to the seat. Captain Brown and Mundo sat behind me and the other guard. The train was destined for Mandalay, we were told. The captain and I were not allowed to converse, but Mundo seemed to have plenty to say to the captain. The other guard hardly spoke, not even to Mundo.

My main fear on the train was the thought that if we were attacked by our planes I would not be able to get out, being handcuffed to the seat. So I made excuse after excuse to go to the toilet. After about the third time, Mundo asked me to promise not to try and escape if he did not put the handcuffs back on. I did so and rode the rest of the way much easier in my mind.

At Mandalay we were marched to the river, as the train could go no further. Our engineers had done a good job on the Ava Bridge across which the railway ran. One huge cantilever lay half in the water of the Irrawaddy. We were rowed across the river in a sampan. Mundo had drawn his sword before sitting down facing me, with Captain Brown behind and the guard with the rifle behind him.

Once on the other side we were marched to a large building, a kind of hall, where we slept the night. The next morning we were handed over to other

收 容 所 Camp	馬來 昭和 19 年 3 月 15日	番 號 No.	馬 VI 93
姓 名 Name	Frederick Charles GOODE. フレッド リーク チャールス ゴッド	生 年 月 日 Date of Birth	1918.7.22.
國 籍 Nationality	英		No. 5108868.
階 級 身 分 Rank	Corporal. 伍 長	所 屬 部 隊 Unit	Duke of Cornwall's Light Infantry.
捕 獲 場 所 Place of Capture	緬甸 シャドン ミートキナ 西北スス哩	捕 獲 年 月 日 Date of Capture	昭和17 年 8 月 3 日
父 ノ 名 Father's Name	William GOODE.	母 ノ 名 Mother's Name	Gertrude GOODE.
本 籍 地 Place of Origin	BIRMINGHAM, England.	職 業 Occupation	自動自転車機械工
通 報 先 Destination of Report	16, Templeton Road, Great Barr, BIRMINGHAM, 22, England.	特 記 事 項 Remarks	

Japanese prison record for Fred at Rangoon Jail. (Courtesy of Kew)

guards, and to my utter surprise Mundo came and wished me goodbye. As he did, I said quite a few words under my breath.

At about ten in the morning we were marched to the old fort. There we were taken along a dark passage and pushed into one of a number of barred cells. There were no windows, the only light coming from the passage. There was no toilet either and nowhere to wash. It was literally a dungeon.

The other cells were occupied by other prisoners. Who they were we did not know. As the sun went away from the front of the long hall, darkness came to our cell. The blanket that I had brought with me from the hospital now came in very handy and I spread it on the floor for both of us to lie on.

This being the first opportunity we had had of talking together, I asked Captain Brown how he had injured his arm.

He began by starting from when his party had left us, when Bland had hurt his foot. There had been some disagreement about the speed they were going, and they had split into two parties, then met and gone on together again. He told how Bob Sharp had met his end. It seemed that there was a time when they too were starving, and when they eventually got hold of some food Sharp ate so greedily that he had choked to death.

He went on to tell me how Lockington had died. He, like Lacey, had developed beriberi. After being carried by the others he collapsed and died within five miles of Sadon. Captain Brown continued to tell me how he had gone down with fever at Sadon. The others stayed with him for the required two days, then had pushed on, leaving him in what they thought was a safe place. Two days later he felt fit enough to go on alone, but a few miles from Sadon he was attacked by bandits. As he lay on the track he turned to go for his revolver at his left hip and one of the bandits slashed his arm with his dha. The bandits then robbed him and left. He was found later by a Gurkha villager who took him back to Sadon. There his arm was temporarily bandaged and put into a sling, and Mr Kin-Maung ordered him to go quietly and surrender to the Japanese.

When he had finished I asked him if there were any Japanese troops in Sima when he passed through. I could not see his face in the dark, but his answer was no. I then asked him when he went through there. 'About the beginning of August,' he replied. It was now becoming clear to me why the Japanese had sent troops up into Sima at the end of August and beginning of September. It was to stop any more stragglers like me and Lacey from getting through, and they were expecting a signal from Sadon when I arrived.

I then told him of my exploits and of the meeting with the three captains who brought Lacey and left him with Bland and me. I told him how we had lost Bland on our journey back to Man Ying. In fact I told him the whole story from when they had left us up to my capture, and what had happened at the hands of the Kempeitai.

Eventually we both fell asleep. The light was coming down the passage when we were awakened by the noise of the other prisoners as they were maltreated by the guards. Then it was our turn. We were ordered out into the dark passage and into the bright morning sunshine, which made us cover our eyes, having been in almost complete darkness. We came out on to what seemed to be a courtyard. There was a single tap. We were given a few minutes to drink from it and swill our faces. We were then led to a toilet where given hardly any time at all before being ushered back towards the passage. There we were given a ball of rice from a tray held by an Indian and led back into the cell.

We spent about five days in that place, then early on the sixth morning we were marched to the railway station where we joined up with about three hundred Chinese prisoners and six American airmen.

The Americans looked at us in amazement when they heard that we had come from Myitkyina, as they thought that their troops had captured it. Captain Brown, two of the Americans and I along with about fifty Chinese were loaded onto steel cattle-trucks. Two of the Chinese were already in a bad way and had to be carried on. There was hardly any room to sit down when the two Chinese were laid flat. We had to squat down as best as we could. Realising that we would be travelling during the heat of the day, I got Captain Brown to stay as near to the sliding doors as possible so that we would be able to get some air. Before the train started the Japanese came along and closed the doors, leaving just a small gap for air to get in. The trucks were already hot as they had been standing in the station, waiting for our arrival.

As the train moved off a slight breeze did come in through the gap in the doors, but as the journey went on and the heat built up with the crammed bodies those furthest away from the door began to move nearer to the doors for a breath of fresh air. It was only with the timely intervention of Captain Brown, the two Americans and myself that fighting among the Chinese was prevented.

Except for the two men who were sick we managed to work it so that ten men stood near the doors for about five minutes at a time, before we all moved around to the right. We had to keep our eyes on one or two men who tried to dodge their turn.

The train kept stopping for some reason or other, but the doors were never opened. The heat really built up inside the compartment when the train stopped, making it stifling hot.

Darkness descended while the train was at a standstill. We wondered what the holdup could be. It seemed ages before we got on the move again. In the wagon it was pitch black. One could not even see who was on either side. Word was passed around that it was thought that one of the sick Chinese had died and that the other would not last through the night.

I tried to go to sleep in a standing position, but my knees kept giving way under me. Captain Brown was on my right. He suggested that we work our way into the corner nearest to his right. With the cool of the night we had abandoned our moving around. Slowly we edged our way into the corner. There, with him taking one angle and I the other, we managed to squat on our heels. After some time we decided to get down into a sitting position by crossing our legs over each other. In this manner we did manage to get a little sleep, but the stopping and starting of the train kept waking us up. We must have managed to nod off, for when I opened my eyes it was daylight. Most of the others had managed to get down into sitting positions like us.

Hunger and thirst was now our main worry. The heat had not yet affected the corpses of the dead Chinese. The second one had died just before dawn. As the morning wore on and the heat built up we became aware of a distinct smell from the dead bodies, a smell that grew stronger and stronger.

At about midday the train was brought to a halt at a station called Wunto and the guards came along opening the doors. They issued us rice and water and we told them about the dead men.

After some time, the guards told us to get the two corpses off and take them onto the platform across the track. I helped to carry one of the bodies, and as we laid it down a large crowd gathered around to look at them. Quickly I vaulted up onto the platform on the outside of the ring of onlookers and walked along it, trying not to arouse any suspicion. I just ambled towards a corrugated toilet at the far end, keeping a watch out for any Japanese who might be standing around, but everyone seemed more interested in the dead Chinese than a thin bearded man dressed in a white shirt and white trousers. I neared the entrance and was about to enter when a Burmese came out. He looked at me and bowed his head. It was then that he looked back at my face. He had seen that I was barefooted. He stopped aside and let me pass. Out of the corner of my eyes I saw him walk away in the opposite direction from the crowd. I moved out of sight and into one of the cubicles, and squatted down as if I was relieving myself.

Then I began to plan what I would do when the train had gone. I knew from maps that this town was about two hundred miles from Taunggyi. There I could search for some of the money we had buried and also get to the home village of Hohi, the nurse I had befriended in the civilian hospital, at White Crow Lake, so-called for its shape. I squatted there in that tin toilet, sweating more from the excitement than the heat of the sun on it. Here I am, I thought, planning to make a break for it, when half an hour ago I had no plan at all. The chance had come and I had taken it.

The sweat began to pour from me as the sun played down onto the tin roof and made it like an oven, but I still kept my position and waited. It seemed ages and ages that I had been there, then I heard the shrill whistle of the engine ready to move off.

My heart began to beat faster and faster. I began to quake with nervous excitement, asking myself if I had succeeded. Had they missed me? I began to congratulate myself and for a moment I completely forgot that I was almost roasting to death.

The sound of the engine came to my ears as it moved forward, causing the wheels and piston to turn. Steam was let out and the thump-thump, choo-choo began as the great iron horse began to move out of the station. Then I heard a shout and more shouts. There was a squeal of brakes and jangle of the wagons going into each other as the train was brought to a halt. Running footsteps came towards where I squatted. The footsteps stopped and in walked two Japanese. They began to shout and swear at me. I bent double and said, 'Byoki, byoki,' and tapped my stomach. They forced me out of the toilet with their rifles and between them took me across the track and up the line where the doors of our wagon were opened. They made me climb up and inside, and the doors were closed and the train was once more on its way. Inside, Captain Brown said, 'Hard luck. It was a good try.' The Americans also praised my attempt and told me they had thought I had made it.

We arrived at the Rangoon terminus at about nine in the evening. We were then marched through the streets of the town. There must have been some form of curfew, for the streets were deserted except for a few Japanese troops walking about. We were marched up Commissioner Road until we came to the jail. There we were turned in, inspected, counted and separated. The Chinese were marched away, leaving the Americans, Captain Brown and me, and a civilian who was a magistrate and had been out in the wilds when the Japanese came along and nabbed him. With two guards we were marched up what seemed to be a road between two compounds. We went past a sentry on duty near a large tower, then on to a larger building. We were marched into this, then up a flight of stairs onto a balcony, and placed in separate cells.

In the darkness I laid my blanket on the floor. In one corner near the bars of the doorway was a square tin. This was for toilet use. The next thing I did was to look through the barred window opposite the door. Through this I could make out other buildings. When all was quiet and it seemed that we had all settled ourselves down for the night, we heard a man shout out of the darkness from below. It seemed as if the noise was coming from the bowels of the earth. In very good English he shouted, 'Who's up there?' None of us answered. The shout came again. 'Hello! My name is Chi, General of the Chinese army.'

At this, one of the Americans answered, 'Hello General.'

There was some exchange of talk which was very difficult to follow as you could not always catch the full words or sentences. Eventually all went quiet and I fell asleep.

It was still dark when I was awakened by something moving near me. I jumped to my feet just in time to see the dark shape of a rat as it ran out through the door and onto the landing. Once again I settled myself down, but now the tiredness of the journey had gone and the pangs of both hunger and thirst kept me awake. It was some time before I again fell to sleep. The next time I woke it was daylight. Outside the birds were chirping and singing. I went to the window to see what the other noises were, those of men shouting to each other. I could make out phrases in English. I pulled myself up so that I could look out. I saw a yard that was separated from our building by a high wall, which ran up the pathway that we had been brought up the night before.

Looking down into part of a square I saw a number of very thin and poorly dressed men. They were forming into ranks. I watched as they passed through an iron-studded doorway, down the pathway that we had come up between the two compounds towards the main gate. Some of them limped, some found it hard to walk without any footwear. All were in rags. Some wore hats of all types that would have gone well in a pantomime. The audience would have laughed their heads off. I watched until they went out of my vision. There were still some men left in the compound. I saw them as they moved about.

Not long after the parade I heard noises from below. Footsteps were coming up the steel staircase. Quickly I moved away from the window. A Japanese came and motioned me away from the door. Then two Chinese came. They ladled out some rice into a flat saucer-like bowl, together with some green tea, and pushed the bowl under the door. The Japanese motioned me not to touch the bowl until the Chinese had gone away from my door.

After they had gone we heard another shout from the general down below. We tried to make some conversation with him. Although the distance between us was too great, we did understand that he was kept in complete darkness, except when his door was opened to give him some food. From what we could gather he was taken out now and then and tortured. He said that he had been kept like that for about four months.

With the thought in my mind that we might be kept in this solitary condition for some time, I rationed myself out and saved some of the rice, leaving just a little in the bowl for later on. I took off my shirt and covered the bowl with it and put it onto the windowsill, but I soon had to remove it. A couple of mynah birds came and began trying to pull the shirt from the bowl. I took it from the window and put it down on the floor beneath the window. I had not put it there for long before a rat came and poked his nose around the doorway. So I ate the rice and settled myself down to sleep.

Night followed day. We were still kept in solitary confinement. All that we could do was to try to hold a conversation with the man in the next cell. I exercised myself by walking around my cell. By day I watched the thin ragged ranks of men as they went out on what I imagined was work parties. We had the usual call from the Chinese general below, most of which we could not understand anyway.

I watched the thin and ragged men go out in the morning and return in the evening. Some looked as if they were going out to their deaths, or when they came back, to the same thing. It dawned on me that most of them had been prisoners for nearly a year and subjected to all sorts of ill treatment, just by judging on the treatment that I had received in my own short time. It was no wonder that they had little or no clothing or footwear.

For seven days we were kept in the cells and not allowed out, not even to empty our makeshift toilets, which were beginning to smell. On the seventh day a Japanese officer who wore a sword came with a guard, unlocked the cell doors and told us to bring out our toilet tins and any kit that we had with us. In file we were marched down the stairs and out into the bright sunlight and clean fresh air.

Out once more into the sunlight. What a relief from the stench of the cell! We were ordered to drop our belongings and take our toilet tins to a large open sewer, some thirty yards away. Into this we tipped the contents, left the empty tins and went back to collect our belongings. We were then marched to the iron-studded door through which I had seen the men go out and come back each day.

Inside the compound we were handed over to the senior British officer, who was a brigadier called Hobson. Other officers and NCOs greeted us as we stepped forward. Captain Brown was taken away by the officers, and so were the American lieutenant and the civilian. I was handed over to Company Sergeant Major (CSM) Finnerty of the Royal Inniskilling Fusiliers, who took me into a large room. The room faced a large garden at the rear of the compound. Here I could see men digging and hoeing the ground. I was informed that this was how the officers were kept employed. I was given a place on the concrete floor against the wall and in between two barred windows that reached from the floor to the ceiling. The room was bare of any furniture, except for a number of tidily folded sacks which were placed around the room at intervals. On some of these sat thin, almost skeletal men. They were obviously sick and starved. Some found it very hard to stand, they were that weak. They just stared at me.

The CSM left me and went out of the room. I sat down on my few possessions. After a while I got to my feet and went to the nearest man to find out what the routine was. He told me that he had been taken at the Sittang River battle early in March. He told me how they were marched with the Japanese, who used them for carrying their equipment, and how many of his friends had been bayoneted when, exhausted, they had fallen under the heavy loads they were forced to carry, how other men were then given their loads.

Others came and sat with me, asking me for the latest news. As I was about to tell them, Japanese came down the passage and into the room. One of the men jumped to his feet and shouted, 'Kiotsuke!' Everyone got to their feet. Not knowing the procedure I was a little slow in coming to attention. The Japanese came straight to me, and before I could prepare myself I was flat on the floor under a series of blows, with the Japanese standing over me shouting what I imagine was abuse. Slowly I got to my feet only to be sent back down again. I rose again. This time I was ready and steeled myself. I stood up to the beating, gritting my teeth and pressing my hands and clenched fists to my sides. Without a word the Japanese turned and left the room.

The men then told me what I should do when Japanese came anywhere near the compound or into the room. They also told me not to give them the least chance or excuse to beat anyone up. They suggested that I get out into the sun as soon as I could, for as I was lily-white I would be earmarked for punishment at the slightest thing. Some of the guards were worse than others. They had got nicknames for them. One was called 'The Lasher' because he carried a whip – and used it. Another was called 'Slapsy' simply because he could not resist slapping anyone who came near him. Then there was the 'Admiral,' so-called because when he took the salute before dismissing a working party he always stood on the water trough and looked down as the prisoners marched past him. I was told that the only Japanese allowed to speak English was the one they called 'Billy Bunter.' There was another whom the POWs called 'Lavatory San' because his name sounded like that. The men who were telling me all this were too sick to go out to work, and so did the necessary chores inside the compound.

The working parties that I had seen going out from my solitary window went out just after daybreak and returned just before dusk, which meant twelve-hour-day work. We were given two meals a day; one in the morning before the workers went out and another when they returned in the evening. The morning meal consisted of a handful of boiled rice and a cup of green unsweetened tea. The evening meal consisted of an issue of rice with thin cabbage or vegetable soup and the green tea.

After the evening meal all ranks were made to parade for 'Tenko,' or roll call. The man in the front rank numbered off, and the Japanese guard checked that there was a man behind him. All orders and numbering were done in Japanese, so I was advised to get myself into the rear rank until such time as I could count in Japanese. I asked where I could get a wash. I was told that I could get a swill down from the water trough which was situated in the centre of the compound, but only when the workers returned. The only persons allowed to take water, other than at that time, were the cooks.

One of the men, an Irishman, said that he would show me around the compound. The first thing was the water trough, then the toilet, which was just an open shed where one squatted down and did what one had to do into an ammunition tin. There were about twelve tins placed opposite each other. I asked who emptied them when they were full. 'That will be one of your jobs until you go out to work,' he replied. 'The sick and unfit normally do all that sort of work. The Japanese insist that everyone must earn their keep.'

'Is there any sick room? Or hospital?' I asked.

'Not yet,' he answered, 'but we have a colonel of the Medical Corps (Colonel K. P. Mackenzie, RAMC) and also a major who is a doctor (Major R. Ramsay, RAMC). They are trying to get the Japanese to turn one of the rooms into a sick ward.'

As we walked around the compound I saw living skeletons suffering from dysentery making an effort to keep their balance as they took one shaky step after another. Some of them carried their own toilet tin so that if they should need it they just put it down and sat upon it where they were and then got up and made their way under their own speed to the toilet without any hurry. There were men with advanced stages of beriberi trying to walk around. Their legs and bodies were swollen out of all proportions – a condition of which I was well aware, having seen Lacey in the worst possible state.

The workers returned and I made a beeline for the water trough. I found a piece of sacking and used this as a sponge, then, wringing it out as tight as I could, used it as a towel to dry myself.

We had hardly eaten our meagre meal when we were ordered out to 'Tenko.' Remembering what I had been told I made my way into the rear rank. All the men made room for me but before I could get settled the Japanese who was going to take the roll call came straight towards me. Not being out in the sun for a long time I stood out against the others. I was made to stand in the front rank with the Americans. The men on each side of me said what number I was to say, while others said, 'Don't speak, and we will say your number.' I was in a quandary what to do, and then it was too late. The command 'Bango' was given. The noise of numbers came nearer. I listened to the man on my right shout out his number, then I too made some sort of noise. The numbering stopped for a few seconds. The man on my left tried to pick it up, but the Japanese stopped it and came over to me. Standing directly in front of me with his legs astride and his hands on his hips he began to rave, then with both hands one after the other smacked me across the face, sending my head first one way and then the other. He then gave a push and sent me back into the rear rank. The numbering began again. This time it was the American newcomer's turn, then another newcomer's, and so on until all the newcomers had been dealt with. We were then allowed to dismiss. I was informed by my roommates that this was the normal procedure for all newcomers, but not to fall for it again. I had to learn to count at least up to ten, and go up the scale as I went along. So, my first night out of solitary in that prison, I learnt the Japanese numerals from one to ten.

Every day it seemed that someone died, sometimes two, sometimes three men. The men had got so used to seeing their comrades die that they could point out who was going next.

I was warned that every time I passed where the sentry outside could see me I was to turn and bow, even if he was not looking. It was not worth the chance of getting beaten up, so I complied, as did all the other prisoners.

There was no one in the compound that I knew except for the Americans, and they seemed to stick to themselves. The only man whom I did recognise was an Australian from the Bush Warfare School at Maymyo, who had been in the Singapore contingent. His name was Buck Bryson. I got acquainted with him and some other Aussies from out of the Air Force. We sat together at night near the water trough after 'Tenko' and told our different stories and talked of films that we had seen.

A full week went by before I went out on a working party, and that was only to carry our human excreta in dustbins. This was done by two men carrying the bin on a bamboo pole round to the rear of the prison. There some of the prisoners were doing 'gardening'. Our job was to walk up the rows of vegetables while one of the 'gardeners' ladled out the excreta and poured it around the base of whatever was growing. As soon as the bins were empty we returned to the jail to get another load of 'fertilizer,' this time from the Chinese compound, then the next from the Indian compound. To stop the mess from spilling over, the two men had to get into a kind of jog step and keep in time with one another. Unfortunately not all the carriers were fit enough to do this jog-trot for very long and there were a number of mishaps. We also got a tirade of abuse from the Japanese guards.

It was early 1943 before I was selected to go out on a full working party. The friends I had made told me to steal anything I could lay my hands on, especially food. I thought to myself, I will watch you old hands and see what methods you use first.

It did not take long for me to manage to get what I wanted. It was a matter of life or death how good one became. There were many working parties where it was impossible to even scrounge a bit of paper to make cigarettes with, whereas there were other jobs that offered an abundance of both food and medicines, sometimes even clothing.

It was amazing the ruses and methods we used for getting the contraband past the guards when we re-entered the jail. A man collapsing just in front of the sentry was one ruse we used on a number of occasions. We marched past the guards with ½ lb tins of meat tied under our legs and armpits, or army water bottles filled with maize. The maize was ground down into flour by the sick and made into cakes.

The months went by, and then we were into April and the beginning of the monsoon season. One of the downstairs rooms was allotted as a medical ward where the sick could be collected together, but the irony of it was that there was no medical kit of any kind issued. All the sick could rely upon was the stuff that was stolen by the outside working parties.

One night we heard a great commotion as if an army was being marched into the jail. By devious means over the next few days we found out that a large contingent of Dutch service prisoners had been brought in from Java and Sumatra. The exact number was 1,500. These men had suffered most terribly. More than half were at death's door with all kinds of diseases and infections, besides being starved.

For a great number of weeks it seemed that our compound supplied the grave-diggers for those who died, and it was not one a day. It was sometimes twelve or fourteen. We had to dig graves large enough to take six or seven, and the stink from the bodies, which were wrapped with only two sacks sown together, was overpowering.

During this time we had other intakes of prisoners. These were also kept apart from us but it was not long before we found out that they were part of a force that had penetrated far into the middle of Burma under the leadership of none other than one of our old friends from the Middle East, Wingate, but who was now a general. Another name also came into the conversation, Brigadier Calvert, our explosives teacher at the Bush Warfare School. Others were brought in at different intervals, but most of these had been taken around the Akyab, Arrakan area. They were all kept for some time in solitary. However, we still managed to get bits of information from them, and from civilians outside when we were in the working parties.

With the hospital ward coming into being, and with so many dying and leaving the other rooms almost empty, there was a reorganisation of the whole of the accommodation blocks. Men from the same units were put in one room, men from the West Yorkshire's, the King's Own Yorkshire Light Infantry and the Cameroonians. The Duke of Wellington's and the Gloucestershire regiments were put in together in one room as there were not many of them left. I was put into a room with the odds and sods: Australians, Americans, RAF and others from small units. We were in the room next to the hospital ward on the ground floor.

As the months rolled away we in our compound were beginning to get more organised, with no help from the Japanese. We did it only through our own ingenuity and stealth in obtaining stores, otherwise unavailable to us prisoners, when out on work parties. Through this the death rate began to drop considerably. We made potions, and cultivated certain medicinal herbs, which helped many men survive who were completely covered with ringworm and jungle sores that otherwise would have surely killed them. To rid ourselves of any form of dysentery we ground up burnt bones and swallowed the powder. One of the herbs cultivated in the garden was of the spinach family. The senior medical officer organised this and the herb was boiled like cabbage, strained, the green water drunk, and the vegetable eaten with rice. This, the MO said, would stop the ringworm. Another of our standby chemicals was the blue stone (copper sulphate). This we ground up into powder. By adding water to the powder we made bottles containing different strengths. This was found to be good to help heal sores. But it had such a sting, even in the most diluted form, that many men were put off using it.

Towards the middle of 1943 bombing raids were becoming more frequent. On a number of occasions bombs from Allied aircraft fell quite near the jail, knocking down some of the outer walls. Then it was our task to rebuild them. Another task that was given to us was the removal of unexploded bombs. On many occasions we had very narrow escapes.

One of these was when an unexploded bomb was reported after a night raid on some waste ground about a mile from the river. Eight of us were sent in a lorry to the scene with four Japanese guards. On arrival the Japanese gave us orders and stood well back. The sergeant in charge was an RAF man. The bomb was sticking out of the ground and showing the tailfin, and he told us to clear all the dirt from around the body. This we did, stopping to listen every now and then to see if we had set off any mechanism. When we had uncovered the whole of the bomb casing the sergeant called the Japanese for further orders. One of them said in broken English to hoist the bomb onto the lorry. All of us lifted it together and managed to get it onto the lorry. It was about four foot long and about eight inches in diameter. One of the men jumped onto the lorry and rolled it into the middle. He put his ear to it, shook his head and sat on it as we all climbed aboard. Two of the Japanese got into the cab and the other two stood on the running-boards. They drove us down the river to where a wall kept the tide back and reversed the lorry against the wall. On the sea side there was a drop of about twenty feet to the water. We rolled the bomb over the back of the lorry, gave it a mighty push, and it disappeared from view. We heard the splash as it entered the water, then a second later there was a terrific explosion that almost threw us out of the lorry.

After we had gathered ourselves we looked for the Japanese. They were walking towards the lorry as if there was going to be another bang. They were all wide-eyed and shaking, their faces a deathly white. We all stood on the back of the lorry, laughing at them and calling them to get us out of the place. Looking rather sheepish, they did.

The prisoners who had been taken in the Chindit expedition of 1943 were allowed out of solitary and occupied another compound. From information gathered from both the Indian and Chinese who had to feed them, sickness and disease were rife among them, as it had been in our units.

Both Brigadier Hobson and the medical men made representations to the Japanese and asked for some of the fitter men in our compound to cook and tend the sick, thus saving at least a few lives, but the Japanese would hear nothing of this, saying that they were soldiers and should be able to meet any eventualities that faced them. However, some weeks later a number of the fitter men were allowed to come out on a working party with us. Among them I found a man from my hometown of Birmingham. Eager for fresh news I asked him how things had been at home. What he told me was a little depressing. I wondered if I did manage to return, would I know where to go, and would any of my family be left.

Bombers over the city were becoming more frequent and were also coming over in greater numbers. The Japanese, who were now getting a taste of their own medicine, did not like it and were beginning to call those who flew the bombers 'murderers and criminals.' So when any planes were shot down it was in a shocking state that the crews were brought in, and they were not allowed to mix with us but were kept in solitary confinement.

One such crew of Americans had been shot down in flames. Out of the crew only four were alive. Three of them were so badly burnt that they were almost dead when they were brought in. These four were brought into our compound. They were bandaged about the head with dirty bits of rags which, it was presumed, the local natives who had got to them first had provided to cover the burns from the flies. Their hands and legs had also been badly burnt. In different parts of their bodies it was evident that either bayonets or knives had been used to cause injury, for there was dried blood on the wounds. Volunteers were called to assist in the medical room to help change the dressings and clean them up as best as possible. So I volunteered to help. The Japanese must have felt some remorse, for they sent bandages and cotton wool and white lint.

The burns were the most terrible that I, and I am sure everyone else present, had ever seen. Three of the men had nothing but charred stumps for hands, and at the back of their knees one could see the blackened burnt bone. How they had managed to walk, if they had walked, was a mystery. They had been brought in on makeshift stretchers made from bamboo poles.

The medical officers stood one on each side of the rough prison bed. As they proceeded to remove the wrappings from the head of the first injured flyer 'the rags' were handed to us. The last cover was removed very slowly, revealing the most horrible sight that I had ever seen. The first thing that hit me was the swarming mass of yellow maggots in the eye sockets of the blackened fleshless skull. Each one of us let out a gasp of horror at the scene before us. For a moment I was completely stunned and stood there staring. It completely baffled me that this was a living human being. The MO just wiped away any loose burnt flesh. He had nothing with which to bathe or to dress the wound, so the head was again wrapped up, leaving the maggots to continue their gruesome task. One of the MOs, Major Ramsay, told us that the presence of the maggots would keep away any gangrene. The stumps of the hands were treated as best as could be and wrapped up.

The second and the third injured men held no horror for us, as the first had made us well aware of what we were to find beneath the covering of those 'rags'.

The fourth was not so bad either. His hands were badly burnt but he still had his fingers, though he was unable to hold anything. The back of his knees were burnt as well, but not as badly as the other three. He was able, after a few days, to get about in a half crouching position. All of his hair had been burnt and his forehead was badly scarred, but he could see, and his chin had been burnt. Someone had to escort him out into the compound because he could not see the sentry and as a result might have got a beating for not bowing. Within three days the other three badly burned airmen died, leaving him the sole survivor of his crew.

Chapter Nineteen

Cholera and Bombs

Towards the end of 1943 we managed to form a concert party. We held the plays on an upper floor as this gave us more time to disperse if any Japanese came into the compound to snoop around. We were getting one day a week off. This was on a Thursday, as the Japanese in our area had every Thursday as a rest day. But some men still had to go out on work parties if they worked in another area of the jail.

Lieutenant Field and Corporal Caton were the two most responsible for putting on the concerts and plays. All that we had as regards costumes were some old bits of blankets and mosquito nets loaned out by the men and officers. However, using a little imagination the audience seemed to enjoy what was being performed. But on no account could they applaud or clap, as that would have brought the Japanese down upon us. All they could do was tell the performers after the show whether they had acted well or otherwise.

Owing to the more frequent bombing raids on Rangoon the Japanese did not want us to see the damage that had been caused, so there were periods when there were no work parties outside the perimeter of the jail. It was during these times that we became extremely bored. Nothing was brought in to replenish our meagre rice rations and we were back to the basic rations of weak vegetable gravy to go with the rice.

Just before Christmas we were told to hold ourselves ready for work on the docks, but owing to the amount of bombing this would have to be done at night. So at about eight in the evening we were marched out of the jail down the main road to the docks.

Two Japanese freighters were berthed and ready for unloading. By the time we were ready for work it was quite dark. We were split into four parties, two to each ship. With very little lighting except around the unloading area the parties on the dockside had little trouble in taking one of the unloading cases to the rear of one of the massive warehouses. The case was opened and the wood of the case was easily discarded by getting near the water's edge and letting it fall gently into the river.

A number of cases were opened and found to contain ½ lb tins of meat, peaches, pears, pineapples and some mixed fruit. Some cases also contained small dolls and trinkets, which were made up in bags like Christmas stockings. This, of course, created quite a bit of merriment, to think that we were going to rob the Japanese of their Christmas toys. Some of the cases went into the river by 'accident.' Our return to the jail in daylight was very quiet, as each man was concentrating on getting his hoard through and past the guards.

Fortunately everyone got through without mishap. As we entered the compound those who had not been out stood waiting to see what we had smuggled. The goodies were immediately hidden in various places. The total for that night's work was about 200 tins of meat, sixty tins of peaches, twenty tins of pears, ten tins of pineapples and a number of bags of trinkets. It worked out that on average each man had brought in about three tins each.

During my stint on the deck of one of the ships I had time to snoop around, looking over the riverside of the ship. I saw a small sailing boat tied alongside. When I went back the next night I made sure that I was on the same ship. I had a plan that if I could get the person on the sailing vessel to help me down the river unnoticed, then I could sail the boat out to sea. Everything was right for such an adventure. The food was there and so was the water. All I wanted was someone who could sail a boat. If the person on the boat would not go we could do it alone.

During the day I approached an Australian friend. He had sailed a junk to escape from Singapore but was captured when he entered what he thought was a friendly port only to find it taken over by Japanese troops. I thought he was the ideal person to accompany me on such an adventure. He said that he thought it a mad idea to try anything like that, but would I give him some time to think about it? I told him that I would try and contact the man on the boat that night, and would see him when I returned the next day. Again we marched to the docks, and I managed to get to the same ship, but this time I was not thinking about how much swag I could get, but waiting for an opportunity to go over the side to talk to whoever was on the small boat alongside.

It was about two o'clock in the morning when I slipped away from the crowd of workers. I got near the water's edge and, in between some drums that were stacked on the quay, slipped off the bits of rags we called clothes, rolled them into a bundle and stuffed them between the drums. Naked, I swung my legs over the water's edge and clung with my hands until my feet found one of the uprights. Then, getting my feet onto one of the horizontal beams I managed to get beneath the quay. The tide was coming in. The water was only about four feet from where I stood. I got down and let my feet and legs dangle in the water.

The night was warm, and the water not too cold as it lapped against my legs. I let go my hold, and with a little splash dropped into the water. The tide pushed me against the rough timbers. So, putting out my hands, I pushed away and struck out with an overarm stroke. I kept well under the shadow of the quay, but at the same time kept away from those rough stanchions. I had a little difficulty in making for the ship as the river current took me downstream. Using my hands on the side of the ship, I edged my way along until I came to the bows of the small wooden craft. I dogpaddled until I was opposite the canopy, which covered the rear part of the vessel.

For a moment I waited, holding on to the boat with the tips of my fingers as the current tried to pull me away. Then with my one free hand I slapped on the canopy. There was no sound. I waited a while and patted again, this time a little harder. Now there was movement from under the canopy. A dark head appeared with two white staring eyeballs.

'Urdhu jonta hai?' I asked in a whisper.

The dark face looked at me in amazement as I poked my head higher above the side of the boat. 'Kia mongta sahib?' it asked.

'Doe admi calco jaeger mongta, un bara Engliss sahib, doe lack rupee lager, teek hai? Teek hai nay?' I prompted him. 'Dae lack rupee, atcha hai, toom rajah hain!' I asked him again, 'Galdee geldee! Calco teek hai?'

For some time he pondered, then passed a dark brown hand over his face. He looked around to see if anyone was watching, then back to me. The whites of his eyes shone in the darkness. With a broad grin he said, 'Teek hai sahib.'

I pulled myself further out of the water, drew my forefinger across my throat and said, 'Nay boltah, jonta hai?'

He shook his head and said, 'Teek hai sahib, may boltah.'

I sank back into the water. I found it a little more difficult to swim my way back, as the current was against me, but as the tide had come in it made it easier for me to clamber up the wooden stanchions and onto the quay. It did not take me long to find my 'clothes,' put them on again and go back and join the rest.

I still found some time to get a stock of tins. I looked mainly for the fruit as they contained liquid. These I hid at the rear of the warehouse.

On our return to the jail I did not go straight to the Aussie, but went and got my head down. I wanted to give him time to think it over. Our time was all topsy-turvy. We were aroused for our meal at two in the afternoon. We got a really good meal of the red meat with rice, followed by peaches and floured cakes.

The Australian was called Lofty because of his height. He was over six-foot tall. He was in the same room as me, and while I ate my food I called him over. He came and sat on the floor opposite me.

'Well, have you made up your mind?' I asked him.

'It's no good, Fred. You wouldn't stand a chance,' he said.

'Look, I got it all fixed with an Indian. We'll go tonight. We can be on the high seas and around the coast before daylight,' I continued without waiting for him to speak. 'If you want to dump the Indian, that's OK by me. I only wanted him in case we needed him at the mouth of the river.'

'What about food and water?' he asked.

'Lofty, I have got food stacked away at the docks, and we can get the lads to empty some of the tins and fill them full of water,' I replied eagerly.

'But I'm not even on the working party!' he said, as if looking for any excuse to cry off.

'That is the least of our worries. All you have to do is go to the officer in charge of tonight's working party and say that you wish to change with someone.'

'What about the winds and the tides?' he then asked.

'That's where I need you,' I replied, getting a little impatient, 'otherwise I wouldn't have asked you.'

'Well, if I'm on the working party tonight, I'll think about it,' he answered.

Word got around that I was going to make a break. Captain Brown came to me and asked if it was true. I told him that it was but that I did not want too many to know about it.

'Well, I have been ordered by the brigadier to ask you not to go ahead with it,' he said.

'Why should he give you that order, sir?' I asked. 'And why should I not have a go?'

'The brigadier thinks that you may cause extreme hardship and suffering to the rest of us. Besides that, you may not succeed.'

I began to get a bit ruffled, and replied, 'Nothing succeeds if nothing is tried, Sir.'

'Am I to take it that you intend to go through with it?' he asked.

'Yes Sir,' I answered.

His manner changed completely. He took hold of my hand and shook it, and said, 'I wish you all the luck in the world!'

Other officers came and wished me luck and gave me small items that I might be able to swap for either money or food.

As we marched out I glanced at the brigadier who stood at the gate. His eyes glared at me as I went past him. Lofty was not on the working party, so now I had to put all my trust in the Indian.

The two parties settled down to the work of unloading. I carried on as usual, trying my best not to be noticed. Some of the men brought me some empty tins and some tins of meat that were already open for me to take with me. At about midnight I sneaked on board the freighter, passing the man working the donkey engine and across the steel deck to the side of the ship. I had wrapped my foodstuff and tins in my shirt and tied them around my waist. I climbed over the side and slid down the rope that secured the smaller vessel. As my bare feet touched down on the wooden deck it gave a lurch that sent the small craft bumping against the side of the larger vessel. The dark shape and white eyeballs appeared at the open end of the canopy. For a moment I stood still, leaning with my back against the side of the ship. The head of the Indian came out first, followed by his crawling body. He stood erect and began to shout. He got one word out and I was upon him. I had my hands around his throat, stifling any other sound he tried to utter. Quickly I drew him back into the dark and against the side of the ship. He was clawing at my fingers as I held him tight. My whole body was shaking. I looked into his terrified eyes and pulled his head close to my mouth. I whispered into his ear, 'Mutt boltah! Mutt boltah! Teek hai?' He forced a nod and I eased my grip. Perhaps the donkey engine had covered the shout. No one had come to look over the side, so I thought I was safe in that respect.

The man looked pitifully at me as I stood there still holding him. He too had changed his mind. I loosened my hold on him and he slunk back beneath the canopy. I still stood there, quaking in every muscle. I could not lift my arms to grip the rope. I do not know how long I stood there, but at last I turned and with a last look at the dark face that was watching me from the canopy gripped the rope and with my feet on the side of the ship climbed back on board and made my way back to join the others.

No one on the working party asked any questions, but as we marched back towards the jail I felt like making a dash for it, I was so depressed and let down. I felt that I could not face those who had given me stuff and wished me luck.

Upon entering the compound I found the brigadier standing there. His face widened into a broad grin when he saw me. Then as I entered into our room I was met by Lofty standing with his hands on his hips and his feet apart. 'What went wrong, Fred?' he asked, 'wind in the wrong direction?' Without hardly looking, but more by judgement, I swung my right clenched fist at his jaw. It caught him right on the point and he went over backwards and down. I then turned and went to my bed space.

I heard someone say, 'He asked for that.'

I hardly spoke to anyone for a couple of days after that, except to take orders. Early in March 1944 the Japanese decided to separate the two English compounds and make one into a sick compound, with some fit men to do the heavier work and cooking. This is what had been suggested a year earlier by the MO to make our compound free of sickness.

A few weeks later we had two separate working parties in two different parts of Rangoon. Shortly after arriving back from one of these parties one man was taken violently sick with both diarrhoea and vomiting. This went on through the night. As soon as the Japanese were informed he was transferred to the sick compound. Before the working party could go out another man went sick with the same symptoms. At this the medical officers got their heads together and came to the conclusion that we had got a cholera outbreak in our midst.

The Japanese were immediately informed, and all working parties were stopped. By the evening the first man had died and the second was not expected to last the night. Having sent the sick men into the sick compound, both compounds were now infected.

Strict measures were introduced in regards to hygiene, but the only cleanser we possessed was chloride of lime. With this we made swill basins. Every time one went out of the rooms and into the compound area we had to wash our hands and feet in the solution.

By the second day of the infection four men had died, two in each compound. We could not bury the dead because the Japanese would not allow us outside the prison. All they allowed us to do was wrap the dead bodies in sacks, open the gate of our compound, carry the bodies to an unoccupied compound and leave them there.

Everything that had come into contact with the dead men had to be burnt. It became a nightmare. Men were afraid to speak even to their closest friends in case they passed on the dreaded disease. Before the outbreak we used to sit in groups and talk at night. This did not happen now. Each man had to collect his own food so as not to make contact with anyone else. We were told that we must go for ten days without anyone showing any symptoms before the compound could be regarded as clear of the outbreak.

The medical officers made representations to the Japanese, but all they would do was look over the wall by standing on a ladder, as they would not come anywhere near us. The medical officers told the Commandant through an interpreter that they held him responsible for all the lives in the camp, and demanded that we be given anti-cholera injections.

Meanwhile three more men had died in the other compound, bringing the total to seven dead in three days. We in our compound were more fortunate. We had suffered no more deaths. We had only one who complained of a small pain in the stomach, which did not develop further. Another three died in the other compound in the following three days, while in our compound we had gone five days clear.

The other compound was still getting deaths and their total had gone up to twelve in eight days. We were on our seventh free day when we were told that we were all to be inoculated. The other compound was also given the serum, but not before their total of deaths had risen to fourteen. We had gone our ten free days, while the others had to go another eight days at least. The tension eased slightly after the tenth day, but still the Japanese would not come near us.

We were not allowed outside the jail, but it was decided that the best job we could do was to burn the bodies of those who had died during the isolation period. The Japanese gave us the materials and then locked us inside the compound to carry out the task of cremation.

We made a base of bamboo. This was dowsed in petrol. We then put two bodies at a time on the bamboo and covered them with anything that would burn. We ripped up floorboards from the rooms upstairs to put on top of the pyre. These were also soaked in either paraffin or petrol. We stood well back and made torches out of straw and flung them at the mound. In a swoosh the whole lot went up in flames. After a few moments it amazed us to see the bodies sit up as though ignoring the heavy planks that we had laid across them. We dug a large pit and buried the burnt remains in it.

The names of the burnt men were noted down by an officer. And so what we considered the worst period of our captivity ended.

All thanks must be given to those men who gave their lives tending the sick. No medals or mention in despatches for them. Just a hole in the ground in Rangoon Jail!

Meanwhile the aerial attacks were becoming so frequent that we were hardly taken out to work. We were nearly always forced to take cover from our bombers, with sometimes as many as two hundred planes of the B29 type flying over. These the Japanese called 'flying hotels,' and by the look on their faces we knew they made them feel a little sick, especially when their Zeros took to the air in an effort to attack back, which we noted was not very often now.

In late June of 1944 some more prisoners were brought in. Again these were men from a 'deep penetration' expedition, only this time they had come in by gliders. Those that were captured told us that they had overshot the landing areas and were then picked up in isolated areas. They were kept in solitary for about a week. When they came into our compound and told us about the second front which had begun and the counterattacks on the Eastern front by the Russians we all went berserk.

These men in our midst were so full of confidence that we fed off their belief, and we became elated. For the very first time in three years men who had hardly had a smile on their faces were now beginning to laugh again. Everything changed. Instead of walking around as if death was just around the corner, there was a spring in their step.

The new prisoners told us how the Americans were counterattacking in the Pacific on land and at sea. All this gave us a new lease on life. Working parties did not cease altogether but they were certainly curtailed. The Japanese themselves seemed to be getting friendlier. It was also noticed that the crueller elements of our guards had been moved away. There were fewer beatings for minor offences. Out on the working parties there were the odd arrogant Japanese who still thought that they were invincible. It was these who gave the odd kick and slapping now and then. But on the whole the majority of them must have realised the end was coming.

The general talk among us after 'Tenko' now was how the Japanese would deal with us when the crunch came. This had been the one question we had always asked. Would they try to take us with them, or would they dispose of us first and then go, or would they just go and leave us? If we were to resist any attack we must have food and water, so it was agreed that we should collect as many kerosene tins or anything that would hold water and store them up in the ceiling of the rooms, along with sacks of rice that had been amassed over the last few months. We also had tinned food hidden away if the Japanese were put under siege by our troops. They certainly would not give us any food or water.

All that we could do now was to wait and see and listen out for any scraps of information that we could get. We were also told, when we went out on work parties, to watch out for people who were still pro-British who could give us some signal or sign.

Very few new prisoners were now coming in. The remaining Dutch survivors had been taken away somewhere. One NCO and I were selected for a working party around October. We were put to work in a woodwork factory which was situated at the rear of the jail. The factory consisted of a number of wood-turning lathes. On these we were shown how to turn out wooden rifles from rough planks. There were two young Burmese youths with us in the factory, one of whom could speak a little broken English. It was through these youths that we obtained news of our forces in Burma and other information to keep those in the jail happy. Besides, we both got plenty of what we called 'tailor-made' fags and good food.

It seemed that the Japanese were going to copy the British idea of having the locals train with wooden rifles, similar to our own 'Home Guard,' plus the fact that they could put the dummy rifles with dummy men at certain locations to confuse our troops. The two youths informed us of the capture in the north of certain towns and how our forces had defeated a Japanese thrust towards India.

A day in November began with an early air raid warning. This stopped any working parties going out. We just hung around the compound in groups, waiting for the Japanese to fetch us. The all clear went, our officers formed us up and we got ready to go out of the gate, when the alert sounded again. No sooner had the sirens stopped than the bombers were overhead. They had come in very low over the sea, thus giving the Japanese very little time or warning. The Japanese HQ was only about a mile to the rear of the jail. We thought that it was this that the bombers were after. The second wave came over a little higher and let their bombs go slightly earlier, and one salvo fell right across the jail. One bomb completely demolished the cookhouse and killed one of the cooks. Luckily, most of the bombs fell in the garden and the unused compound, but still the casualties were very high. We had twenty-three killed and over two hundred wounded. The Indian compound also suffered a great number of dead and wounded.

The Japanese made the most of this by bringing in the press and taking photos for their propaganda. They forced prisoners to kneel by the craters as if saying their prayers. After clearing up the rubble and burying the dead, we once more tried to get back to normal.

Three days later the air raid sirens sounded again, but this time it was at night. It was the twenty-third of November 1944 and it was a cloudy night. The air was a little chilly. I had been suffering with a slight bout of malaria and I wrapped my blanket around myself and made my way to the slit trenches we had dug for protection against falling bombs. We could hear a plane circling above, but as there was so much cloud I doubt if the pilot or the bomb aimer could make out the target. After what seemed a long time someone shouted from one of the other trenches, 'If you are going to drop 'em, drop 'em!' As if in answer to this the bombs came screaming down.

As I sat there with my blanket around me I felt a drilling sensation on my left-hand side. The wall of the trench seemed to be closing in on me. I leaned against it and as I did I heard my shoulder go crack. At the same time earth and dust was falling over me. I tried to lift my left arm but it would not respond. I tried with my right and reached up. Earth was piled up on top of me. I was buried. In front of me was an American. He shouted through the wall of earth between us that he was going. 'Hang on!' I shouted back, 'I'll come with you.' Every time I made a movement earth came down, closing my air gap which was getting less and less. The man behind was wriggling about so I told him to keep still as he would have no air to breath. I began to shout at the top of my voice. After what seemed a hell of a long time I heard scraping above my head, and through a small hole fresh air rushed down to me. I took great gulps as the hole was made bigger and my head was cleared of earth. 'Quick!' I shouted, 'Get the man behind me. He must be nearly a goner!' They left me and began to scrape away the earth with their bare hands, but had to stop as another plane came over. But this time it went further down the river towards the docks and let go its bombs there. The rescuers dug frantically at the place behind me. The man must have had his head well down, for they located his back first. By the time they got him out he was dead from suffocation.

The rescuers then finished getting me out. They had no tools and had to work with their hands. The American in front of me who had shouted had gone silent. When they dug him out he too was dead. There were twelve of us in that trench. Only three of us got out alive. All three of us had suffered dislocated shoulders. Mine was the left shoulder while theirs was the right. Being at the other end of the trench they had faced in the opposite direction. I was put into the sick bay for the night, fearing that I would be suffering from shock.

The next morning I got up and went to look at where I had been. To my utter amazement I could not have been more than ten feet from the centre of the crater, and I never heard the bomb go bang! I stood there, looking down, with some of the men who had dug me out. They turned to me and said, 'Fred, you must have had someone praying for you.'

'Yes, I have,' I said, thinking of Father McGovern.

Chapter Twenty

Forced March to Freedom

Christmas 1944 came and went. The new year came in with a flourish. We could tell by the number and frequency of the air raids that the end would not be long in coming, but how would it come to us?

The Japanese were putting on a brave face as if nothing was happening, but the little bits of news and information we obtained told us otherwise. Even the locals were getting braver. Those who had always been loyal to the British were coming out into the open, but we still had to be very careful as we did not want to cause them any danger.

We were taken much further afield on working parties. We saw the troubles the enemy had gone to to camouflage the areas of the city and its suburbs. Even the main roads were covered with camouflage nets.

The Yorkshire NCO and I got our little job back in the wood factory, but this time we were making food bowls. It was there that we got news, quite by accident from a Japanese guard himself, that the 14th Army were at the gates of Mandalay. He casually asked us how far Mandalay was from Rangoon. We told him the estimated mileage. Then he asked how long it would take an army to get from there to Rangoon. Here one of the youths broke in and with his fingers crisscrossing to denote fighting, said, 'Engliss, boom, boom, Mandalay.' The Japanese shut him up and sent him away, while the other youth winked his eye and walked back to his machine.

The Yorkshire NCO and I could not get back to the jail fast enough to deliver the latest and best news that we had received.

After that we barely went outside to work. We were given jobs to do inside. This included digging a huge air-raid shelter beneath one of the compound buildings near the guardhouse and the guard quarters. They got all the Yorkshire men who had been miners to dig under the building and use wooden props to make it like an underground bunker, while others acted as labourers to take away the unwanted earth in baskets.

Herds of cattle were also being driven down from the north and brought into the spare compound. Most of them were in a sorry state for they must have been driven for at least three hundred miles.

BUCKINGHAM PALACE

The Queen and I bid you a very warm welcome home.

Through all the great trials and sufferings which you have undergone at the hands of the Japanese, you and your comrades have been constantly in our thoughts. We know from the accounts we have already received how heavy those sufferings have been. We know also that these have been endured by you with the highest courage.

We mourn with you the deaths of so many of your gallant comrades.

With all our hearts, we hope that your return from captivity will bring you and your families a full measure of happiness, which you may long enjoy together.

George R.I

September 1945.

Letter from King George VI to all FEPOWs.

This gave us new hope. It told us that the Japanese were driving them down before our troops could get them.

The interpreter came to our compound and asked for carpenters. One or two stepped forward. From the two compounds, there were six volunteers. These men were taken away and returned for the evening meal and 'Tenko'. Naturally they were questioned by all. On the first day they could tell us very little, but two days later they told us they were making big long boxes, like coffins, only wider. This had the rumours going well and truly!

The first rumour was that the boxes were to put all our officers in after they had been killed. But we argued that the Japanese would not waste time and wood. They would just bump them all off and dig a big hole to put the bodies in. The mystery of the boxes went on for some days. A theorist came up with, 'Perhaps they are going to get the twenty most senior officers, tie them up, put two in each box and cart them away.' The carpenters told us that there was no lid, but the theorist said they would be open to the air and would be seen. After all we had a brigadier (British), a colonel (British), another colonel (American) and quite a few majors of all nationalities, as well as squadron leaders and wing commanders. So there could have been something in that.

It was one day early in April that a number of us were taken with a sergeant in charge to the guard room, but instead of going past as was usual for working parties we were turned right towards the condemned cells. Through the bars that separated the yard from the cells we could see a line of fresh Japanese troops whom we had not seen before. They were standing in a line with bayonets fixed. About twenty or thirty feet from them lay the wide boxes, all set out in a line. We were made to stand by the bars while the guard went to get the key to unlock the gate. Everyone in the party was looking a bit worried and looking at each other. My throat had suddenly got quite dry and I found it difficult to swallow. All sorts of things went through my mind. Eventually the guard returned with a key and we all trooped in sheepishly behind the sergeant. We were led to the line of boxes. There we had to wait. The sergeant went with the Japanese into a kind of outhouse. After a while he came out and called for six of us to come into the outhouse. There we had to bring out long shafts and large wheels. The Japanese drilled holes into the boxes and the shafts, and some of the men fitted the shafts onto the boxes with nuts and bolts. Axles were fitted and the wheels put on. We could now see that they were huge carts that could be pulled along. Not only had the mystery of the boxes been solved but there was also a great sigh of relief when it was realised that the line of new Japanese troops were having morning drill rather than execution drill on us prisoners!

Of all the Japanese guards that were on duty in the jail at this time there was just 'Billy Bunter', the interpreter. All the others had gone. These new troops who had taken their place were much easier with us and they hardly ever came into the compound, except for the usual 'Tenko' or to request working parties.

On April the 23rd 1945 we were assembled in the compound. All who were considered unfit to walk were sent to the sick compound. All the fit men from the sick compound were brought to us. At six o'clock that evening we were marched out of the gates of Rangoon Jail with what few belongings we had, led by the Commandant. We had been issued with bits of old Japanese uniforms and shoes which they insisted we should wear, but most of us still had our bush hats on our heads in preference to the cloth caps they had given us. Also in the column were some RAF air crews who had not seen the light of day for some weeks. They had been starved and were very weak. We, the fittest, were asked to keep a look out for them and to watch that they did not fall out, as we were not sure what would happen if they did.

The six carts were pulled by four men in the front and pushed by two men at the back. There were about four hundred of us in the column. This included Chinese, Indian and others. The carts were spaced apart along the column. We all had to take turns pushing or pulling.

The carts as far as we knew at the time contained most of the guards' kit and gear. The foodstuff was sent on ahead by a lorry.

Once out of the jail we were directed onto the main road towards Mingaladon Airfield. This was in a northeasterly direction. We had no idea where we were being taken, but we did know that our forces were coming south. We were going north, so that made our march easier to handle. It was estimated that the airfield was about eight miles away, and some of the men who had fought around that area in the first campaign had an idea that we were being taken over the Sittang River and into Thailand.

Our first stop was in a wood well off the road. We were herded together like cattle in a pen so the guards could keep an eye on us. The first thought in everyone's minds was to make a break for it, but it had to be in the right place and at the right time, as some of the more senior sergeants said. It was no use just dashing off anywhere only to run into some Japanese who would just shoot us on sight. We would have to wait until we were further north and then decide when to move.

We moved off again in the dark. It was about eight in the evening. We were all very keen to make it well past the airfield as we did not want to be in the open if a night raid was made on the airfield by our planes. The 'old hands' that had been this way before thought that the best place to make a break for it, if there was a chance, was at the junction of the Prome Pegu road. It was here that they thought our troops would make a push, to cut off the retreat of the Japanese from the south.

We passed the aerodrome during the night and were very glad to see it behind us. As we marched we thought that we could hear the rumble of gunfire in the distance. Behind us there were also a number of explosions, and pink glows appeared in the sky. The Japanese were doing their demolition work.

On April 25th, at 8.20 am, we were halted at the thirty-fourth milestone from Rangoon. Camp was made in a clump of bamboo at the side of the road. A handful of rice was our meal, the first since leaving the jail. We tried to get some sleep as best as we could. Some men had already collapsed with exhaustion. With the lack of food and water we could only wait for our best opportunity to slip away.

Our bombers passed overhead many times during the day as we tried to sleep, but we dared not move for fear of bringing them down upon us.

We began again at about seven in the evening. It was my turn to go on the carts. The six of us were all companions in the jail and we worked it so that we took turns in front, then at the back. We were regarded as the best fiddlers in the compound, so it was not long before we found that our cart not only carried the Japanese kit but also some tinned food. We also managed to smuggle one of the weak RAF men under the load of kit, which helped us, for while he was lying hidden he got hold of some of the tins and passed them out. We passed this information to the other carts, so they did the same. When we stopped, the man had to get off and mix as quickly as he could with the others. About ten minutes after one of these stops the word 'kouushuu' was passed by the Japanese. This meant an air raid.

Almost immediately a lone plane, a Mosquito, swooped down from the dark sky above the road. We scattered to each side of the road into the brush and undergrowth. Its guns chattered as it went by. It turned quickly and came back down the road again. I swear that it was no more than fifty feet above the ground. The moon was well up. We were sure that the pilot had seen the carts parked on the road. On the fourth run he dropped a bomb about four hundred yards further up the road. After the all clear was given we again moved off. Where the bomb had dropped we could see that a number of bullock carts that the Japanese had been using had suffered serious damage.

A little further on, we came to the Prome Pegu road junction. Here there was plenty of commotion. Japanese troops were moving about. At each side of the two roads there were burnt-out vehicles. We went for about three miles up the right-hand fork before we were again halted for the day's camp. A handful of rice was handed out for our meal. Water was our main problem. At this point there was none to be had anywhere.

To be truly safe it was felt that our troops must intercept us before we reached the next road after passing through Pegu. Some of the officers had insisted that we all keep together and not make a break for it. Brigadier Hobson tried to make this an order, but most of us said that if the chance came we would take it.

The majority of us took it that now it was every man for himself. After all, we did not know what lay ahead of us, even if the Japanese got us to the railway line and to Bangkok. What then?

On April 27th, about eight in the evening, we began to march again. It was not long after starting that one or two men and officers were falling at the side of the road totally exhausted, only to be kicked and beaten to their feet. Those of us who were comparatively fit tried our best to give them some help, but we were shoved away and told to get back in line. Some of them never got to their feet again.

At about eight in the morning of the 28th the Japanese told us to leave the carts and get under cover. They appeared very agitated. The place where we stopped was partly gorse and partly bamboo. We had not been off the road for more than ten minutes when we heard the roar of planes. There were four Spitfires, a grand sight under any circumstances. They passed right over where we were, saw something and came back. The noise of their engines and the chattering of their guns, together with the boom-boom of their cannons, made a terrific noise. They kept this up for about half an hour.

It was at this time that most of us decided that the best time to make a break for it was while there was an air raid on, but others disagreed with this option, saying it was sure death to even breathe heavily during an air attack, let alone run.

The planes went away, and the Japanese were shouting to us to fetch the carts and put them under cover. It was not long after that the planes returned.

After the planes had gone again we were told that we could help ourselves to what was on the carts, as they were not being taken any further. My companions and I made a beeline for our cart, knowing more or less what it contained. Although we had already depleted the stock considerably I packed as many tins and packets of cigarettes as I could into an army pack which I had picked up before leaving the jail. This as good as told us that the end was now very near and that we must watch our every step.

We made a meal using the juice from the tins of fruit to quench our thirsts. We were about seven miles west of Pegu and about twelve to fourteen miles from the junction of the Tangoo road. Here the Japanese made us leave the road and go across country. It was dark as we picked our way through the rough undergrowth. I looked around to see if any Japanese was watching and sidled off to the right, going in a northerly direction. I was going by the North Star. Then in front of me I could hear voices. I got down on my hands and knees so that the light of the sky was behind whoever was in front of me. I could make out the shape of a Japanese steel helmet. I also heard the sound of that hated language. So as fast as I could I made my way back the way I had come and re-joined the ranks of weary and tired men.

We went back onto the road just before we entered Pegu. As we passed over the bridge to enter the town we saw the Japanese placing charges ready to blow it. We did not stop but went on through the town which was more or less just a pile of rubble. There was not one whole building standing.

About four miles out of the town we rested for about ten minutes. After the short rest we struck off the road once again and followed the railway line. Everyone by this time was extremely thirsty, as we had only the fruit juice which we had shared and tried to make it go around as best as we could. We had not had water to drink for two days. Beneath the railway lines there were some pools, but they were covered with green slime. The only way to get anything from these was to make a grab and let the drips fall through the fingers and on to the tongue.

We marched on and on along the railway line through the darkness. The fitter men helped those who were not so fit. Quite a number of times we were forced to stop because our planes were flying overhead. Perhaps it was as well that we fitter men had stayed with the column. Otherwise many of the weaker ones would surely have died.

Dawn of April 29th came with a crash and a bang as the Japanese blew up the bridge at Pegu. There was a great flash to our rear. We were guided towards a large clump of bamboo. There were a number of huts among the trees. From some of the 'old hands' we learned that this was a small village called Waw. In the middle of the village there were two wells. We clambered around to wet our parched throats. The Japanese then allotted areas for us to rest.

We estimated that we had covered just over one hundred miles in six days and in bare feet. We all got down into our own little spot to get some rest for the night's march. To where was anyone's guess.

We were told by the Japanese that this day the 29th April was the birthday of Emperor Hirohito, whose ancestor was none other than Jimmu Tenno, son of the Great Sun God and ruler of the mighty Nippon, the Land of the Rising Sun. None of us cheered. As a matter of fact we had our own ideas about that subject.

I had barely got my head down to get a bit of sleep when I was roused by the man next to me. He told me that we were all to assemble at the wells. I got up and made my way with all the others. There standing on one of the wells and surrounded by all the men and officers was Brigadier Hobson.

He waited until we were all close enough to hear what he had to say. There was a general hubbub going on. The brigadier shouted 'Quiet!' at the top of his voice. He put up both hands and in a quieter voice said, 'Quiet and listen.' Everyone fell silent. His face broadened into a smile. 'Men! I have the news that you have been waiting a long time to hear.' He paused and looked around at the faces below him, took a deep breath and shouted, 'We are free!' It took some moments for the words to sink in, and then everyone shouted. Some did a jig. Some just sank to their knees and cried. Men were shaking hands with each other and slapping one another on the back and saying that they had never thought that it would happen like this. 'Quiet!' It was the brigadier speaking again. 'The Japanese have gone. I have here a letter that says to other Japanese units to allow us to go free.' We all looked around us to make sure that there were no Japanese about and to make sure that they had really left us and gone. There was some mumbling among the gathering, and I voiced my opinion about that letter. We had been with the Japanese too long to rely on a piece of paper. If any Japanese did come along I for one would not give them even a chance to read it, but would be off. Knowing them and the way things were going for them at the moment, showing the letter would simply be asking for either a bullet or a bayonet.

It was with this that we dispersed to our own areas. It was decided among the officers that we should put out some sort of signal to warn our planes that we were in the vicinity and needed help. As it was now about ten o'clock in the morning there were many of our planes passing over.

All the white cloth that we could collect was mostly underclothes from the Japanese and off the carts. These were placed out to attract the attention of any aircraft coming near. A number of us set ourselves outside the white signal when any aircraft did come near, and we waved our hats and arms to attract them towards us.

I had taken up a position with a squadron leader, Duckenfield, who had organised the setting out of the signal. He drew my attention to four specks in the sky coming from the northwest. 'They are Spits and they are coming straight this way,' he informed me.

We both began waving our hats like mad with both arms waving wildly. Suddenly Duckenfield began shouting, 'Get up, you daft bastards!' As the planes began to peel off, he was still waving. 'Take cover! They're going to strafe us!' he shouted to me. I made for the nearest tree. Turning in my flight, I saw the spurts of dust coming up as the shots hit the ground. The chattering of the guns made a terrific din as they came down towards us. The scream of the engines was deafening as they neared the place where I found refuge, behind a huge tree. I glanced back to where the squadron leader was still standing and waving. I saw him jump into the air and go sideways as the spurts of dirt approached the spot where he stood.

The four planes came over the trees with their guns and cannons blazing, turned and came down again. The next time they changed course and came down in the opposite direction, so I moved to the other side of the tree. On the fourth run down they came with their guns firing. The first one dropped a bomb at the front of the wood, and the last one dropped a bomb on the back end. It was as if they were trying to panic us into running to that side of the wood.

All went quiet as the planes flew off. For a moment I remained where I was and thought of the squadron leader. He dusted himself down with his cap and walked towards me.

'That was a near thing, Sir,' I remarked.

'Stupid bastards!' he spat out. 'Don't they recognise an RAF officer when they see one?'

The aircraft were Spitfires from the Indian Air Force.

We both walked back together to the village, expecting to find many casualties. We asked a cluster of men how many men had been injured.

The reply astounded us. 'Only one, Sir.'

'Who was that unfortunate man?' the officer asked.

'The brigadier, Sir. Killed instantly by a cannon shell in the back.'

The brigadier had set up his HQ in one of the huts in the village. This was like all other huts in Burma, raised off the ground on stilts. He had been standing up when the attack happened and caught one of the first bursts of fire.

After the air attack we were all doubtful about the safety of staying where we were, as those planes might think that we were some enemy troops and could return at any time. It was therefore decided to disperse into the jungle until such time as we could make contact with our ground troops. We left on the understanding that we would return at dusk to find out if any contact had been made.

I along with some others went off into the jungle in search of food. At the same time we kept our ears and eyes open for both friend and enemy. I managed to find some bamboo shoots, which I shared with the others. When the sun began to drop and darkness was upon us, we made our way back to the village, guided by the light of a haystack that had been set on fire by one of the bombs. Many of the men were there. Some had stayed there all the time and they told us that quite a number of Japanese had gone past but they had kept themselves hidden. After hearing this we gathered tree branches and bamboo sticks from the buildings in the village. We then formed a perimeter around the village and lay in wait, just in case we were challenged by any Japanese stragglers.

No contact had been made with our frontline troops, but after about an hour four Japanese armed with rifles came near. When they were about ten yards away we all jumped up together and shouted, showing our sticks. They stopped, turned, and ran as fast as they could into the darkness.

I told my companions that I would give it about one hour. If no contact was made by that time I was going to make my own way. They did not try to stop me when I said that I was going.

Leaving the village I went in a westerly direction. I did not hurry. I just took my time, going very quietly and carefully. Picking my way through the undergrowth I listened for any sound and stopped now and then to look skywards for the stars to give me a guide. I found the Plough and from that the Pole Star. I stopped and rested often and listened to the different insects as they made their own type of noise. Except for these there was hardly any sound.

I must have been on the move for well over an hour when to my ears came the sound of voices. They were being carried on the slight breeze which was also stirring the tops of the trees. I froze, standing perfectly still, listening and straining my ears to catch one syllable that might tell me who they were.

The sound came from my left. Slowly I sat down among some brush and turned my head first to the left, then to the right in an effort to catch another sound, but there was none. All was silent again. After a while I decided to go towards where the sound had come from. I moved slightly to my left, going as carefully as I could and moving from tree to tree until I came to some open ground. The only light was coming from the stars. I dropped down onto my stomach and lay flat for a time, not moving a muscle. I could see before me the black outline of trees against the skyline on the other side of a paddy field. As I lay there viewing what was in front of me I saw some figures pass across my vision. I was almost sure that they were wearing British steel helmets. My heart gave a flutter but I still hesitated. I was not going to throw caution to the wind. Not now, I thought. I did not want to get this far and then miss the boat, like the brigadier. Keeping flat I edged myself over the paddy bund and began to wriggle forward. Stopping now and then I must have gone thirty yards on my belly when I heard voices again, this time more distinct, and I was sure that they were either Hindi or Urdu. I was about to go on a bit further when there was a prod in the small of my back. I went hot, I went cold, and I began to shake. I kept perfectly still, lying flat on my stomach with my hands outstretched in front of me. The thing was still pressing into my back. Sweat was pouring from me.

Then a voice in broken English said, 'Get up and keep your hands above your head.'

When I heard this I felt so relieved that I wanted to jump up and hug whoever it was. A pencil of light shone on my back and as I rose to my knees I could see my own black shadow thrown onto the ground in front of me. I raised my hands into the air. No other words were spoken. Hands began to search me, and I saw that I was almost surrounded by armed Indian troops. The man with the small torch came around in front of me. He shone the light first onto my face and then up and down my poorly clad figure. I could just make out a large burly sort of person and in the light I could make out three stripes on the khaki shirt. I could also see that he was shaking his head as he looked me over.

I had two men standing behind me. They began to speak in Hindi and gently propelled me forward with the officer leading the way. I followed with my hands still in the air. As we crossed the paddy field I could now see other men and some vehicles parked alongside the trees. As we passed the men there were gasps of astonishment and some murmuring as it was seen what sort of prisoner had been taken.

I was marched to one of the vehicles. In front of it was an English officer, a captain wearing the soft type of hat. His look of amazement when he saw me made me almost burst out laughing, but I managed to keep a straight face.

'Where the hell have you come from?' he asked wide-eyed, as if I was from another planet. 'And where are your boots?' Before I could give an answer he asked in one breath, 'And your arms, man?'

I began to explain to him who I was and what had happened. As I did, his jaw began to sag open, and he stopped me talking.

'Hold it, hold it. Jemadar!' he shouted. The NCO came forward, and they talked in Hindi. I was immediately given a blanket and seated in the back of one of the trucks. Food and drinks were brought to me together with cigarettes. I told the officer about the others and warned them that some of them were in a much worse state than I was.

I slept soundly in the back of the truck. As soon as dawn came I was sent back to Brigade HQ. There I joined up with all the others who had been found very early that morning and had suffered no casualties. We were sent further back to Divisional HQ. Here we were issued with fresh clothing and toilet things such as soap, towel, razors and shaving brushes. We could also take a bath!

General Slim came and greeted us and shook each one by the hand and told us that it would not be long before we were back in 'Blighty'.

After some days we were flown to India. We were put into the Military Hospital at Secunderabad. Here we were given our first pay. So we went down into the town and celebrated.

Sometime after that I received news from different sources that out of the fifty men of my unit who had begun the journey from Taunggyi in the southern Shan state of Burma, only five had survived.

The first party to move out from the copse at the Irrawaddy River was Sergeant McAteer and his men. They were caught in an ambush and all killed.

The second party to move out was ours. Three survived. Sergeant Friend was picked up by a missionary and taken to Kunming. Bland was picked up by some communists and also taken to Kunming. And myself.

Captain Brown was the sole survivor of his party. The rest died on their way to Sumprabum or further on.

Of the colonel's party, only one made it across the Irrawaddy to the other side and safety. The rest perished in the water.

Kin-Maung, the traitor, was hanged by the military in Rangoon Jail after a trial in 1946.

The two young white girls who witnessed me being tortured in Washung were reported to be roaming about Burma with two or more offspring of the Japanese army.

This is the end of my true story that spanned three years.

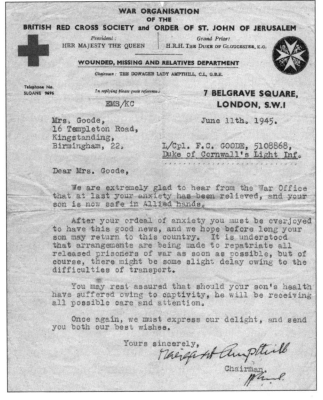

Third letter from the Red Cross informing the family of his being alive.

Postscript

by Peter F. Goode

In July 1983 I was a member of a police team investigating the murder of a banker who was found strangled with a bathrobe belt and dumped in a banana plantation in a remote area of the New Territories, Hong Kong. Investigation proved that the murder took place in the five-star Regent Hotel in Tsim Sha Tsui. One of the Assistant Managers of the hotel, a Japanese national named Faith Yayoi Numa, was assigned to assist us in the enquiries. A suspect was soon identified and arrested, the case went to the Supreme Court in Hong Kong, and the man was eventually found guilty of murder and sentenced to life imprisonment.

During the investigation, Faith and I realized there was a chemistry between us and we shortly afterward became engaged. The following spring we travelled together to England so that she could meet my parents. I had told Faith about my father's experiences as a prisoner of war of the Japanese in Burma. As in other families whose menfolk had been prisoners of the Japanese during the war, no Japanese product ever crossed the threshold of our house, and the Japanese were never spoken of. However, I hoped that my parents would accept Faith, especially my father, and even learn to love and appreciate her.

So it was with some trepidation that Faith and I took the British Airways Jumbo from Hong Kong to London. To my great relief, my father was courteous and kind to Faith, though my mother was cold and distant. I explained to Faith that my mother had been this way since I was a teenager, thinking no girlfriend of mine good enough for me!

Another trial for us took place when we went to the ex-Servicemen's Club in Birmingham for a drink and dance. Some of my father's friends who had been captured by the Japanese in Singapore and served on the notorious Burma railway were there. To our surprise these men were civil and friendly with Faith, which I think gave my father an opportunity to break the ice with her, and he seemed more relaxed in her company. Faith gradually brought my father around with her charming way to the point that one day he asked her whether, if he wrote a letter, she would send it to a national daily newspaper in Japan. He said that he would have liked to meet up, if possible, with one of his ex-guards who had actually been very kind and friendly to him and other prisoners in Rangoon Jail. Faith readily agreed, and on our return to Hong Kong sent a copy of his letter to the Asahi Shimbun newspaper. We still have my father's letter today. Unfortunately, Asahi Shimbun could not help my father. At that time, the Japanese government was trying to help repatriate all the Japanese 'War Orphans' left behind in China by their Japanese parents at the end of the war, and Asahi Shimbun were putting all their efforts into this project.

In October 1985 Faith and I were married at the Cotton Tree Marriage Registry in Hong Kong and we made arrangements for the wedding reception to be held at the Regent Hotel the following month. This was to be the big test as my parents and Faith's parents would meet for the first time. Faith's mother and father were of the same ages as my parents, and her father had served in the Imperial Japanese Army throughout the war in northern China. Faith's parents were courteous and friendly towards my parents, but my parents were extremely cold and avoided them as much as possible. Now that I have read my father's memoir and appreciate what he had to go through, I can imagine how difficult it had been for my father to accept that his one and only son was going to marry a Japanese national. All the horrible memories must have flooded back to him as he faced Faith's father, a Japanese man. Throughout the reception Faith and I were on tenterhooks, but thankfully it went without incident.

After we returned from our honeymoon, I received a letter from my parents telling me that they were disowning me and no longer considered me their son.

This naturally hurt and upset me a great deal, but it was actually worse for Faith, who blamed herself for my parents' behaviour.

Two years later when we were back in Europe on leave, Faith told me that it would mean the world to her if my parents and I reconciled. She told me that my parents would have been missing me terribly and most probably they must have been sorry for what they said in their letter. She then urged me to go and pay my parents a visit, and assured me that everything would turn out alright. So I went, reluctantly as I was still hurt, but sure enough my parents welcomed me back. They also wanted to see Faith.

After that day in 1988, my parents started coming to Hong Kong to stay with us once every two or three years. At that time, satellite TV was not readily available in Hong Kong, but they did broadcast an hour-long Japanese drama series on Sunday, which was called the Japanese Hour. Every Sunday Faith watched a Japanese home drama called 'Wataru Seken ha Oni Bakari' which literally means 'Demons the World Over'. The series featured a typical Japanese family, their loves, ties and daily problems. One Sunday my father joined her and was soon engrossed in the drama, so much so that when back in England he wrote to Faith and asked her to update him on what happened in subsequent episodes.

Over the next five years my father and Faith became very close, and he told her once that he thought the world of her, which meant a great deal to us. He also told everyone around him that Faith was the best thing that happened to his son. He always kissed her goodbye when we visited them in England or when they came to Hong Kong, and he loved to spend time talking with her.

In October 1993 I visited my parents and as usual at the end of my leave my father came with me from Birmingham in my hired car to Heathrow, where I treated him to lunch before putting him on the coach back to Birmingham. On this occasion I asked him why he always insisted on coming with me to Heathrow to see me off when it meant a tiring four-hour journey back home by coach. I told him that I would have been happy for him to say goodbye at the house, as my mother did. He responded with these words. 'When I used to go to the train station in Birmingham to return to my regiment after leave, no one ever saw me off, and I don't want that for you.' Then, when he was about to board the coach, he did a strange thing which he had never done before. He turned around, hugged me and said, 'I love you,' to which I replied, 'I love you, too, Dad.' He went up the steps and the coach drove off. That was the last time I saw my father. He died on December 1, 1993. I later found out that he knew he did not have long to live.

I would like to think that in his heart he had overcome his hatred of the Japanese.

I buried Burma gold, says Fred

THAT extraordinary tale of the treasure trove buried in the Burmese jungle during the war continues — and the small fortune could still be there.

"I helped to bury sacks of gold coins, with 2,000 coins in each sack, in a graveyard," says Mr. Fred Goode, of Great Barr, Birmingham. "They could still be there."

Mr. Goode, was with another Brummie, Lance Corporal Bill Bland, which as regular readers of this page will remember, is where our story began some weeks ago.

A small group of men were dropped into Burma in 1941 to take charge of 300 carts of rupees and charged with the responsibility of getting them out of the country and out of Japanese hands.

LEFT: Mr. Fred Goode is pictured on the right of the back row, in Burma, in November, 1941, with fellow Brummie Bill Bland on the left of the back row. RIGHT: Mr. Goode today with the bush hat which was all that remained of his uniform.

Taken as a prisoner of war by the Japanese after eight months in the jungle, Mr. Goode informed the War Office of his part in burying some of the money when he returned to Britain.

"The answer I got was that they had no knowledge of any money being buried. I know there were 2,000 rupees in each sack because an officer and myself had the task of counting them," he added.

But more than that, Fred may have saved his fellow Brummie's life.

Bill Bland had injured his foot and this was hampering the group's escape from the Japanese forces which had encircled them.

"At the next village we reached, a vote was taken that Bill was to be left behind. Being a fellow Brummie I voted against this and remained with him until his foot was healed."

Having originally picked up the newly-minted coins and bank notes from a treasury house in Taungyi, in the southern Shan States, the group was cut off. They burned much of the paper money and split up. Bill and Fred later went their separate ways after meeting with another small group from their original unit. Bill, after 12 months in the jungle, reached safety.

Fred meanwhile, struck off with another soldier called Lacey.

After eight months Lacey fell ill and sometimes the pair only covered four miles a day. They reached a village thinking they were safe, but were betrayed to the Japanese.

Lacey died later and Fred went to Rangoon jail. He made two unsuccessful attempts to escape.

MIDLAND PARADE ——— Edited by DUNCAN BAKER ———

The 'spy master' drops in —with a bubbly message

Maurice Buckmaster

Eleventh hour for 11th time!

With his 11th General Election just a few days away, the Midlands' oldest and longest serving MP is working harder than ever to get

Fred's interview with the Birmingham Mail & Post, April 1979.

Notes

Place names: Many place names have changed since Burma gained independence in 1948. The ones used in this book were those that were customary during the period described in my father's manuscript.

Chapter One

Major General Orde Wingate DSO (and two Bars) was a British officer famed for his eccentricity. His belief in the establishment of 'deep penetration' operations behind enemy lines resulted in the formation of the famous 'Chindits', who first saw action in late 1942. Wingate died in a plane crash on 24 March 1944 when his aircraft flew into a jungle-clad hill in present day Manipur, northeast India. He is buried in Arlington National Cemetery, Virgina, USA.

In 1941 Henry Courtney Brocklehurst, commander of SSDII, was actually too old at 54 to be on active service but, through family connections, he had managed to persuade the War Office of his capabilities. He had served in the Royal Flying Corps in WWI and had spent the interwar years as a big game hunter in Africa and China, being the first Westerner to bag a giant panda and bring back its skin.

Chapter Two

The attack by members of SSDII on two locations inside Thai territory near Chiang Rai, on gun emplacements manned by combined Japanese/Thai forces, is disputed by the British government to this day. However, it is mentioned in *Burma: The Longest War 1941–1945* by Louis Allen (J.M. Dent, 1984). Allen repeatedly asked the government for confirmation, but did not receive any. It is likely that my father was the only eyewitness to these raids, as those others selected by Brocklehurst to go with him died attempting to escape into India later that year (1942). My father is very specific, and points out the route they took back to Taunggyi via Mong Hsat and Kentaung.

Chapter Three

Bombing raids by Japanese aircraft killed and injured many civilians in and around the town of Taunggyi, which was one of the largest in central Burma. Lighting fires to guide bombers, and other such actions by fifth-columnists who supported the Japanese, were widely reported in the press at the time.

Chapter Four

Colonel Brocklehurst received instructions to blow up installations at Heiho Aerodrome and other facilities to hinder or slow the advance of the Japanese towards Mandalay. The aerodrome itself was located in central Burma and would have been of great use to the Japanese airforce for raids on India if left intact.

Taunggyi was a centre for the British military and civilian administration, hence the large amount of currency held there and given over to the protection of Colonel Brocklehurst, whose instructions were to get it back to India to prevent it falling into Japanese hands.

Fred said when interviewed by the *Birmingham Mail* in 1979, 'I helped to bury sacks of gold coins, with 2,000 coins in each sack, in a graveyard. They could still be there.' As well as that there were gold chalices from the church, and also bank notes, most of which were burnt. When he returned to Britain, Fred informed the War Office of his part in burying the treasure. 'The answer I got was that they had no knowledge of any money being buried. I know there were 2,000 rupees in each sack because an officer and myself had the task of counting them.' Fred also wrote to the Burmese Govt, but received no reply. At the time of writing, it is not known whether the treasure has been retrieved.

Chapter Five
My father recounts in this chapter that as they made their way northwards they came across a small group of mounted Indian troops. These were possibly the remnants of the final British Empire cavalry charge which took place on 21 March 1942, when a sixty-strong patrol of the Burma Frontier Force encountered Japanese infantry near to Toungoo Airfield, located south of Taunggyi. Led by Captain Arthur Sandeman of the Central Indian Horse (21st King George V's Own Horse), they charged in the old style with sabres drawn. Most were killed, including Captain Sandeman.

Chapter Six
The town of Mogok is still famous for ruby-mining, and Gokteik Gorge nearby has an old viaduct railway bridge which in 1942 was of strategic importance. After the closure of the Bush Warfare School, Calvert was sent with twenty-two men from the school and a few hundred men seperated from their units to guard the Gokteik Viaduct. The Allied C-in-C, General Wavell, believed that Calvert would use his initiative and demolish it, despite orders to the contrary from the civil administration to keep it intact. But for reasons known only to himself, Calvert retreated from the viaduct without destroying it. He later stated that it was one of the biggest mistakes of his military career.

Chapter Seven
It is at this point in my father's story, when the men split into four groups, that basically SSDII ceases to exist as a cohesive fighting force. The dates for this are a little confusing, as two of the survivors suggest it was May 15th, whereas another suggests the end of the month. From research, the groups initially, on separation, appear to have been as follows:

Group 1:
Lieutenant Colonel Henry Courtney Brocklehurst, 135896, 10th Royal Hussars
Captain William Lancaster, 104108, York & Lancs Regt

Captain (Dr) A.R. Banajee, ABRO
Corporal Wilfred Isgar, 5182058, Gloucestershire Regt
Lance Corporal Charles Edwards, 1896442, RE
Private Thomas Morgan, 4977740, Sherwood Foresters
Private Cornec, 5498109, Hampshire Regt
Private Francis Cawsey, 5499203, Somerset Light Infantry
Signalman Jewan Singh, 8079, Taunggyi Wireless Station

Group 2:
Captain Dennis Brown, 108389, King's Own Yorkshire Light Infantry (KOYLI)
CSM Arthur Richardson, 5281845, 17/21st Lancers
Lance Corporal George Amey, 7910219, RAC
Gunner R. Couldrey, 830703, RA
Trooper Arthur Lockington, 324447, RAC
Trooper Donald Sharp, 323789, RAC
Naik Mohammed Ismail, Kentung Wireless Station

Group 3:
Sergeant John Friend, 7912265, The Queens Bays
Corporal Robert 'Jock' Johnson, 2931826, Queens Own Cameron Highlanders
Lance Corporal Frederick Charles Goode, 5108868, DCLI
Lance Corporal Alexander Ballantyne, 2934334, Queens Own Cameron Highlanders
Lance Corporal William Bland, 5571603, Seaforth Highlanders
Private Harry 'Ginger' Hancock, 4748143, York & Lancs Regt
Trooper William Smith, 7909151, RAC
Private Leonard Lacey, 5669104 Somerset Light Infantry (met up with this group shortly after the separation of the members of the unit at the river)
Two Indian soldiers (Gurmukh Singh, Sarwan Singh)

Group 4:
RSM McAteer, 6976837, Royal Irish Fusiliers
CQMS Reginald Gillingham, 543209 RAC
Corporal Murray, 6976274, Royal Inniskilling Fusiliers
Lance Corporal Richard Homans, 5948673, Beds & Herts Regt
Trooper Lewis Scanes, 321274, 1st Royal Dragoon Guards
Three Indian Sepoys

The groups would occassionally meet up again in the jungle, and the men would change groups as they saw fit.

Chapter Eight

The construction of the Burma Road commenced in 1937 and was completed in 1938. It took some 200,000 Burmese and Chinese labourers to build. It is 717 miles (1,154 km) in length and starts in the town of Lashio, Burma, running through mountainous terrain to terminate in Kunming, Yunnan Province, China. It played a big role in the early years of its existence, before Japan was at war with Britain, as the British used it to transport materials to China in assisting Chiang Kai-shek's forces against Japanese occupation of China.

Chapter Nine

My father describes in this chapter being surrounded by jackals as they crossed a plain at night. These were golden jackals, or Burmese 'wolves.' The Burmese wolf (*Canis aureus*) is found across the Indian subcontinent and ventures into habitable areas to scavenge for food. It is very common in the evergreen forests of Burma and Thailand and, where food is scarce, attacks cattle and other domesticated animals.

My father credited Father McGovern with giving him the strength to survive during his later time of incarceration. Father McGovern was of the Jesuit Order and there was a large group of such Jesuit missionaries in the border areas. I have attempted to identify him, alas without success, despite contact with the Jesuit Fathers in Hong Kong and Penang, Malaysia.

Chapter Eleven

From the description of the symptoms given to my father it would appear that Johnson died from dysentery, or as my father says 'the squirts'. Amoebic dysentery is an infection of the bowel caused by an amoeba which causes the victim to have very bad diarrhoea and if untreated can lead to death. The causes are dirty food or water. A large majority of deaths in the POW camps in Asia were from this type of disease where food rations were of poor quality and the water was from polluted wells or rivers in or near the POW camps.

Chapter Fourteen

Fort Sima, very close to the Burmese/Yunnan border, was established by British forces during the Burma wars of the nineteenth century. From a historical point it is of interest as a Victoria Cross was won there on 6 January 1893 during the Kachin Expedition. While an attack was in progress by local forces on the British garrison within the fort, Owen Pennefather Lloyd, then a Surgeon Major in the Army Medical Service (later the RAMC), went with an Indian NCO to the assistance of the commanding officer who was wounded outside the perimeter of the fort. Surgeon Major Lloyd stayed with the officer while the NCO went back to fetch further help in carrying the wounded man back into the fort, where he died of his wounds. The enemy were within 10 to 15 paces during this time, keeping up heavy fire, and Surgeon Major Lloyd was wounded while returning to the fort. Lloyd later achieved the rank of Major General and was knighted. He died in St. Leonards-on-Sea, Sussex on 5 July 1941. His VC is displayed at the Army Medical Services Museum, Aldershot, England.

Chapter Fifteen

Sadon (formerly Fort Harrison) was a typical hill station, established by European colonials as a cool retreat from the heat of the plains in the summer months.

The McRaes had been resident in the area for some time before the Japanese invasion.

Sumprabum, some twenty miles from Sadon, was occupied by Indian troops throughout the war and would have been the nearest allied base for my father to reach from the hill station.

Edith Cavell (born 1865) was a nurse who is famed for saving the lives of Allied and German soldiers alike in WWI. After helping 200 Allied soldiers escape from German-occupied Belgium she was arrested by the Germans and executed by firing squad in 1915.

Dha which can also be spelled 'dah' or 'dhaw' is a Burmese word for knife. Kachin dha is a long bladed knife, about 18 inches long. Shan dha is also similar in design with handles made from hard wood and covered in rattan or sometimes with metal bands.

Kin-Maung is a fairly common name in Burma to this day, and efforts to identify Nita and her father have been unsuccessful.

Chapter Sixteen

Beriberi is a Singhalese word meaning 'I can't, I can't'. The disease is brought on by lack of vitamin B1, and causes the victim to be confused, have less mental awareness, and suffer, like Lacey, severe swelling of the legs or other extremities. It is fatal if untreated.

Chapter Seventeen

Myitkyina was at that time the northernmost HQ for Japanese forces in Burma and the location of the Kempeitai whose role was infamous throughout occupied territories in the Far East. Like the rest of the Japanese armed services, the Kempeitai were indoctrinated in the 'Bushido Military Code,' which called for Japanese troops to die rather than suffer the shame of surrender. The five codes of bushido were righteousness, courage, humanity, propriety and sincerity. However, it is apparent that humanity went out of the window. The Chinese were especially picked out as being sub-human. Japanese brutality also applied to prisoners of war, who were thought to have lost all honour in surrendering and were thus treated with great cruelty. The Kempeitai regularly searched POWs for diaries kept by them and administered brutal beatings on anyone caught keeping one. Pilfering was usually punished by execution.

Mr Kin-Maung, the father of Nita, was reported by my father to have been tried and convicted of war crimes in 1946/7 (see Chapter 20). I have, however, been unable to locate any transcript of the trial.

Chapter Eighteen

Mandalay was the old royal capital of Burma and is located on the Irrawaddy River. The railway line runs from Myitkyina to Mandalay and the station of Wunto (Wonetho) is approximately halfway between the two cities in the state of Sagaing.

The royal palace in Mandalay was converted into a fort and renamed Fort Dufferin in 1885 (after the then Viceroy of India). There was a major battle for the town, with stubborn resistance from Japanese defenders, but the fort subsequently fell to Allied Forces on 20 March 1945, led by General William Slim and his 14th Army.

Rangoon Central Jail (also known by the Japanese as Malay VI Camp in POW records) was built by the British and completed in the late 1930s. It was built in the shape of a wheel with the central water tower as its focal point and 'spokes' emanating from it as the prison cell blocks. It was known for its brutal regime.

The senior POW commanding officer at Rangoon Central Jail was Brigadier Hobson, assisted by two Royal Army Medical Corps officers, Colonel K.P. MacKenzie and Major R. Ramsay. The two medical officers were assisted by other POWs. Medical equipment was handmade and medicines either pilfered while prisoners were on outside work details, or produced through herbal gardens within the compound by the prisoners themselves under the guidance of the MOs.

The American aircrew that had been badly burned as a result of a forced landing were brought into Rangoon Jail on 15 November 1943. They were taken heavily bandaged to the solitary block where they remained for five days without medical attention. The crew consisted of: Major Werner (unhurt), who had managed to pull out his crew from the burning wreckage, with the exception of the rear gunner who died in the aircraft; 1st Lieutenant John C. Kelley; 2nd Lieutenant Thomas P. Hogan; S/Sgt Thomas E. Hopes; S/Sgt. Francis B. Jordan; T/Sgt. Urvan A. Aubuchon; and T/Sgt. Francis M. Daly. It was only after five days that Colonel MacKenzie and Major Ramsay were allowed to examine them, but they were instructed by the Japanese Commandant not to speak with them. MacKenzie requested that the men be taken to the Japanese-run Rangoon Hospital, but this was refused by the Camp Commandant. A second request that the men be allowed to be brought into the main compound was agreed upon. Of the crew, one, believed to be Lieutenant Hogan, was not moved due to his extremely poor condition and he died the next day. Of the remaining crew only Major Werner and Sergeant Daly survived and lived to return to the USA. The other crew members died of their injuries, despite the efforts of both MOs.

On the 11 May 1946 the sole surviving senior Japanese Imperial Army officer from Rangoon Central Jail, IKEDA Kumejiro, Sergeant Major, was formally charged with committing a war crime, namely the ill treatment resulting in the deaths of Lieutenant Kelley, T/Sgt. Hopes, S/Sgt. Jordan, Lieutenant Hogan and T.Sgt. Aubuchon, American prisoners of war in Rangoon Central Jail. The trial commenced on 21 June 1946 and concluded on 25 June 1946 with a 'Not Guilty' verdict. (Kew WO235/930 refers)

During my research into Rangoon Jail, I was supplied with a copy of the 'Death List' from Block 3. Sheet 2. This document was compiled by Captain Brown who had been with my father in Mytkyina and given the responsibility by the Senior British POW to record such deaths in the Block. The record was headed with Army No. Rank, Name, Unit, Date of death, Cause of death and finally Remarks. It was noted that on the second entry for that page and out of sequence by date was that of an individual, with no army number recorded, name of Lacey. Unit is recorded as SLI (Somerset Light Infantry), date of death is given as 15.9.42, the cause of death as Malaria and in the remarks column, MY (Mytkyina). This could only be Leonard Lacey, Unit is correct and location of death and date. It can only be assumed that either my father or Captain Brown noted these details down to ensure Lacey was recorded somewhere. On the same page, and the last entry, is recorded the death of 35305336, S/Sgt Hopes T.E., Unit recorded as 493HB Sqn. USAC (United States Air Corp) 14.11.43 of burns.

Chapter Nineteen

The cholera outbreak is well recorded in the 1954 book *Operation Rangoon Jail* by Colonel MacKenzie. A record was kept by a POW officer on those who died and were cremated inside the jail. Those named are on the Rangoon War Cemetery Memorial stone, which is located within Rangoon City.

Chapter Twenty

At great risk to himself my father kept a diary on his person during the 'forced march,' as it was the belief that at some stage the POWs would be executed before the arrival of Allied troops. He had not kept a diary at any time before this.

Group Captain Ronald Duckenfield died on 5 December 2010, aged 93. In 1942 he was appointed to command 615 Squadron, flying Hurricanes from Jessore, India. On 27 December 1942 he was leading a flight of eight Hurricanes to attack the airfield of Magwe, Burma. Over the airfield his engine failed, and he was forced to crash land in a creek 200 miles behind enemy lines. He was captured and taken to Rangoon Central Jail. While incarcerated, he taught himself Japanese and produced a Japanese/English dictionary. He retired from the RAF in 1969, after which he joined Rolls-Royce and was appointed to the position of Marketing Manager for Japan.

Brigadier Hobson is buried in Rangoon War Graves Cemetery.

General William 'Bill' Slim was born in Birmingham on 6 August 1891. He joined the Royal Warwickshire Regiment and served in the First World War where he saw action in Gallipoli. A very highly respected officer, he led the Allied Forces in the defeat of the Imperial Japanese army at both Kohima and Imphal in 1944. These defeats for the Japanese ended the belief that the Japanese were invincible in the jungle environment of Burma. His belief in support drops from the air gave considerable advantage to the troops on the ground. Slim died on 14 December 1970, a hero to the solders of the 'Forgotten Army' and members of the Burma Star Association.

'Return of Former Japanese Prisoners' www.youtube.com/watch?v=o0WkG_fgMec shows a large group of American & British prisoners from Rangoon Central Jail that were force marched from Rangoon to Pegu, Burma then abandoned by the Japanese. My father can be seen among them (left of screen, just behind the officer, in bush hat, grinning, at about 6 minutes and 54 seconds).

From my own researches, the fate of the men of SSDII who separated on the banks of the Irrawaddy was as follows:

Of Colonel Brocklehurst's group, only Private Cornec and Signalman Jewan Singh survived to reach India. Lieutenant Colonel Brocklehurst and Captain Lancaster drowned when the raft they had built capsized in a fast-following unknown river. All the others perished of disease, exhaustion or starvation.

Of Captain Brown's group, only Captain Brown and Lance Corporal George Amey survived, the former being incarcerated in Rangoon Central Jail and the latter reaching India. All the others perished of disease, exhaustion or starvation.

Of Sergeant Friend's group, only Sergeant Friend, my father and Lance Corporal William Bland survived. Friend made his way to Kunming with the assistance of missionaries. Bland made his way to Kunming with the help of guerilla bands. All the others perished of disease, exhaustion or starvation.

Of Sergeant McAteer's group, all were killed in an ambush by Japanese troops, except for Corporal Murray, who escaped to reach India.

Further Reading

Operation Rangoon Jail, by Colonel K.P. Mackenzie, R.A.M.C (Christopher Johnson, 1954)

The Long Trek, by John Friend (Muller, 1957)

Burma: The Longest War 1941–1945, by Louis Allen (J. M. Dent, 1984)

All Hell on the Irrawaddy, by John 'Tim' Finnerty (Anchor Publications, 1985)

The Middle East Commandos, by Charles Messenger (William Kimber, 1988)

Return via Rangoon, by Philip Stibbe (Leo Cooper, 1994)

Index

Admiral, the, 201
Akyab, 204
Alexandria, 5
American airmen, 196
Americans, 196, 198, 202, 203, 205, 206, 215
Amey, George, 31, 42, 234, 240
Arrakan, 204
Assam, 135
Australians, 205
Aubuchon, Urvan A., 238
Ava Bridge, 194

B29, 214
Baker, Corporal, 3
Ballantyne, Alexander, 59, 60, 74, 105, 106, 107, 108, 109, 111, 121, 235
Banajee, Captain, 234
Bangkok, 222
Bataum, 136, 138, 139, 144
Beddall, Sam, viii
Bell, Mr, 35, 36
beriberi, 169, 195, 202, 237
Billy Bunter, 201, 220
Birmingham, vii, viii, 206, 229, 231
Birmingham Mail, 233
Bland (William Bland), 6 20-2, 27- 30, 43, 59, 60, 62, 64, 68-83, 85-8, 91-3, 95-101, 105-6, 108-112, 114, 119-122, 129, 195, 228, 235, 241
Brahmaputra River, 59, 135
Brocklehurst, Colonel, 1-3, 7, 8, 11-13, 15, 17, 18, 20, 22, 25-30, 37, 38, 40-9, 49, 51-9, 69, 72, 97, 108, 111, 120, 129, 228, 232-4, 240
Brown, Captain Dennis, 3, 8, 23-4, 39, 5-9, 68, 69, 70, 91, 96, 97, 129, 135, 142, 175, 176, 194-6, 198, 200, 211, 228, 234, 239, 240
Buck Bryson, 203
Burma Rifles, 54
Burma Road, 1, 46, 50, 69, 235
Burma Star Association, ix

Bush Warfare School, 1, 3, 44, 74, 128, 203, 204, 234
Bushido military code, 237

Calcutta, 1, 62
Calvert, Mike, vii, 2, 3, 4, 204, 234
Cameroonians, 205
Canton, 5
Caton, Corporal, 208
Cavell, Edith, 163, 237
Cawsey, Francis, 234
Ceylon, 1
Chapman, F. Spencer, DSO, vii
Charlie Chaplin, 44
Chi, General, 198
Chindits, 201, 206, 232
Cobham, 1, 2
Commissioner Road, 198
Cornec, Private, 234, 240
Couldrey, Gunner R., 234
cholera, 209-17, 239

Daly, Francis M., 238
dha, 137, 160-1, 164-5, 195, 237
dragon's teeth, 9, 10, 15
Duckenfield, 224, 240
Duke of Wellington's Regiment, 205
Dutch, 204, 215
dysentery, 202, 205, 236

Eastern front, 214
Edwards, Charles, 20, 234
Emperor Hirohito, 223
Errol Flynn, 38

Farrier, Mr, 35
Field, Lieutenant, 208
Finnerty, CSM, 200
Friend, Sergeant John, 3, 8, 12, 13, 30, 34, 39, 58-60, 62, 64, 65, 68, 70-1, 74, 77, 82-3, 88, 91, 100, 105-10, 116, 120-2, 228, 235, 241

Gardener, Captain, 1, 3, 6, 7
Geneva convention, 173
Ginger (Harry 'Ginger' Hancock), 6, 17, 21,
    22, 24, 27, 30–6, 57, 59, 60, 62–5, 70, 72, 74,
    105–11, 121, 235
Gillingham, Reginald, 235
Gloucestershire regiment, 205
Gokteik Gorge, 49, 234
Gurkha, 19, 20, 34, 141, 195

Hancock, see Ginger
Heiho Aerodrome, 37
Hobson, Brigadier, 200, 206, 211, 222, 224,
    225, 238, 240
Hogan, Thomas P., 238
Hohi, 32, 33, 34, 35, 36, 40, 197
Homans, Richard, 13, 14, 15, 235
Home Guard, 215
Hong Kong, 5
Hopes, Thomas E., 238

India, 54, 59, 97, 111, 120, 127, 137, 142, 159,
    175, 216, 228
Indian Air Force, 225
Irrawaddy, 37, 38, 40, 46, 47, 48, 50, 52, 53,
    54, 58, 129, 143, 182, 194, 228
Isgar, Wilfred, 234
Ismail, Mohammed, 234

jackals, 21, 80–1, 235
Jesuits, 236
Jock (Robert 'Jock' Johnson), 6, 10, 14, 15, 19,
    24, 43, 55, 56, 57, 59, 60, 61, 62, 64, 66, 67,
    70, 71, 73, 74, 75, 104, 105, 107, 109, 235
Jordan, Francis B., 238

Kachin, 40, 41, 66, 67, 83, 236, 237
Karennis, 83
Kempeitai, 171–2, 176, 180, 191, 193, 195,
    238
Kentaung, 6, 7, 18
Kelley, John C., 238
King, Captain, 25
King's Own Yorkshire Light Infantry, 24, 205
Kin-Maung, 159, 161, 164, 191, 195, 228,
    237–8
KOYLI, 24, 26
Kumejiro, 239
Kunming, 228

Lacey, Leonard, 57–9, 68–70, 72, 74, 76–8,
    80–1, 85–8, 91, 93, 95–101, 105–6, 108–139,

142–155, 157, 159–167, 169, 171–3, 176–9,
    182–4, 186, 188–193, 195, 202, 235
Laihka, 42–4
Lancaster, Captain William, 1, 3, 8, 12, 39, 59,
    234, 240
Lashio, 38, 45, 50
Lavatory San, 201
Lieu Chang, 177–8, 183, 185, 188–9, 193
Lloyd, Owen Pennefather, VC., 236
Lockington, Trooper Arthur, 157, 195, 234
Lofty, 210, 211, 212

Mackenzie, Colonel K. P., 202, 238–9
Man Ying, 89, 94–5, 98–100, 111–12, 114, 116,
    120–1, 127, 134, 195
Mandalay, 1, 44, 194, 218
Maymyo, 1, 2, 44, 46, 50, 175, 203
McAteer, 1, 2, 7, 8, 11, 19–21, 23, 37, 39, 44,
    54, 55, 59, 60, 228, 235, 241
McGovern, Father, 80, 82, 84, 86, 88–92, 95,
    97, 109, 217, 236
McRae, 159, 162, 163–4, 237
ME Detachments, 2
Milman, Major, vii
Mingaladon Airfield, 220
Mogok, 47, 50, 234
Molo, 52, 53
Mong Hsat, 6, 7, 15, 17
Mong Kung, 45
Mong Mit, 51, 52
Moore, Mr, 2
Morgan, Thomas, 6, 9, 10, 19–22, 24, 27–36,
    43, 51, 57, 59, 234
Mosquito, 221
Mundo, 179–185, 187, 194
Murray, Corporal, 31, 34, 37–8, 235, 241
Myitkyina, 59, 69, 162, 171, 182–4, 186, 188,
    190, 196
Myitnge River, 47

New Delhi, 3
Nita, 159, 161–4, 191

Pacific, 215
Pearl Harbor, 5
Pegu, 16, 222–3
Prince of Wales, 5
Prome, 16, 221
Psipaw, 40, 42, 43

Radio Delhi, 89
RAF, 37, 205, 220–1, 225

Rajputana riflemen, 58
Ramsay, Major R., 202, 207, 238
Rangoon, 1, 16, 193, 198, 208, 213, 218, 221
Rangoon Central Jail, 198, 214, 220, 228
Repulse, 5
Richardson, Arthur, 234
Robinson, Mr, 2, 3
Rommel, 5
Royal Inniskilling Fusiliers, 200
Russians, 214

Sadon, 69, 97, 135, 149-152, 154-160, 162,
    165, 170, 174-6, 195
Salween River, 6, 17
Sam (Samantebo), 88-90
San Chien, 177-8, 188, 193
Sato, 188-9, 193, 194
saubur, 33, 111, 115-120, 127, 128
Scanes, Lewis, 9, 10, 19, 20, 26, 235
Secunderabad, 228
Sharp, Trooper Donald, 30, 38, 45, 48, 52, 70,
    133, 134, 195, 234
Shell-Mex, 2-3
Shwegu, 53-4, 58
Shweli River, 52
Sima, Fort, 135, 137-8, 140, 142-6, 148, 150,
    154, 162, 195, 236
Singapore, 5, 203, 209
Singh, Signalman Jewan, 234, 240
Singh, Gurmukh, 235
Singh, Sarwan, 235
Sinlum, 78, 82-3
Sittang River, 200, 220
Slapsy, 201
Slim, General, 228, 238, 240
Smith, William, 59, 60, 64, 74, 109, 111, 121,
    235

Spitfires, 222, 225
SSD I and II, vi-ix, 232, 234, 240
Sumprabum, 135, 159, 191, 228

Taiping, 89, 95, 102, 134
Taiping River, 89, 102, 134
Tamura, 183, 184, 185
Tangoo road, 222
Taunggyi, 5, 7, 15, 17, 18, 20, 22, 24, 26, 28,
    37, 38, 40, 141, 170, 174, 197, 228
Tengchong, 97, 123, 124, 126-8, 130, 132-4,
    137, 143
Tenko, 201-3, 215, 219-20
Thailand, 5, 220
The Lasher, 201
Thompson, Captain, 25-6, 76-7
Tiu-Tien, 100-4, 110
Tobruk, 5
Tulip Force, vii

Washung, 143, 171, 228
Wavell, viii, 3, 234
Waw, 223
Werner, Major, 238
West Yorkshires, 205
White Crow Lake, 197
Wingate, Orde, 1, 2, 3, 4, 204, 232
Woodward, Dorothy, viii
Wunto, 197

YMCA, 96-8, 100-1, 121, 122
Yunnan province, 75

Zeros, 214